FIGHTING MELANCHOLIA

CONTENTS

ABOUT THE AUTHOR

Françoise Davoine obtained an *Agregation* in classics (French literature, Latin and Greek) in 1966, followed by a doctorate in sociology in 1981, before becoming a psychoanalyst. She worked for thirty years as a psychoanalyst in public psychiatric hospitals in France, and as an external consultant and is currently in private practice. She was a Professor at the Centre for the Study of Social Movements, École des Hautes Études en Sciences Sociales (EHESS) in Paris, where she and Jean-Max Gaudillière conducted a weekly seminar on 'Madness and the Social Link'. She has also made numerous presentations at the Austen Riggs Center in Massachusetts (USA), as well as elsewhere in the US, in England, Sweden, Finland, Greece, Mexico, Brazil, Argentina, and Switzerland. Dr. Davoine is the author of many articles and books, including *La Folie Wittgenstein*, *Mother Folly*, and *History Beyond Trauma* (with Jean-Max Gaudillière).

WARNING TO THE READER

How to survive a hostage-taking

At the end of October 2007, after Anne Dufourmantelle had been entrusted with the manuscript of this book, in which I use Don Quixote as a guide in the psychoanalysis of madness and trauma, a providential event reassured me just when I started to be assailed by doubts about the text I had written.

Taking on Don Quixote, that may be all very well, but with no knowledge of Spanish … What was I thinking? What would Hispanic Cervantes scholars say? Freud had at least learned Spanish in his youth to be able to read the book in the original (Freud, Ernst L., 1970). He even identified with the knight's boyish idealism. But in the end he chose Oedipus as the founding myth of psychoanalysis, having no way of knowing that the "diverting scrutiny" in Chapter V1 would catch up with him. In the 1933 Berlin book-burning, his books were destroyed by fire, just as Don Quixote's library had been. So, is it not another folly to ask the hero to assist Dame Psychoanalysis today? Fortunately, chance came to my rescue when I least expected.

After submitting the manuscript, Jean-Max Gaudillière and I left for Cornell University in the United States. We had been invited by Cathy

Caruth (Caruth, 1996) to speak about our book *History Beyond Trauma* (Davoine & Gaudillière, 2004), in the Comparative Literature Department. That evening, when we were all gathered in her home, with her cats, she handed me a book entitled *Cervantes in Algiers. A Captive's Tale.* (Garcés, 2002) The author, Maria Antonia Garcés, was a professor of Hispanic Studies at the same university. As soon as I read the first few pages, I understood that she had opted for reading Cervantes from the perspective of his wars and his captivity, the very viewpoint I had found inescapable.

This exceptional book, which I read like a thriller that delves into the archives of the Inquisition, provided me with a wealth of historical information explaining Cervante's motivation for writing about war and his life of captivity in prison. The power of Maria Antonia Garcés' writing confirmed me in my belief that Cervantes' novel has therapeutic value. In fact, Don Quixote and Sancho Panza are engaged in a veritable psychoanalysis, during which Don Quixote even becomes the analyst of the madman of Sierra Morena, and eventually makes it possible for his creator, Cervantes, to inscribe the epic tale of his wars and his captivity in Algiers.

Maria Antonia Garcés is of Colombian origin. From the start of her book, she recounts her own experience. "I was kidnapped by an urban guerrilla group in Cali, Colombia [...]. During my seven-month confinement, I remained locked in a tiny, windowless cell, constantly guarded by armed jailers"—who were also hooded, she told us. "My love for literature kept me alive [...]. This traumatic experience first kindled my interest in Cervantes' captivity, an interest fuelled by my fascination with Cervantes' creations and my profound understanding of the rigors of human bondage, from that of [...] Cervantes and Antonio de Sosa, to that of the Holocaust victims and contemporary casualties of kidnapping and terrorist activities in different parts of the world. [...] Having been visited by death, *having lived it in some way* during this unspeakable tribulation, I am personally aware of the vicissitudes of telling undergone by survivors [...], difficulties eloquently discussed by Dori Laub (Feldman and Laub, 1992) in various articles. [...] my writing on Cervantes' captivity and correlated fictions has indirectly aided me to work through my own experience in the interminable process of recovering from trauma. (Garcés, 2002, p. 6)

Thus, Cervantes and his *Don Quixote* helped her to overcome her own devastating trauma, and to write, in her turn, a book endowed with the power to draw the reader away from the fascination exerted by the spheres of death. I set out to write with the same intention.

Psychoanalysis, it seems, has had its day

Of course, psychoanalysis is over one hundred years old. But, with great regularity, schools and institutions engage in passionate clashes in which the venerable old lady still displays admirable vitality.

And yet, the situation is serious. Another war is raging—a multinational war—in which the new brain is about to triumph over the psyche. Psyche herself, far more ancient than psychoanalysis, is in danger of becoming outdated. Even in psychiatric hospitals, dedicated to her care, as their name implies, she is being neglected. Rumour has it that Eros is cheating on her, the world over, with Neuronal Man.

Poor Psyche! Am I to help her sing her Swan song? Am I not a psychoanalyst? But it is time for the *Nunc Dimittis*, time to let go. The wise choice is reconversion. Eric Kandel, Nobel Prize winner for medicine in 2000, argues in its favour brilliantly. The era of interminable analysis is over, Kandel declares, and his statement is based on relevant experience. His book *In Search of Memory* (Kandel, 2006) "describes how certain events of his childhood—the arrival of the Germans in Vienna, anti-Semitism, expulsion from the family home and the family's last-minute escape to the United States—have remained imprinted, in great detail, in his memory. As a result, he began to ask himself very early how different memory systems function. For a time, he even considered becoming a psychoanalyst. But, somewhat impetuously perhaps, he soon abandoned psychoanalysis for neurobiologic research, which was to make him famous.

At the Centre for the Study of Social Movements at the Ecole des hautes études en sciences sociales where Jean-Max Gaudillière and I conducted a weekly seminar called "Madness and the Social Link", our work focused on traumatic memories, precisely the type of memories that surprised Kandel by re-emerging like ghosts. In the madness of war, everyone discovers that there is reason to go insane. But this does not stop people from holding on to basic certainties. For instance, in 1914 people were convinced, as they are today in Iraq, that when soldiers and civilians "lose their minds", it is because they suffered a tiny brain concussion, an invisible injury at the synaptic level. The underlying idea is still "shell shock", updated to suit the latest explosive devices.

In the meanwhile, psychoanalysis, trained on the front lines, had obtained, as early as the First World War, results that, while not quantifiable, were significant enough to cause this approach to be applied to subsequent wars. In peacetime, this "forward psychiatry" was discarded.

But let us recollect at least one of its principles, recognised as early as *The Iliad*: psychic survival requires the presence of a "therapon", to use Homer's term, an attendant with whom it is vital to speak. Achilles had Patroclus, and Don Quixote had Sancho Panza.

CHAPTER ONE

Andante!

The psychoanalysis of knights-errant …

This is what gave rise to the idea of a reading of *Don Quixote* in this seminar—Don Quixote and his wandering knights who might come to the rescue of our duenna. For today old Dame Psychoanalysis seems unable to defend herself from the invasion of her domain by her rival, the brain. In truth, the brain lends itself without hesitation to the standard protocols: biochemical, electric, even psychological with videotaping, one-way mirrors or two-way mirrors for that matter. Moreover, its value keeps increasing on the world's stock markets, despite recession, while when all is said and done, the psyche only yields peanuts.

Indeed, when wounded psyches possessing these profitable neuronal networks come knocking on our door, they are a sorry sight to see. Bleary-eyed, their faces empty as if all their energy had been sucked out of them by a vacuum pump, their discourse, like a broken record, endlessly repeats that their fate is sealed. Above all, they do not believe in psychoanalysis. They insist that their future is completely predictable. When things are going too well, they will get worse, you can count on it. Besides, they have been told that their disease appears to be genetic—what isn't, these days? Nothing can persuade them otherwise. The disease was passed down by their parents and is transmissible to their descendants forever and ever, Amen; their family and friends sing the same refrain. But, thankfully, their mood is stabilised by the latest discovery of the ancient humoral theory, be it drops, pills or electroshock.

These psyches come to talk to us, but insist that they have nothing to say. They demand answers, but they no longer hope for anything. And yet, they succeed in carrying out impossible missions in which they fight windmills, as evidenced by the following story.

One day, we had a call from someone who introduced himself as a psychiatrist, and said that he had heard of our seminar on *Don Quixote*. He added that he would like to send a knight-errant to us. I acquiesced, thinking all this was a joke. Soon afterwards, a young man made an appointment and, when he arrived, he introduced himself as "the Knight". After four centuries of roaming the earth, and his adventures becoming an international best-seller, he wandered into my office, to my astonishment and secret delight. With the simplicity of someone returning from a fabulous journey, he recounted his adventures, how he dodged the CIA and the French DST (Directorate of Territorial Surveillance), and how he predicted the war in Iraq. But he was perplexed and wondered why he had come to see me. I told him about our seminar and about his doctor's call concerning Don Quixote, adding that I was willing to be his Sancho Panza.

I had to explain to him in detail how Don Quixote's madness delves into the traumatic revivals of his creator, Cervantes, who in 1571, at the age of twenty-four, enrolled as a soldier for five years in the war against the Turks, and spent the next five years as a slave in the prisons of Algiers. He did not return to Spain until ten years later, in 1580. Our psychoanalytic adventure, initiated in this fashion, produced results. Without going into details, suffice it to say that I was led to ask myself, as was he, if forward psychoanalysis had not been discovered well before the First World War, by the old one-handed soldier of Lepanto, who wrote *Don Quixote* as a manual for psychic survival.

This is what gave me the idea of writing this book in the form of a psycho-dynamic talking cure between Don Quixote and Sancho Panza, using their exchanges after each episode of traumatic revival, since these are the episodes which reactivate in subsequent generations the kinds of physical and emotional wounds Cervantes had suffered as an elite soldier and later a captive. This also gave me the opportunity to show how Don Quixote then became the psychoanalyst of a madman identified as such, in turbulent sessions that served as lessons for my work.

... and wandering souls

But was I not committing sacrilege? At the end of the Second Part of the book (De Cervantes, 2001), published one year before Cervantes' death at the age of sixty-nine, in 1616, an explicit prohibition is formulated. Having given his son, at long last, a splendid death, like that of Socrates, Don Quixote's father hung up his quill—which, he says, is also his lance—, forbidding anyone from taking it up again. He had had enough of literary hostage-takers, like Avellaneda, a native of Tordesillas, who vandalised the first *Don Quixote* by writing a spurious and stupid sequel (Canavaggio, 1991, p. 280). This is why he had his hero die, to prevent plagiarists from profiting by the hero's marketing throughout Europe and even America.

In Chapter VI of the novel, the books in the knight's library are thrown into the flames. When Don Quixote wakes up and looks for his books (De Cervantes, 2013, p. 41), his caregivers comfort him with platitudes, telling him not to fret, and that the whole episode was only a dream, as Helen of Troy sings on the eve of the Trojan War, in Offenbach's operetta composed shortly before the 1870 Franco-Prussian War (Offenback, 1864).

Sometimes, through the years when Jean-Max Gaudillière and I conducted our seminar, I had the impression that the Ecole des hautes études en sciences sociales was haunted by what Aby Warburg called "surviving images" (Warburg, 1923, pp. 277–292). Warburg, who was mad about books as well, and an expert on Renaissance art history, became delusional in Hamburg in 1914, declaring himself to be general-in-chief of the army. Hospitalised in the early 1920s in Switzerland, at the Binswanger Clinic, he kept shouting that the Jews would all be exterminated. At last, he was "cured" of his madness, just as the knight had been, a few years before his death in 1929.

Warburg's gigantic library was comprised of books that his brothers kept providing throughout his life, in exchange for his birthright, that he conceded to them at the age of thirteen, for the bank owned by the family. This childish pact was concluded between the Warburg siblings in 1880, the year when the first Anti-Semitic League was founded by Wilhelm Marr in Hamburg. Aby Warburg's library was secretly relocated in London in 1933 to escape destruction by the Nazis (Chernow, 1994, p. 25). Since then, it has been enormously augmented. Known as the Warburg Institute, it now operates as a research centre. But all this makes me ask myself if Aby's surviving images (*nachleben*) might not be the errant forms of books and people long-vanished, imbued with energy, persisting in their effort to escape annihilation.

From Lepanto to Algiers

I learned everything that follows by consulting Jean Canvaggio's biography of Cervantes (Canavaggio, 1991) and his translation with commentary of Don Quixote—subsequent to Jean Cassou's translation into French. Born in 1547, Cervantes spent ten years outside Spain, between 1570 and 1580. In 1571, at the naval battle of Lepanto, he was hit with three harquebus shots in the chest, and lost the use of his left hand. He served another four years as an elite soldier (*soldado avantajado*) on Spanish galleys off Sicily, with his brother Rodrigo.

In 1575, when they were finally returning to Spain, in sight of the Catalan coast, they were kidnapped by Turkish pirates near Cadaques, put in chains and carried as slaves to Algiers, to one of the infamous bagnios of the Ottoman Empire. Miguel was twenty-eight. He would spend five years in Algiers, shackled for several months as a result of four attempted escapes, threatened with beatings and impalement— a fate that befell many of his companions. He was ransomed *in extremis*, on the eve of his transfer to Constantinople, where all trace of him would have been lost.

All this is recounted in a book published in 1612, around the same time as *Don Quixote*, by an author using the pseudonym Fray Diego de Haedo, whose work is entitled *Topographie et histoire générale d'Alger* (De Haedo, 1998). In fact, this book had been written twenty years earlier by one of Cervantes' fellow captives, Doctor Antonio de Sosa. (Garcés, 2002, pp. 67–77). He wrote about his friend: "The life and exploits of Miguel de Cervantes would deserve a particular narrative."

The book describes four attempted escapes, all of which failed, year after year, bringing the threat of death decreed by the Dey of Algiers, Hassan Pacha, a Venetian converted to Islam who eagerly tortured his former co-religionists and condemned to death all those who tried to escape with Cervantes. As for any questions that might arise in connection with Cervantes' survival, the testimony of his fellow captives is unanimous. During the mandatory investigations following the return of prisoners to Spain, they all declared that Cervantes always took responsibility for the escapes and never collaborated (De Cervantes, 2001, p. xvii).

But trauma always strikes twice.

In 1597, seventeen years after his return to Spain, Cervantes finds himself imprisoned again, in Seville, where he conceived *Don Quixote*. The second trauma is provoked, in classic fashion, by betrayal of his own people. This time, the trauma prompts him to write again. He had, in fact, stopped writing after the publication of his pastoral romance *Galate* and a collection of plays (including *Naval Battle* and *Algerian Customs*). Thus, writing became vital for him immediately after returning to Spain. In his endeavour to extricate himself a second time from the sphere of trauma, *Don Quixote* contributed new elements still lacking in the cathartic process initiated earlier but interrupted in 1587, around the time when his father, the apothecary-surgeon named Rodrigo (like Miguel's younger brother), died.

When he returned from war and captivity, Cervantes was, in fact, a thirty-three-year-old war veteran. Like many veterans, he was no doubt looking for a way to talk about his hellish experiences, and for a possible audience. He was poor, maimed, his parents had become destitute after paying the ransom needed to free their two sons; Rodrigo was freed first, after two years, for a smaller ransom. At the age of thirty-six, Miguel married Catalina, but acquired, at the same time, her parent's debts.

He thought he might try to change his fortune by immigrating to the West Indies in 1590. He could imagine holding a post as paymaster of the Territory of New Granada, governor of Soconusco in Guatemala, auditor to the galleys in Cartagena, or chief magistrate in the city of La Paz (De Cervantes, 1949, p. xxi). All his petitions were rebuffed by the royal administration.

For over ten years, Cervantes worked as a commissary agent of provisions and travelled through the Spanish countryside requisitioning supplies and collecting taxes destined for Spain's military ventures, such as the impending disaster involving the Invincible Armada in 1588. His functions caused him to be imprisoned again in 1592 in Castro del Rio, where his requisitions had angered some monks. In 1597, the cause of his imprisonment was of a different nature. He was betrayed by the

Sevillian banker to whom he had entrusted the sums he collected, to be paid to the treasury in Madrid; the financier became bankrupt and Cervantes was denounced and incarcerated.

Second trauma

At the age of fifty, twenty years after his return from Algiers, Cervantes relives once more the uncanny situation of a soldier coming home from the front as a stranger in his own country. Ousted from the world of the living, which he had been on the verge of leaving more than once, he can no longer find his bearings in civilian life. Since he first left at the age of twenty-three, society has completely changed, and so has he.

Jonathan Shay remarks in his discussion of contemporary wars (Shay, 1995), that when your own people betray you, a real deconstruction takes place, an "undoing of character". Most of Cervantes' friends had built successful lives, they no longer had time for him. Something about him repulsed them, his stories upset everyone. He had aged prematurely and was haunted by the ghosts of his comrades' unlived lives, interrupted in full swing. In addition, as his biographer confirms, Cervantes, like many veterans, was "innocent in his honesty" when it came to business (Canavaggio, 1991, p. 158).

Perhaps, like Don Quixote, he rushed into zones of chaos familiar to him, to restore justice after having been wronged, and to attack the scoundrels that everyone else tolerated. His battles and attempted escapes had long since sharpened his senses and taught him to focus on the essential. In Spain, a country he no longer recognises, he analyses the signs predicting a "paralysis that was to immobilise [the country] in torpor for several centuries" (Vilar, 1971, pp. 3–16).

Now, he found himself thrown in jail by his own countrymen, in a place "where every misery is lodged and every doleful sound makes its dwelling". It was there that he conceived "a dry, shriveled, whimsical offspring, full of thoughts of all sorts and such as never came into any other imagination" (De Cervantes, 2013, p. 3). Cervantes even admits paternity, only to disavow it later, preferring to declare himself the hero's stepfather.

Cervantes' apologetic confession awakens my reminiscences. "You are not my daughter", my mother would say when she found me too tough. By coincidence, I also spent my first months as an embryo in prison, between October 1942 and February 1943. My mother was arrested when she was caught crossing the demarcation line. The guide was killed and my mother was imprisoned at Chalon-sur-Saône and later at Autun, where "every misery [was] lodged", since the cell was crammed with women, hostages like us, expecting to be shot at dawn every morning, and where "every doleful sound [made] its dwelling", because the torture chamber was next door.

For Cervantes, trauma struck again in 1600, five years before the publication of *Don Quixote*. His younger brother Rodrigo, whom he had joined in Italy when he had been only twenty-three, his companion in combat and slavery, was killed in the first Battle of the Dunes in Flanders, in which the Duke Maurice de Nassau inflicted a severe defeat upon the Spanish troops in 1600.

Thus, Don Quixote, an old child "approaching fifty" came onto the world scene on the occasion of his bereaved creator's fifty-seventh birthday, in 1605, carrying the traumas of his lineage.

The black moleskin notebooks

White-haired children, those we call patients, regularly bring me texts written in pencil in black moleskin notebooks, found at the bottom of drawers or in attics, like those written today by soldiers in Iraq or Afghanistan (Carroll, 2006). A small number of these texts were published after the war.

This is how I came to read the notes of a young physician taken prisoner and assigned to the sewers of Cologne (Garin, 1946) to pick up the debris after Allied bombardments: he was looking after fugitives from death camps at the risk of his own life. And then there is the letter—carefully rewritten in clear handwriting for his grandchildren— from a British soldier in the First World War to his fiancée: the hours spent playing dead in the no man's land, under enemy fire, drawn out endlessly, unforgettably, while he crawled at snail's pace towards his own front lines. We also have the testimony of a young Navy pilot who steered ships to Dunkirk amid floating mines dropped by German planes (Dubard, 1945). There are also the war diaries of an Air France pilot who became a fighter pilot in the RAF, with the future writer Jules Roy as a bombardier. And the recollections of two grandfathers who lost their legs in Verdun, and so on.

As I read these illegible scrawls, I ask myself what to do with the phantom limbs that hop around in my office. And what should I make of the former prisoners who were sent back to prison in peacetime, like the sixty-five-year-old soldier who, in 1979, was imprisoned and then found innocent, not understanding what was happening to him any better than Cervantes did in Seville. Questioned by the examining magistrate, the veteran reminded him of his service record in the last war, the shame of defeat, the prison camps, the deportation of his brother Emile, the fact that his father had been gassed in Péronne, that his father-in-law was a stretcher bearer in World War I, that he himself had organised provisioning for the Tarentaise underground in order to stop the retaliations between the Resistance fighters and the mountaineers. The answer of the young, inflexible judge, son of the Nazi collaborator employed as porter at the hotel where the Nazis were housed during the war was: "Nobody forced you to do it."

CHAPTER TWO

Cervantes, an old warrior

In imminent danger

Cervantes was perhaps a *converso*, a descendant of converted Jews. Canavaggio states that these origins can be traced to his father's maternal grandfather, a physician in Cordoba. Cervantes was born in 1547, the year Spain issued a purity-of-blood law, causing the exodus of the Spanish Jews to all the countries of Europe and as far as the New World. At the end of his life, Cervantes was a member of the Third Order of the Slaves of the Most Blessed Sacrament, as a tribute to the Trinity Brothers who ransomed him and his brother. Miguel de Cervantes died as a Tertiary Capuchin monk, after having taken vows to enter the Order of St. Francis, following the example of his sister Andrea and his wife Catalina. But all this does not constitute proof concerning his family's origins. Be that as it may, according to Cervantes' biographer, he showed "great interest in Islam and its rites, with no preconceived ideas or deference, and was a clear-eyed observer of the different communities [...] living side by side in this Noah's Ark that was Algiers at that time" (De Cervantes, 2001, p. xvii).

In the Preface of the Second Part of his book (De Cervantes, 2001, p. 397), Cervantes defines himself simply as an old soldier. He was proud of having fought, at the age of twenty-four, as a novice harquebusier, on October 7th, 1571, "in the most memorable and exalted occasion that bygone ages ever saw or coming ages hope to see", as he proclaimed at the age of sixty-seven, in the Prologue of the Second Part of *Don Quixote*, and he was proud of the three harquebus wounds he received aboard the galley *Marquesa*, forty metres long and only five metres wide, with over four hundred men on board (Canavaggio, 1991, p. 57).

He kept reliving the moments when he fought, at his post, in spite of his fever, as his comrades testify, above the bloody sea, "by the launch berth, as his captain had ordered him to do, refusing to take cover below deck and look after his health" (Canavaggio, 1991, p. 57). His captain and forty men died; one hundred and twenty others, like him, were wounded.

Indeed, the context of actual war brings into question the general Freudian interpretation of a homosexual bond between men in the military. The care that soldiers can only provide for each other, and the intensity of feelings awakened by danger, create bonds that cannot be measured by the standard of everyday life. Ancient Greeks called *philia* such unfailing ties of affection as those between Don Quixote and Sancho Panza.

The plural body of survivors always includes fallen friends. And the fact is that our voyeurism while we watch televised atrocities intensifies the guilt of those who return, and their shame, less about the horrors in which they were involved than about having stayed alive. *Lucky You Died Young* is the title of the book written by Chronis Missios, imprisoned in Greece by the Colonels. Missios learned to write (Missios, 1985) specifically for the purpose of bearing testimony in his book, as did Captain Coignet (Coignet, 1850), an officer in Napoleon's Old Guard.

"Why am I still alive? It's beyond understanding", my father keeps saying—this hundred-year old veteran, each time he returns from his regular trips to the cemetery, where he visits my mother's grave and then the military section. He adds: "They were still kids, like your sons, do you realise that?" The kids buried there would be his age, but for him they will always be twenty; both he and his father were twenty-five when the latter returned from the "Chemin des Dames" wearing the blue jacket of the Dragons, to get to know his infant son before going back again, then returning for a short leave and finally coming back for good in 1920, long after the Armistice, when everyone thought him dead. Still, he had inhaled less poison gas than the infantry men he saw from atop his horse, falling "like a mowed down field of wheat", as he used to say, along a border that kept shifting.

A book on the border

When Cervantes, nearly sixty at the time, says that he fathered this "offspring full of thoughts of all sorts and such as never came into any other imagination", I ask myself if these thoughts were not of the sort to take shape on just such a border. On Catalan shores, for instance, or between Algeria and Spain, on a border that cannot prevent the entry of surviving forms, whimsical yet persistent.

As it happens, I was born in 1943 on the border between France and Italy, in one of the cheese cooperatives created at my father's initiative during the war. Until the age of two, I was present at the meetings of underground fighters, held in the kitchen opening onto the terrace above the ripening cellars, which were an escape route in case militia men or German soldiers should burst in.

And so, in this everyday life, the only one I knew, amid showers of bullets, bombs and artillery shells, I learned to speak and to know whom to trust, from among the underground fighters gathered around the kitchen table, some of them strangers to my parents. I was told that I would listen attentively to the conversation, clutching a book that never left me. There was no danger that I would repeat what was said.

Not long ago, while clearing an attic, I came upon the book that never left me at the time, and that I called "bada". The other book that played the same role had been a telephone directory. The book I found was a bright red colouring book telling the story of Don Quixote, followed by the adventures of Robinson Crusoe.

One of the strangers in our kitchen came with a taller man who wore the blue uniform of Petenist organisations. The other members of the Resistance were uncomfortable seeing him come to our house, until ...

Vitek

When I was over sixty, the questions I asked my father finally uncovered the name Vitek, son of a Parisian furrier, and resolved the mystery of his blue uniform. "When he would come to our cooperative, where the customary comings and goings covered up secret meetings,

he always took you on his knees, perhaps he had a little girl your age",
I was told.

So it had been him, the man in blue who visited me—a true surviving image—, after we moved away from the mountains to the plain, at
my mother's request. One day, in primary school, I invented a story for
my schoolmates, convincing them that I had secret rendez-vous every
Sunday with a young man in a blue uniform. Week after week, I would
recount our walks together until my imagination was exhausted. My
ability to lie with such flourish astonished even myself.

When I saw the photograph of an Alpine infantry officer, I believed
for a long while that it was Captain Bulle, killed in 1944, whose parents,
the postmasters, lived in the Post Office building on the street next to
the fruit cannery.

Over time, the memory of the cooperative on the border and of the
man in blue faded. But it reemerged intact the day I read an article that
obliterated the role of these cooperatives during the war, to restore the
reputation of a man who had belonged to the French Militia created by
the Vichy regime.

I was determined to set things straight, but was dissuaded by the
usual paternal admonishment: "What good can it do to stir up the past?
This boy went wrong, let bygones be bygones. Besides, amnesty has
been granted, and his father was a decent man". And then came the
most convincing argument of all: "During the war, you would have
been killed for less … At the time he was only twenty. It was really
strange when I saw him one day wearing the Militia uniform, with one
of my schoolmates, who was such a nice boy. I could have called out to
them, but I looked the other way, since he could have informed on me.
All of these things went on then, all sorts of strange situations. Families
where one brother was a Resistance fighter and the other … Later when
I was part of a Liberation Committee, I threw away hundreds of signed
letters of denunciation—think of it, there were enough to imprison half
the population of the town."

Much later, my father finally told me: "Vitek was a Jew and he was
an informant for the Resistance under cover of his blue uniform. He
was taken away in a round-up. "He's on our side, it was really true",
kept saying the man who came running to warn us that we had to hide.
Later, I caught a glimpse of him at the Chambery train station. On the
platform, I saw him for the last time between two German soldiers, his
face beaten to a pulp. Our eyes met; I am sure he recognised me. They

executed him soon afterwards. I keep seeing the look in his eyes, every day I keep seeing that look."

So the visitor I had invented in primary school was the embodiment of the gaze that haunted my father.

Still other voices echo in my ears, stories disconnected in time, which come rushing back especially when I walk along the mountain pass above my home town. In the wind that sweeps the descending slopes, I hear the voices of the lives that stopped here, of those no one mentions any more, and of whom I find no trace in history books.

Only Don Quixote brings back the spirit of those times—a messenger from the province of La Mancha, famous for its goat cheese, the Manchego, fresh or aged, enjoyed with fresh bread and local wine, which was one of his delights. In Chapter XVII of The Second Part, when Don Quixote puts on his helmet, in which Sancho has placed some curds bought from a shepherd, the knight thinks that his brain is melting when the squeezed curds run all over his face (De Cervantes, 2013, p. 490).

In the Middle Ages, cheese was the quintessential symbol of folly, as illustrated by an illumination of the Psalm *Dixit insipiens*, depicting a fool holding cheese. In a vision of Saint Hildegarde, eleventh century builder and healer from Bingen, in the Rhine Valley, human souls appeared to her in the form of various kinds of cheeses, with different tastes depending on their degree of ripening (Jéquier, 1993, pp. 42–54; Fritz, 1992, p. 53). Was Cervantes a "refiner" of the psyche? Even admitting that he was, there is no justification for concluding that his work is based on some alchemical code, or that it cannot be understood without knowing the Kabbalah.

So I decided to let Don Quixote be my guide in the sphere of trauma, as he had been portrayed in that ugly, red comic book thanks to which I was as good as gold while I listened, without understanding, to the members of the Maquis seated around our table during the war, on the border. They would stand up to sing together "Le Chant des partisans", "Le Vieux chalet", and other songs. Don Quixote, like the old chalet in the song, builds himself up again after every fall.

"There are tears [in] things" (Virgil, 1952, p. 19)

One day, in 1991 in Stockholm, we were taking part in a symposium organised by Christian Müller and Gaetano Benedetti, on the analytic psychotherapy of schizophrenia. I was making a presentation on the Gradiva (Freud, 1907a), in a session dedicated to psychic trauma. That is where I met Svere Vervin, a Norwegian analyst whose father had fought in the battle of Narvik, like my uncle Emile.

After the conference, we visited the outdoor museum in Skansen, showing traditional wooden houses from all over Sweden. A sudden shower forced us to take shelter under a porch, with the other visitors, young and old, who did not know each other. Suddenly, several voices in unison burst into spontaneous song; the chorus of voices rang out clear and strong. To my great surprise, because I do not cry easily, I burst into tears—a shower more violent than the downpour around us, which lasted for hours and whose cause I did not understand until recently, when I learned about the songs sung around the family table during the war.

A noteworthy event

When Cervantes published *Don Quixote* at the age of fifty-eight, thirty years after he had enlisted in the Holy League against the Turks in Italy, the battle of Lepanto, fought on October 7th, 1571, was almost forgotten.

Of course! Now that I am in my sixties, who remembers the massacres of the Pass of Petit-Saint-Bernard, where twenty-eight hostages had to dig a mass grave, before being shot at the edge of the pit? Where? Somewhere on the mountain. When? Was I already born? Who remembers the evacuations to a village down the river, to stay with the communist mayor and his wife, happy to welcome the refugee little girl, since they had no children of their own. Who can still remember the round-ups, the rapes, the fires, the stealthy returns under cover of night, between the river and the train tracks, the wartime cooperatives, uncle Emile's deportation when he returned from the battle of Narvik? After being used as a human Guinea pig, he had been among the concentration camp survivors at the Hotel Lutetia, where his own brother, my father, had trouble recognising him. He sent all his decorations back to Paris and his name was never again found in any registry.

And yet, Cervantes employed all his genius to prevent this erasure, not only of the events that took place in Lepanto, but also of slavery in the Ottoman bagnios around the Mediterranean. But, sad to say, dates, wars, heroes, with their songs and poems, are no longer taught in schools today.

Still, I would really like to know who was the man they called Lieutenant de France, killed like the others, whom my father and I used to meet at night, before I was two, when during their talks I would eat handfuls of honey from a jar, and spread it all over the interior of the car. I remember their whispers, the honey in the night, the black car … What kind of car was it? And my question in the dark on the winding road along the Isere: "Where are we going?—To Aime". A beautiful place name for *philia*.

In his masterpiece *The Mediterranean*, Fernand Braudel asserts that such events are the "ephemera of history" (Braudel, 1995). All that matters is the history of peoples, mentalities, economic relations. British historian Julian Jackson (Jackson, 2000) holds a different opinion; he places the focus on specific events, just as Cervantes did. Comparing the two star historians of the Annales School—Marc Bloch who founded it with Lucien Febre in 1922, and Bloch's post-war successor, Fernand Braudel—Jackson points out that Braudel wrote *The Mediterranean* in captivity.

Marc Bloch had a different experience (Bloch, 1999). He had been an Intelligence Officer during the First World War and joined up again in 1939, despite the fact that he was fifty-three and the father of six children. After the defeat, he enrolled in the Resistance in Lyon, with the whole kit and caboodle of sacrifice, patriotism, and spilled blood. Another one of those who did not have to do it. He was tortured by Barbie, and consoled the young boy crying next to him, waiting to be executed in a ditch, saying: "Don't worry, they will shoot us, they are not going to hurt us."

Jackson concludes that for Marc Bloch dates and places are sacred. What hurts is to erase them. The overall perspective dilutes events; for instance, that month of May in 1940 when French battalions were surrounded like cattle, a month which Braudel probably has no wish to remember, any more than Don Quixote wanted to remember "the name of […] a village in La Mancha […] which [he has] no desire to call to mind" (De Cervantes, 2013, p. 11).

Today, this opening sentence of *Don Quixote* serves as a logo for all the commercial enterprises carried out in the villages of La Mancha. Still, Cervantes needed thirty-nine chapters and three hundred pages to record and pass down the battles of Lepanto and La Goulette, in which he fought, as well as the places to which he was deported in Algiers.

Cervantes is so attached to his battle that he depicts it in relief, like the battle of Atlanta of the American Civil War, reconstituted in a diorama that can still be seen in that city. Whatever the war, survivors all say the same thing, formulated by the analyst Wilfred Bion, at the age of seventy in these words: "I died at Cambrai in 1917. [...] We were old men before having lived" (Bion, 1991).

"If I had known, I wouldn't have come"

The phrase made famous by Petit Gibus, Pergaud's remarkable character in *La Guerre des boutons* ("The War of Buttons", fought among country kids), is on every recruit's lips. Louis Pergaud (Pergaud, 1942) himself was one of the first soldiers killed in the First World War. If they had known ... But they were there, on the front lines, and the reality to which they testify must be heard.

A "real" still present for the old soldier who looked death in the face on the bridge outside the Dijon train station in 1940, when he was twenty-six, after his first escape from the camp where his company was surrounded in the Ardennes. He and four others, who had just met, decided not to submit to their fate, but rather to cross the river when the lights of the motorcycles passing on the road on the other side would leave a space of darkness.

He did not know how to swim. One of the others was ready to abandon the idea. A third, the one who had had the idea and had devised the plan, was paralysed with fear. But at the crucial moment they all jumped into the water in concert, linked together as one, and somehow arrived on the other side and ran blindly in an unknown direction. For a month they roamed aimlessly, walking at night, finding food on abandoned farms, until a German soldier stopped him, when he was alone, on the bridge outside the Dijon train station, and placed a handgun under his chin, without firing. "Why?" he still asks today.

He was forced to walk down the Grand-Rue in Dijon, aptly renamed "rue de la Liberté", kicked from behind by his captor, until they reached the Longvic airbase. Luck and circumstances would help him escape from prison once again. But in his nightmares he still sees the young girl he crossed on the sidewalk of the famous street, whom he asked in a whisper: "Where are our troops? What news do you have?", and whom her friend prevented from answering, saying: "You know we are not to speak to French prisoners." At times like that, it is as if you die, he often tells me, and you keep reliving those times.

Cervantes, like Bion, could have written: "I died at Lepanto in 1571, or in slavery in Algiers in 1576, 1577, 1578", when he saw his companions being tortured, particularly after their last attempted escape, when their guide turned them in. *Don Quixote* resuscitates these bygone times. Like a good genie, he brings us out of the lethargy of an era when "sloth triumphs over energy, indolence over exertion, vice over virtue, arrogance over courage, and theory over practice in arms" (De Cervantes, 2013, p. 406). According to historian Pierre Vilar, Spain's obstinate refusal, in the sixteenth century, to adapt to emerging capitalism, brought the country to bankruptcy three times, and isolated it from the rest of Europe (Vilar, 1971). At the end of the sixteenth century, "the black plague ravaged Castilla, chronic famine, rural exodus, a multitude of delinquents and errant vagabonds were the consequence of the pathetic triumph of an idleness that both aristocrats and rogues, in different ways, set up as an ideal" (De Cervantes, 2001, p. xxiv).

This lethargy is not merely economic. Every day, we encounter war veterans who have become homeless, and not only in the United States, where one third of the homeless are veterans who were given an honourable discharge. They are all thrown into the street by the contempt born of a self-satisfied pacifist philosophy that makes no distinction between murder and self-defence.

When I see the children of these "unbearable" soldiers in my office, their symptoms revive covertly obliterated lives, despite the proclaimed duty to remember; their memory preserves the front lines and the sea depths where their fathers were tortured, torpedoed, shipwrecked, amputated, left for dead and above all stunned to find themselves still alive. Such a dark night of heroic times—the term grates on our ears—is trivialised by diagnoses that "ridigulate" them, to use the delusional language invented by a woman in a psychiatric hospital where I worked, a woman who called herself Sissi, the Austro-Hungarian Empress (Davoine, 2014).

So I tell the children of the soldiers the story of *Don Quixote*: "In a village of La Mancha, the name of which I have no desire to call to mind, there lived not long since one of those gentleman that keep a lance in the lance rack, an old buckler, a lean hack, and a greyhound for coursing." His surname is subject to controversy: "Quixada, Quesda, Quixana", whose meanings are as diverse as jawbone and apple tart. "This, however, is of but little importance to our tale: it will be enough not to stray a hair's breadth from the truth on the telling of it" (De Cervantes, 2013, p. 11).

CHAPTER THREE

PTSD*: post-traumatic son Don Quixote (the post-traumatic son of Cervantes)

From one inheritance to another

Before reading Jean Canavaggio's French translation, I had read that of Jean Cassou,[1] published in 1946. Cassou, one of the first to enroll in the Resistance, was arrested and later wounded. After the war, he became Director of the Modern Art Museum. He published *La mémoire courte* [Short Memory] (Cassou, 1953) the year when the last amnesty laws erased the sequels of collaboration. As Cervantes might have done, he attacked the "easy consensus, the blind consent to reconciliation" and, in true Quixotic fashion, he defined the action of the Resistance as "appalling evidence". In his Preface to *Don Quixote*, Jean Canavaggio also draws attention to the solitude of the hero, the same solitude no doubt felt by anonymous Resistance fighters when their action was divested of its meaning in the interest of post-war politics.

This solitude causes their descendants, in whose memory there is no trace of forgetting, to take themselves for fools, to be terrified; yet, they in no way connect these feelings with the notebooks they bring to me.

---

*PTSD: Post-traumatic stress disorder.

They even find it strange that I take an interest in these soiled diaries containing the names of dead comrades written beside the addresses of those who survived and whom it would be unthinkable not to see again, but whom one never sees again.

These notes are in search of an address where they will be recognised, despite the interjection uttered as a disguise when they are tossed on the table next to me: "Look what this idiot wrote!" Others, like the old soldier, are determined not to write anything, so shocked are they by the rubbish that abounds in embellished accounts. Still, when I open one of these notebooks and start to read out loud, I often see tears in the eyes of the children or grandchildren of those who wrote them.

But Don Quixote has the opposite reaction; he takes for granted all the falsehoods he finds in his favourite books: "[he] gave himself up to reading books of chivalry with such ardor and avidity that he almost entirely neglected the pursuit of his field sports, and even the management of his property" (De Cervantes, 2013, p. 11).

Like Aby Warburg was to do later (Warburg, 1923), Don Quixote also gave up his inheritance in exchange for books: "[…] he sold many an acre of tillage land to buy books of chivalry to read, and brought home as many of them as he could get" (De Cervantes, 2013, p. 11). In other words, he invented the concept of the "bada" which I had used at my own modest scale, and which designates a book acting as a shield against the madness of the world.

Cervantes must have done the same thing, especially in Algiers, where books hijacked by the pirates circulated freely throughout the Ottoman Empire (Garcés, 2002, pp. 92–97) and were a highly-prized booty. Cervantes not only passed down to his son the recourse to books as a remedy against melancholia, but considered them the very agent of his writing. With his sharp, lean silhouette, Don Quixote is literally Cervantes' controversial quill and lance, like the discarded notebooks that contain the true story of a disdained social link. Despite counterfeiters, the work resists all fraud. How? Wittgenstein's terse remark provides the answer.

Ludwig Wittgenstein, an old veteran

Let us go back to Jean Cassou. In the face of the general indifference which he criticised in his short text, we must take into account the contempt with which both civil and military veterans are treated.

This contempt was recognised as a fundamental principle by the philosopher Ludwig Wittgenstein, a veteran of the Austrian Army during the First World War. After his heroic action on the front lines, in 1918 he spent a year in captivity in Monte Cassino. Following his demobilisation, for a long time he refused to take off his old uniform and engaged in eccentric behaviour, not the least of which consisted of foregoing a considerable family inheritance.

Visibly traumatised, he abandoned philosophy despite his reputation as a prodigy at Cambridge, where he was Bertrand Russell's favourite disciple. Like so many other men returning from the war, he caused concern to those close to him by his brutality towards the children he tutored in Upper Austria, and his constant thoughts of suicide. In his *Remarks on Frazer's Golden Bough*, there are segments that echo *Don Quixote*, one of his favourite books: "It is indeed important that I must also make my own the contempt that anyone may have for me, as an essential and significant part of the world as seen by me" (Wittgenstein, 1979a, p. 71).

Don Quixote is a concentrate of all the scorn the world pours on the veteran. The hero is constructed like the notebooks in which the incredible truth is laid out sleepless night after sleepless night. The book undertakes a careful examination of the conditions needed for such truths to be heard, despite the scorn. Its success lies in that every reader can recognise himself in the tale, for wars are everywhere. The feat that it accomplishes is to draw attention to the value of stories literally thrown in the gutter, but whose cost is inscribed in the symptoms of the body and the soul. In this sense, the analyst's office is not very different from the Quixotic tavern. At times, events neglected by official history and devalued by public opinion break through in certain sessions, constituting veritable declarations of war.

Thirty years after Lepanto, while being flogged chapter after chapter, like the analyst session after session, Don Quixote lives through Cervantes' traumatic episodes of revival, affirming the reality of facts considered useless and outdated.

And since nothing matters any longer, he asserts that these war stories shall be considered entirely true; "[…] and what with little sleep and much reading his brains got so dry that he lost his wits. […] it so possessed his mind that the whole fabric of invention and fancy he read of was true, that to him no history in the world had more reality in it" (De Cervantes, 2013, p. 12).

The knight's dry brain is the parchment on which the "truth" is inscribed. Now, he has only to test it by confronting it to actual experience, before publishing the results of the experiment. This will constitute Chapter XXXVIII, "which Treats of the Curious Discourse Don Quixote Delivered on Arms and Letters", a discourse delivered in the tavern, which finally opens the narrative space to the partly auto-biographical tale of the captive.

This assertion, inaugural and adamant, amounts to the "yes" required to start an analysis of madness or trauma. "Yes, I truly believe what you tell me. This is not gullible assent, but rather a pledge of good faith. Yes, I trust you, in consideration of the incredible experience to which you testify." But to appreciate the force of resistance of this "construction of dubious and fabulous tales", we must provide an idea of the circum-stances to which they have to resist.

Let us call PMD the appalling evidence to which it is crucial to resist—not to be confused with MDP, manic depressive psychosis, clas-sified as a bipolar disease in the DSM.[2]

PMD: post modern depression[3]

What, then, are the reasons for this chronic post modern depression, evidenced undeniably by the staggering quantities of antidepressants and sleeping pills prescribed to the citizens of developed countries? Why are we so depressed, although we are so much more liberated, tolerant, open-minded, anti-racist, cultured, and literate than people in other parts of the world and in other times?

Don Quixote concentrates all his efforts on inventing a poetic solu-tion to this problem. Little by little, he disperses confusion by construct-ing a space in which the stain—*mancha*, in Spanish—of the trauma can be washed away. This cathartic space must be clearly distinct from the everyday, as the Latin adjective *sacer* (dedicated) indicates.

What, then, must be done, to erase in this designated space the hell on earth that makes the temper gloomy, lifeless, aggressive, foul-mouthed, vulgar, impatient, intractable? What can be done to change this past which clearly cannot change? What can reanimate the life of the mind and liberate speech in a world where the word has lost its value, in a world without poetry?

When Cervantes gives madness "sanctuary in literature", as Jean-Marie Fritz says (Fritz, 1992), to allow it to exert its cathartic function, he follows in the footsteps of his teachers Erasmus and, of course, Rabelais, as well as the theatre of folly (Bigeard, 1972), a ritual performance which, like it did in Greece, serves to exorcise the abuses of the world and the horrors of war. To ward off the Furies let loose after every combat, *Don Quixote* unleashes the comic force, *vis comica*.

Thus, Cervantes launches his old son on the war path of literary creation "for the support of his own honor" and, above all, "for the service of his country" (De Cervantes, 2013, p. 13). Defender of the word, his hero, like Sancho, has a passion for speaking, because words left unspoken, "rot in [the] stomach". In fact, the true object of the knight's adventures is to be recorded in writing, so as to preserve their memory for ever" (De Cervantes, 2013, pp. 130–131). But keeping the story alive is not easy, when no one wants to hear it.

So, Cervantes has let his aged child loose in the limitless zone of the fibs of childhood which challenge the silence in which adults take refuge. These games are not mere fantasies. Often, they reveal what cannot be said, with outdated obstinacy, out of loyalty to the dead, like in a daydream, destitute, awkward beings unaware of social conventions. They remind us of Savinien Cyrano de Bergerac, or of Colonel Chabert.

Notes

1. Translator of *Don Quichotte*, Paris: Gallimard, 1949.
2. DSM-IV (1994). *Diagnostic and Statistical Manual of Mental Disorders*, published by the American Psychiatric Association, Washington DC.
3. In French, PMD: "Psychose maniaco-dépressive".

CHAPTER FOUR

First sally, first sessions

Taking action

One day, without warning, Don Quixote cut the umbilical cord tying him to his nurturing books, and set out to roam the countryside, conceiving "the strangest notion that every madman in this world hit upon, and that was that he fancied [...] that he should make a knight-errant of himself, roaming the world over [...] in quest of adventures, and putting in practice himself all that he had read of as being the usual practices of knights-errant" (Tissier, 1984, pp. 197–235).

It was time to take action. Based on one of the four principles formulated by Thomas Salmon in 1917 to describe the psychoanalytic treatment of war neuroses (Salmon, 1917), immediacy is a common characteristic in this context. Once in a while, it interrupts periods of immobility where time seems to stand still, with episodes of dazzling acceleration providing an opportunity which must not be missed. Sometimes, this urgency emerges in the very first sessions.

Jenin, son of nothing and no one

One morning, the social worker at the health centre where I worked asked me to see forthwith a man found wandering the streets, and who spoke not a word. I tried to prompt him to provide some fragments of his history. He had no father, but this did not matter, and neither did anything else. He had left school in the eighth grade, although he was a good student. Whenever he was employed, he systematically left any job which he performed well. He could not help it, people frightened him. He ran away like a wild animal, and he had been roaming the streets for years.

He bore the name of a grandfather amputated during the First World War, who had refused a civil servant job intended for wounded war veterans, preferring to set up the small farm on which the boy had grown up. He had roamed the countryside with other kids, looking for birds' nests, while his mother worked in Paris. When she married an alcoholic, the boy had had to change his name in eighth grade and move to Paris, where he had been roaming the streets ever since, we might say. At this point, his tale was cut short by an abysmal silence which I was unable to dispel.

While I reflected on the foreclosure of the Name-of-the Father, without knowing what to make of it, I found myself telling him the story of a short medieval play I happened to be reading: *Jenin, Son of Nothing and No One* (Tissier, 1984, pp. 197–235). It seemed to have come along just at the right time, and I felt impelled to tell him the story.

Jenin badgers his mother to find out who his father is. But all his entreaties fall on deaf ears, his mother refuses to say anything. Discouraged, he finally starts to wonder if he is the son of the priest. The latter makes his appearance at this point, and confesses the obvious—since Jenin is his spitting image. But his mother continues to deny the facts, causing Jenin to conclude his quest by saying that he is the son of no one.

As I was telling the story, a slight smile appeared on the lips of the man who was misnamed. Suddenly, he blushed and the weary face of the once betrayed child seemed to grow younger. When he left, I could not tell if he was going to return or not.

The following week he had something to tell me. When he had spoken with his mother on the phone, she had promptly consented to tell him who his father was. What surprised him was that she did not seem troubled. So why had she kept quiet for so long? It was as if he had been responsible for her silence. It seemed, in fact, that he had even seen this father from time to time, before he was three. After that, this man, who was himself the son of an unwed mother, married a woman in a neighbouring village, and fathered other children. Now, Jenin remembered the way people would fall silent in the café when he went in, while his father was there, unbeknownst to him.

But he was really astonished at the ease with which his mother had given him this information. Where was the problem? Perhaps it was he who was not normal. For her, all was well; the shame belonged to him, along with the unshakable fright that took hold of him in the presence of others. My tale had allowed him to discover that he was the son of someone, in Spanish, literally, *hijo de algo, hidalgo*. He then decided to accompany me for a while, and we were able to start our work.

The tale had loosened tongues and augmented the authority of the word, breaking the wall of silence. Augmentation and authority have a common root: *augeo*, to increase. This is also the action of the "author". To face the *mancha* of his forefathers' trauma, Don Quixote starts by increasing language.

Onomastics and augmentation of language

No sooner said than done. With the same haste, Don Quixote quickly constructed a helmet of pasteboard, which a single slash of his sword, used as a test, demolished. But he set to work at once to strengthen it, and adopted it without any more experiments. What Winnicott (Winnicott, 1971) calls a "safe space", a secure space between imagination and reality, was quickly created, to welcome the surviving forms one chases without knowing, in one's wanderings. Once this was done, in "support of his own honor [and] for the service of his country", Don Quixote proceeded to the selection of names, for when the Other, the guarantor of the word and of good will, collapses in the face of the unnamable, one must have the concrete support of new names.

The first name, Rocinante: "He [...] proceeded to inspect his hack [and] [...] four days were spent in thinking what name to give him. [...] And so, after having composed, struck out, rejected, added to, unmade, and remade a multitude of names out of his memory and fancy, he decided upon calling him Rocinante, a name, to his thinking, lofty, sonorous, and significant of his condition as a hack before he became what he now was, the first and foremost of all the hacks in the world" (De Cervantes, 2013, pp. 13–14). This is an exercise of the body and the spirit, where the sound is as important as the sense.

Admirable invention of a signifier! In the meantime, Rocinante is the personification of a theoretical concept. He is, literally, the motor of transference in the motionless time of traumas, which he will very, very slowly set in motion. True to his name designating a former hack transformed into a front line steed, he is the one who leads the way, like a lead climber, and who takes the initiative of choosing the roads his master will travel. Embodied rhythm, he opens a path into depraved eras, *depravadad de nostra eta,* in which before and after melt into one. He stumbles often in the spheres of catastrophe where only madness can chart new paths.

The second name found is Don Quixote. The adventure-bound analyst must now find a name for himself before setting out on the scampering mount of Transference. "Having got a name for his horse so much to his taste, […] he was eight days more pondering […] till at last he made up his mind to call himself "Don Quixote" […]. Recollecting, however, that the valiant Amadis […] added the name of his kingdom and country to make it famous, and called himself Amadis of Gaul, he, like a good knight, resolved to add on the name of his, and to style himself Don Quixote of La Mancha" (De Cervantes, 2013, p. 14).

This name needed no justification. Unrelated to anything else, it was self-evident. And it would take many more adventures for this name by which "he resolved to call himself" to be confirmed by others. The reader has to wait until Chapter XIX for Sancho to name Don Quixote "The Knight of the Rueful Countenance", a name symbolic enough to be painted on his shield as a coat of arms.

In as much as "the name of the father" founding the symbolic order is inadequate, he has to find his bearings through another agency: a lady of his thoughts, whom he soon came upon in the neighbouring village of Toboso; "[…] he came to the conclusion that nothing more was needed now but to look out for a lady to be in love with; for a knight-errant without love was like a tree without leaves or fruit, or a body without a soul." The important thing was to name her. Thus, the third name chosen was Dulcinea.

She was literally his soul, his Psyche, the destination of his thoughts, to whom one could address the unnamable and unimaginable, belonging to a space-time the Middle Ages called the "space of the wonder".

This sphere, inhabited by monsters, fairies, and wild men, is the actual ground of madness, located in spaces outside civilisation, like the forest, the mountain, but also war, a place where one encounters strange, errant forms, "fairylike" creatures. In the *Theaetetus* (Plato, 1955), Socrates calls them *Stoicheia aloga*, the primal elements outside of reason (*aloga*), not yet linked to other signifiers articulated in *logos*.

Don Quixote describes in the following terms the manner in which such monsters come to submit to *logos*: "As he said to himself, 'If [...] I come across some giant hereabouts [...] and overthrow him in one onslaught, [...] will it not be well to have someone I may send him to as a present, that he may come in and fall on his knees before my sweet lady, and in a humble, submissive voice say, "I am the giant Caraculiambro, [...] vanquished in a single combat by the never sufficiently extolled knight Don Quixote of La Mancha" [...]'" (De Cervantes, 2013, p. 14). The name of the giant is linked with that of this vanquisher before the agency of the Lady. She is a place of inscription where lawless beings submit to the laws of the word, *muthos* and *logos*, myth and reason, producing a clear therapeutic effect: "Oh, how our good gentleman enjoyed the delivery of this speech" (De Cervantes, 2013, p. 14).

As befits a true troubadour, on this frontier with the insane, Don Quixote has just made the lucky find of the Lady. She is, above all, a space of discourse where the dual confrontation between the subject and the monsters that haunt him—real or hallucinatory—may be spoken or thought. His inspiration for this figure comes from "a very good-looking farm girl with whom he had been at one time in love, though, so far as is known, she never knew it nor gave a thought to the matter." She is the fiancée or wife, the war godmother in whom the soldier places his trust, to whom he addresses the letters found in his pockets when he is lifted from the battlefield, the woman who cannot betray him.

As soon as he finds her in a reality, Don Quixote disembodies her, to make of her his consort, his female double. She is a place of resonance for never-before-heard harmonics. Indeed, music is needed to rock a child and appease the furies that haunt young and old alike. "[...] upon her he thought fit to confer the title of Lady of his Thoughts; and after some search for a name which should not be out of harmony with her own, and should suggest and indicate that of a princess and great lady, he decided upon calling her Dulcinea del Toboso [...]— a name, to his mind, musical, uncommon, and significant, like all those he had already bestowed upon himself and the things belonging to him" (De Cervantes, 2013, p. 14).

The panoply of Quixotic transference

The "panoply" constituting psychotic, or Quixotic, transference is made up of four elements:

1. The books in Don Quixote's library, containing the existing myths needed to create new paradigms.
2. Rocinante, the agent of transference, erring at random, speeding up on occasion, but most often a wheezy beast, moving as one body with his rider, trotting recklessly at his command, chasing imaginary monsters.
3. Don Quixote, the analyst of time confusion, who changes his identity to acquire a name.
4. Lastly, Dulcinea, whose name, with its tender vowels and consonants soften the name of her consort, to indicate the space of peace and alliance where the unconceived story will slowly find inscription.

The story of a Dulcinea

A fifty-year-old child came to see me, bringing a grievance against her mother, dating back to the time when she was a baby. When she was only a few months old, her mother was hospitalised, she had heard, although no one confirmed the rumour. Her father remarried quite quickly and everything went back to normal, contributing to convince the baby that she was lucky to have a real family again, and to have escaped from the monster locked up in the asylum, who was never mentioned again. The problem was that this mother continued to haunt her.

I don't know what impelled me to dismiss at once the dispersions heaped upon the woman who had been put away, and who was no longer alive to defend herself. I felt entrusted with defending a Dulcinea. No doubt, this was because I had seen other Melusines (Davoine, 2014, p. 31) in psychiatric hospitals, women who had been betrayed, speaking in heart breaking tones of the children they were never able to see again. But this daughter had seen her mother again ten years later, medicated, having been subjected to electroshock, unrecognisable, talking incessantly. Her feeling that she was seeing a stranger was enhanced by the fact that the letters and gifts sent from the hospital had been systematically ridiculed and hidden. For her own good.

What possessed me to place this mother, whom I did not know, in the role of the Lady of Thoughts? Now, it was I who was mad, and who received impassioned grievances in her place, that were perhaps deserved. This mother was impossible, unbearable, authoritative, disturbed. She was also, apparently, brilliant. Imagine that! She had studied during the war. I quickly deduced that she had been in her twenties in 1940. This got me on my hobby-horse.

During the war? What happened? She might have been in the Resistance. Her daughter spoke with a famous member of that network and learned that as a young girl her mother had been known for her courage, intelligence, decisiveness in action, and leadership. She had been nicknamed "the commander". Then, her former comrade boorishly added some crude insinuations regarding the young woman partisan, to my dismay.

Time passed and my patient kept criticising me. Why did I keep protecting this impossible mother, in the most unreasonable fashion? Indeed, I was defending her blindly. Despite all her failings, she had shown herself trustworthy. One day, when I least expected it, I saw a letter that an old friend of this "crazy" mother had retrieved from a bunch of old papers tossed in a drawer, to give to the daughter, who was pursuing her investigation into what had happened during the war.

The heading of the letter startled me: "Dear Françoise"—the name of the friend—as if the letter was addressed to me. Sent from an asylum, the letter spoke of "my war" and recounted very simply but very precisely, specifying places and dates, how on a certain occasion she had saved her network, by going on bicycle to retrieve a suitcase of false papers from a hiding place that informants had just revealed to the Germans. She had gotten away under a shower of bullets, saved by the iron gates of the underground that closed behind her just after she passed through. The letter spoke of all the comrades who were betrayed and executed, of the hiding places, of the woman informer among them, of being on the run, and of how she had refused the overly insistent advances of the famous comrade, whom she found too ugly. The betrayal of some of the network members was there as well, recorded in black and white.

Don Quixote's scanty belongings give us access to phantoms locked up in asylums, and to a true testimony, still discounted today. But this gear, made up of any old odds and ends, is more than just junk. In fact, it operates like an efficient lie detector and trap for knaves, when it comes to unearthing "the touchstone of truth" (De Cervantes, 2013, p. 431).

Cervantes to his son: "you're on your own!"

In fact, the author—and the father—of Don Quixote sends him, totally unprepared, to analyse a confusion similar to what was described above.

One morning, at dawn, the old soldier of Lepanto has his son set off from somewhere in the countryside, dressed any old way, wearing his patched-up helmet fastened with the famous green ribbons, bearing outdated weapons, with no provisions other than acorns and wild grasses, hard bread and old cheese to be washed down with water. The old soldier used to say: "Don't talk to me about picnics and camping." In addition, there was the lack of sleep, the nights in rough conditions, the bad treatment innkeepers inflicted on the penniless, and especially the inadequate logistics, in this case limited to Rocinante's girth which breaks, sending the knight into the dust as soon as he engages in his first attack. "We went off to war wearing puttees and carrying Chassepot rifles from the last war, that were bigger than we were", as the old soldier says.

Whenever he spoke of Arms and Letters, Don Quixote described to his audience the occurrence of random events of war, where everything is constantly changing, where all certainties have come crashing down. He had had a good teacher, since his father, Cervantes, propelled him into the improbable world in which he himself had been plunged at the age of twenty, a world very different than the heroic novels he might have perused in his father's barber shop. This is the common challenge issued by veterans of the previous war to their sons: "Go see for yourself, and try to learn a lesson, by coming back not so much with medals, but with the kind of stories I was not able to tell you. In any case, you have to live through it to understand. Still, you will never know what it was like for us."

For the worst part is the homecoming, ten years later, when everyone has forgotten what you cannot forget. "You are thrown down the toilet and they dump a diarrhea of insults on you every five minutes", cried out a Vietnam veteran one day, to psychologist Jonathan Shay. Wilfred Bion, a veteran of the First World War, says: "We had passed from insignificance (Bion, 1982, p. 286) to irrelevance." The do-gooders who built successful careers during your absence take you for brutes, robots, lowbrow adventurers.

When Cervantes returned from Algiers, he was looked upon with suspicion by the same do-gooders, he disturbed them, he was out of sync. This is the marginal state in which he sends Don Quixote to meet the normal world. And still, health officials, like the governess, the barber, and the curate, ask in all seriousness why these people are unable to reintegrate into society.

This question deserves the answer that was given by the licentiate Marquez Torres to the ambassador of France, Noël Brûlard de Sillery, in 1615, one year before Cervantes's death (Canavaggio, 1991, pp. 300–301). The French nobleman had been sent to Spain with a retinue of learned gentlemen fond of literature, to negotiate the marriage of Louis XIII with Anne of Austria, princess of Spain. They enquired about the famous Cervantes, author of *Galate* "which some of them almost knew by heart", held in high esteem in France. "They questioned me closely about his age, his profession, his quality and quantity."

The licentiate had to disappoint these admirers. "I found myself forced to tell them that he was old, a soldier, a gentleman and poor." The French presumed that such a talented man would be supported by the State. "Then Spain does not make such a man rich and support him from the public treasury?" Another Frenchman retorted with this witty remark: "If poverty will force him to write, then may it please God that he never have wealth, so that, though he is poor, he may make the whole world rich with his works."

About the time this dialogue took place, Cervantes entered the Franciscan Order and took his vows, including the vow of poverty. But the poverty of which the licentiate speaks to Cervantes' aficionados, the source of an impulse to write, characterises the soldier who, despite his meagre wages, is often "liberal and profuse", like the father of the captive in Chapter XXXIX, having, above all, a wealth of stories to tell. Don Quixote always made a clear distinction between courtiers expert in finance who "only know enemies in pictures", and knights who know them "in their own real shapes", but are unable to amass fortunes (De Cervantes, 2013, p. 429).

Still, another poverty exists, hidden under flashy appearances: the symbolic impoverishment that exerts its fascination downward across the social hierarchy, through the worship of idleness. Don Quixote inherited from his father the absolute incapacity to submit to the prevailing attitudes of his era, described by turns as "perverse, catastrophic and depraved". Having set off to carry out the work of a knight-errant, refusing to participate in the ambient denial, he makes his way alone, in warrior's garb, into a world he is going to disturb. In the guise of a madman, Cervantes has a few scores to settle.

Heaven sent

Don Quixote had scarcely sallied forth when he was assailed by doubt about his enterprise. The entire troupe constituted of himself, Rocinante and his far-off Dulcinea lacked symbolic consecration. The Middle Ages are definitely in the past, feudal values are out of date. Therefore, by leaving behind books on chivalry, he abandons literature in favour of reviving the spirit of a social link that is disappearing at the dawn of the modern era.

Astride a steed evoking an image more phlegmatic than phallic, he decides to have himself dubbed a knight by the first one he comes across, putting off until later the inscription of his deeds—the true objective of an analysis of trauma. "Who knows but that in time to come, when the veracious history of my famous deeds is made known, the sage who writes it, when he has to set forth my first sally on the early morning, will do it after this fashion?" (De Cervantes, 2013, p. 15).

Still, when night is falling and one is alone, hungry, without resources, deep in the countryside, and far from home, the first adventure consists of finding a place to sleep and something to eat. In these conditions, the house that offers you a bed and a meal is a castle. It is easy to imagine that, for Don Quixote, the first tavern that undergoes such a metamorphosis revives memories of his readings, and awakens, above all, the nostalgia of a man exiled far from his homeland.

Don Quixote teaches us that the happenstance which guides Rocinante is the master governing all survival stories. Signals strewn here and there, strangers met without reason become reliable guides, heaven sent; the ancient Greeks called them *kledones*, "an unforeseen parallel, a fortuitous consonance that can constitute a providential warning" (Flacelière, 1961, pp. 18–21).

Omens: kledones

The first *kledon* is the sound of a horn that signals a change of atmosphere in the inn where Don Quixote has arrived. Like the herald announcing the start of tournaments, it introduces the entry into the metamorphoses of the Baroque. "At this moment it so happened that a swineherd who was going through the stubbles collecting a drove of pigs [...] gave a blast of his horn" (De Cervantes, 2013, p. 17). Like in the Celtic legend of Avalon, the road of wonders can only be found by chance. It is as if a barely perceptible something altered Rocinante's placid pace to allow a dimension abounding with chivalry to appear. These *kledones* introduce a distortion in time-space perception. "Heaven sent", they allow one world to shift to another.

Not so long ago, I happened to be standing on a railway platform. The cold, the darkness, the falling snow suddenly impelled me to take off along the tracks, determined not to board the train that would have taken me back to Paris peacefully. I was called crazy, but my mind was set. This unexpected crisis, triggered by mere weather conditions, convinced me that this particular train, in this sinister station, would be blown up just as surely as the trains that blew up during the war, and in which I travelled as a baby, cradled in a suitcase, while my father, on the alert, would dash into the toilet to escape through the skylight when German soldiers boarded the train. When I remembered the stories I had been told about these events of which I had no recollection, I went back to the railway station, took the train and had an undisturbed trip.

For Don Quixote, the solemn trumpet call is confirmed by the coincidental arrival, at the very same moment, of "a sowgelder, who, as he approached, sounded his reed pipe four or five times" (De Cervantes, 2013, p. 19). The tone was set. From then on, all the inns would be castles where one could demand that: "[...] whatever it be let it come quickly, for the burden and pressure of arms cannot be borne without support to the inside."

Thus, the tavern becomes a castle for those who are dying of hunger or are in dire need of sleep; the sound of the reed pipe becomes heavenly music; soggy cod becomes fresh water trout; and mouldy bread becomes a sweet bun. Women of easy virtue become gracious ladies, whose worth in fact is greater, since they feed him like a fledgling fallen from the nest, for they cannot sever the ribbons of his helmet. This scene of kindness, literally heaven sent, will be disenchanted later by the easy comfort of peacetime. This scene takes place outside time, in the future anterior, which must be produced to make it come into existence.

The gaiety of courtly love

Contrary to Circe, Don Quixote breaks the spell and transforms wenches into ladies. Without using any of the insulting names that make them social outcasts, he forces them to participate in his defiance of the social order. The inn becomes a place of enchantment, where the mechanisms that reify people are thrown out of gear by the grace of a different perception. The Cervantian remedy reintroduces wonder in everyday life and overturns hierarchies, without falling into a fascination with the seedy, nor engaging in the demagogical discourse that exploits human misery.

Here, Cervantes takes the stance opposed to that of the author of La Celestina (De Rojas, 2009), the first play of the Spanish repertoire, published in 1499, which he admired so much that he could recite entire passages by heart. This masterful play was given various interpretations. Some praised the madam Celestina for her skill in ruining the patriarchal order of the city; others, like Bataillon (Bataillon, 1961), took the text literally and focused on the corrupt social relationships that lead to the death and suicide of young masters and their valets. As for Cervantes, the main role he attributes to "ladies of the night" is entirely different. Of all their functions, he retains only the solace.

These women are nurturing, and the foremost nourishment they offer is gaiety. Don Quixote to addresses them as "maidens waiting on himself", which produces such a fit of joy that the knight feels compelled to make a remonstrance. "[…] when they heard themselves called maidens, a thing so much out of their line, they could not restrain their laughter, which made Don Quixote wax indignant and say: 'Modesty becomes the fair, and moreover laughter that has little cause is great silliness; this, however, I say not to pain or anger you, for my desire is none other than to serve you'" (De Cervantes, 2013, p. 17). Here, we enter the "gay science" sphere of courtly love, thanks to a gift named the "gift of the gab" by the Celts, or the "give away" by the Plains Indians. This gift transforms a tavern, or even a brothel, into a "gateless gate" as Zen philosophy calls it (Collinson, Plant, & Wilkinson, 2000), through which one passes without paying, advancing towards the reconquest (la reconquista) of language.

In contrast to the stifling atmosphere of picaresque novels, the Quixotic universe restores the honour of damsels and allows them to escape from their condition through the freedom they grant themselves to rejoice with Don Quixote, and not at his expense. Thus, they introduce a whole series of therapeutic characters who enter his delusional universe to play opposite him.

The innkeeper as vangard of a psychotherapy

It is, in fact impossible to participate in a delusion without playing one's own part honestly. These Mary Magdalenes whose fits of laughter provoke Don Quixote's indignation, prefigure Maritornes, just as the fat innkeeper, described as "something of a wag", prefigures Sancho. Thus, from the start, a distinction is established between those who play the game with Don Quixote and those who make fun of him.

In this respect, the innkeeper's performance is exemplary. He consents to participate in the hero's delusion, but addresses him as a counter hero, describing himself as a knight who had not lacked for adventure in his younger days, had done "many wrongs, cheating many widows, ruining maids and swindling minors". He finally agrees to "have him dubbed a knight, and so thoroughly dubbed that nobody could be more so" (De Cervantes, 2013, p. 21). Still, the innkeeper enters Don Quixote's delusion in order to protect him from danger, instead of propelling him towards an apocalyptic outcome.

Like Gaetano Benedetti, who warns analysts not to destroy a delusion, but rather to enter it in good faith by transforming its images positively (Benedetti, 1998, pp. 97–101), the innkeeper advises Don Quixote never from then on to travel without money, clean shirts, and ointments, as well as a proper squire to treat his wounds. "He therefore advised him (and, as his godson so soon to be, he might even command him) never from that time forth to travel without money and the usual requirements, and he would find the advantage of them when he least expected it" (De Cervantes, 2013, p. 21).

This ready-made statement is a good illustration of the forsaking of causality, to make room for the emergence of the unexpected. It precedes the first critical episode, in which Don Quixote knocks out two muleteers, one after the other. In order to water his mules, each man had seen fit to remove Don Quixote's armour, which lay on the trough. Thus, the space the hero alone considered sacred was desecrated. The shouts and blows that followed were enough to re-establish the psychiatric diagnosis that does away with his accountability before the law: "The landlord shouted to them to leave him alone, for he had already told them that he was mad, and as a madman he would not be accountable even if he killed them all" (De Cervantes, 2013, pp. 22–23).

This scene introduces a long series of crises that are always triggered by a clash between ordinary reality and the sphere of the sacred. Then, the slightest thing—in this case, a heap of rusty metal—acts as a talisman and magical protection from danger. But when the sphere of reality and that of the sacred collide, sparks always fly. The clash between the banality of ordinary objects and their symbolic power is always explosive.

The same is true of the inn, confirmed as a space of metamorphoses in which stale language games are revived by a good genie that has taken the shape of an old scarecrow endlessly reborn, as illustrated by the early-morning departure of the hero on the second day, at the beginning of Chapter IV. "Day was dawning when Don Quixote quit the inn, so happy, so gay, so exhilarated at finding himself now dubbed a knight, that his joy was like to burst his horse girths" (De Cervantes, 2013, p. 25).

Rocinante caught the scent of oats and trotted more briskly. Here, the steed can truly be said to be the motor of transference: "He hardly seemed to tread the earth." Wanting to heed the advice of the innkeeper, Don Quixote "reckoned upon securing a farm laborer, a neighbor of his, a poor man with a family, but very well qualified for the office of squire to a knight" (De Cervantes, 2013, p. 25).

Thus, a paradigm is created in the midst of a herd of pigs that have been led there to be castrated. The swine are going to return to trample him shortly before his death, in the "bristly adventure" of the second part of the book (De Cervantes, 2013, p. 794). In the interval between these two droves of pigs, the reader finds, in each episode, the same psychodynamic process:

- The slightest thing interferes with the advance of the hero.
- Don Quixote starts to rave, insisting on the existence of another traumatic universe superimposed on everyday reality.
- The reason for loss of reason is found more or less by therapeutic figures, Sancho being the first, while other individuals play a "psychiatric" role.

But each time the sphere of speech is augmented, until the next grain of sand causes the Quixotic quartet to go off the rails again.

First traumatic revival: humanitarian intervention

This can be brought about, for instance, by Don Quixote's falling into the contradictions inherent to humanitarian action. Is it enough to follow one's heart? What price will have to be paid by the one receiving aid for the good conscience of his saviour? Here, the novel grapples with the goodness of compassionate souls, on account of which Cervantes no doubt had occasion to suffer. In any case, this is the first mission he assigns to his son.

This time, the thing which interferes with the advance of the little troupe is totally legitimate and rational. The appeal comes in the form of a plaintive voice, "feeble cries as of someone in distress" (De Cervantes, 2013, p. 25). It is the voice of a fifteen-year old youth, Andrés, flogged with a belt by his master, a farmer. This scene of the flogging of a young man by a brute seems to come straight from the bagnios of Algiers.

Here, Cervantes draws a parallel between political torture and domestic torture, from the standpoint of the one subjected to it. Don Quixote's reaction constitutes a lesson to this day. Listening only to his heart, he frees the boy and commands his master to pay his wages, according to the law. Justice demands nothing less. Then he lectures the brute on the double exploitation of the health and the labour of the youth, and goes off with the good conscience of a liberator and undoer of wrongs.

As soon as his back is turned, the master redoubles his violence against the boy. The defence of victims reveals its limitations, as long as the brute is not neutralised. Wild with rage, the torturer spews humanitarian rhetoric. "Come here, my son, I want to pay you what I owe you, as that undoer of wrongs has commanded me" (De Cervantes, 2013, p. 27). There follows a flogging that leaves the boy nearly dead. He "went off weeping, while his master stood laughing".

This scene is worth a thousand words. It shows that the ritual incantation of ideals of justice exacerbates sadistic impulses. One does not negotiate with a torturer by trying to appeal to his better nature. There is no point in attempting to educate him, move him to pity, humanise him or even understand him. It is wiser to help his victim escape, and render the torturer harmless. This is where we first see that Don Quixote's madness is directed against the perversion of the world. Cervantes points this out several times. He raises a contemporary question: what is the difference between Don Quixote's violence and that of Andrés' master, since both have the same traumatic effect on the child?

The knight explodes in broad daylight, without holding back. Is this explosion comparable to orgiastic violence fostered covertly? As for repentance, is it sufficient? Cervantes' answer is no, as we see twenty-seven chapters later, when Don Quixote meets Andrés again, and the boy refuses to forgive him.

Cursing vehemently the impotence of the knight's complicit humanitarianism, the youth reveals the underpinnings of the brute's narcissism, long before Recamier (Recamier, 1992). gave us his analysis of narcissistic perversion: "[...] when your worship abused him so out of measure, and gave him so many hard words, his anger was kindled; and as he could not revenge himself on you, as soon as he saw you had left him the storm burst upon me in such a way, that I feel as if I should never be a man again" (De Cervantes, 2013, p. 226). The least blemish on the image of an egocrat is fatal. The farmer avenged himself on Andrés for the fact that someone had witnessed his cruelty. Andrés' judgment is irrevocable. Don Quixote can only remain silent in the face of the child's mutilation and malediction: "For the love of God, sir knight-errant, if you ever meet me again, though you may see them cutting me to pieces, give me no aid or succor, but leave me to my misfortune, which will not be so great but that a greater will come to me by being helped by your worship, on whom and all the knights-errant that have ever been born God send his curse." Don Quixote recognises his failure and, despite his own violence, shows he has nothing in common with the pervert, who can never bring his own deeds into question.

Second traumatic revival: the Toledo traders

After Don Quixote continues on his way, leaving behind the scene of abuse of the child, ever in search of something new, an outlandish vision crosses his path. This sight triggers the emergence of another time-space incongruous with reality. In the distance can be seen six people under their sunshades, who were "some Toledo traders on their way to buy silk at Murcia" (De Cervantes, 2013, p. 28). This group, glimpsed against the light, associated with the torture he had just witnessed, revives in his mind's eye Algeria with its itinerant caravans.

The second moment is one of defiance. For the first time, Dulcinea's name is proclaimed *urbi et orbi*, demanding the recognition of the Lady, after the fathers had shown themselves unworthy. "All the world stand, unless all the world confess that in all the world there is no maiden fairer than the Empress of La Mancha, the peerless Dulcinea del Toboso" (De Cervantes, 2013, p. 28).

The third moment is an outburst of insults. The traders play at trading one thing for another, want to see the merchandise to assess her qualities, and depossess Dulcinea of her purely nominal function. "[…] even though her portrait should show her blind of one eye, and distilling vermilion and sulphur from the other, we would nevertheless, to gratify your worship, say all in her favour that you desire" (De Cervantes, 2013, p. 29).

An anti-blason of the feminine body will be used by Sancho to convince us that all that counts is the Lady's name, regardless of reality. But for the moment, she serves as a mirror to the night with a shaky self-image. The self-image of a character who lacks an ego to such a great extent depends above all on the integrity of his consort, his twin, the soul of his life. Soon Sancho will be the one able to watch over his master and take care of him.

Now, we come to the fourth moment, that of immediacy, in which all duration is abolished. He lashed out, saying "[…] ye must pay for the blasphemy […]" and "he charged with level lance against the one who had spoken, with such fury and fierceness that, if luck had not contrived that Rocinante should stumble midway […]".

Again, the clash takes place at the explosive point of contact between the sphere of the sacred, where Don Quixote places his Lady, and the sphere of the traders. Their blasphemy causes a loss of sense that literally evicts him from good sense, and makes him frenzied. This confrontation will be repeated as many times as necessary, to open an ever-widening time-space of war and combat.

We now return to the initial catastrophe: Rocinante is said to "stumble midway and come down" (De Cervantes, 2013, p. 29), and while Don Quixote is stretched on the ground, one of the muleteers began to strike him fiercely, while he "never ceased threatening heaven, and earth, and the brigands, for such they seemed to him." What is at stake now is freedom of speech, and the hero refuses to be silenced.

Finally, we come to the last moment, that of therapy. It is divided into four parts corresponding to the four principles—immediacy, proximity, expectancy, and simplicity—defined for the American Army in 1917 by Thomas Salmon (Salmon, 1917) who after working as a physician at the Immigration station on Ellis Island, completed a mission in the trenches in France.

Psychoanalytic session with the neighbour

Instead of performing diagnostic tests and taking antipsychotic drugs, it is better to turn right away to the comfort of familiar things: "my favourite things" of Julie Andrews' song in *The Sound of Music* (Wise, 1965). In the film, these little things, that are sometimes nothing more than children's songs, can even offer resistance to the Nazis. Surviving songs are, for Don Quixote, songs of heroic deeds and *romanceros*, which he recites to resist hardships. Therapy is found first and foremost in literature. "Finding, then, that in fact he could not move, he thought himself of having recourse to his usual remedy, which was to think of some passage in his books [...]" (De Cervantes, 2013, p. 30).

Instant recourse to this remedy is combined with the arrival of a peasant who tends to Don Quixote. This neighbour, Pedro Alonso, personifies kindness on the battlefield, the kindness of those who do not ask whether the wounded man is mad or not. This principle of proximity and simplicity reaches its full extent with the arrival of Sancho.

Don Quixote proclaims the return of hope, against all odds, just as Erasmus does in his *In Praise of Folly* (Erasmus, 2003). Speaking to Pedro Alonso, Don Quixote declares: "I know who I am and I know that I may be not only those I have named, but all the Twelve Peers of France and even all the Nine Worthies" (De Cervantes, 2013, p. 31). Here, the "I" resonates with the tones of songs of heroic deeds, through what Gregory Nagy calls "identity fusion" with the authors of epic tales (Nagy, 1996). In the same way, when I am getting nowhere in an analysis, to find my way back from the uncanny, I sometimes recite passages of *Don Quixote* to myself.

A "diverting scrutiny" (De Cervantes, 2013, p. 34)

This feeling of strangeness—*unheimlich*—, takes hold of the knight when his neighbour tactfully leads him back to his house, after he "waited until it was a little later that the belaboured gentleman might not be seen riding in such a miserable trim" (De Cervantes, 2013, p. 32). Standing outside the door, both of them hear an animated discussion going on inside between the niece, the housekeeper, the barber, and the curate, all speaking "in a loud voice". The discussion concerns the saving of "the finest understanding there was in all La Mancha", by means of a "public judgment [for the books to] be condemned to the flames [...]" (De Cervantes, 2013, p. 32). Don Quixote and the peasant heard all this. But the knight was exhausted and all he wanted just then was to eat something and be left to sleep, while a plan of extermination was being devised, which entered his dormant state of consciousness.

Here, madness is presented in a rather contemporary organicist perspective. Since the knight's brain is injured by the books he reads, these books must be burned; it must be remembered that all this is taking place before the invention of electrical or chemical means of numbing the mind and making all reading impossible.

Opinions were already divided, between proponents of a final solution and the more moderate defenders of a more selective elimination. The niece and the housekeeper hold a radical view: they blame their own murderous folly on the books. "[...] there is no reason for showing mercy to any of them [said the niece], they have every one of them done mischief. The housekeeper said the same, so eager were they both for the slaughter of those innocents" (De Cervantes, 2013, p. 34). Despite biotechnical advances, these methods are still in use today.

As for the barber and the curate, their scrutiny is more rational. The latter, displaying as much humanism as a Red Guard or a Brown Guard, "would burn with them the father who begot me if he were going about in the guise of a knight-errant." The smell of pyres and other crematoriums overpowers all the institutional might of medicine and academia. The works condemned to be burned include "The Four Books of Amadis of Gaul [...] the founder of so vile a sect" (De Cervantes, 2013, p. 34), the books that were the dearest to the heart of Don Quixote.

At first, the book hunt is undertaken in a mocking manner. The authors who are destroyed are the ones who torture their readers with "the stiffness and dryness of [...] style" (De Cervantes, 2013, p. 34), or with a heaviness of plot that "stands in need of a little rhubarb to purge their excess of bile" (De Cervantes, 2013, p. 36). Translators deserve the same fate, for they rob the author "of a great deal of his natural force" (De Cervantes, 2013, p. 36).

But soon the Gang of Four is overcome with iconoclastic fervour. As the destruction accelerates, they are seized by a murderous frenzy: " [...] not caring to tire himself with reading more books of chivalry, [the barber] told the housekeeper to take all the big ones and throw them into the yard. It was not said to one dull or deaf, but to one who enjoyed burning them more than weaving the broadest and finest web that could be; and seizing about eight at a time, she flung them out of the window" (De Cervantes, 2013, p. 36). This is how cultured clergymen avail themselves of secular manpower.

Delusion is the enemy; its presumed cause must be eliminated. But Cervantes shows that madness does not follow causalist reasoning, unless the outcome is fanaticism, as evidenced in the twentieth century by murderous shock treatments—lobotomy, Cardizol injections, malaria therapy, insulin induced coma, electric shock—that were in fashion consecutively, and were presented by their advocates as scientific advances.

The "process", as it is called in Latin America, is carried out based on a simplistic, inalterable protocol. "And some must have been consumed that deserved preservation in everlasting archives, but their fate and the laziness of the examiner did not permit it [...]" (De Cervantes, 2013, pp. 40–41).

Cervantes insists on the stupidity that causes the books to be tossed out the window, to cries of "into the yard with them!" As a former Chinese Red Guard testifies, a man who flung many books into the yard, and sometimes their authors: "We preached counterculture but knew nothing about culture." When righteous minds deal with culture by the light of torches, they provide proof for the saying: "The innocent pay for the guilty."

Cervantes against the picaros

In Chapter VI, Cervantes sets himself the task of distinguishing between madness and fanaticism. To avoid the fires of hell, the housekeeper tries to subdue her own excitement by the sprinkling of holy water, while the curate and the barber attempt to achieve the same aim through rationalist discourse. But, here again, the choice of doing the deed in secret differentiates the pronouncements of the four accomplices from those of Don Quixote. According to Hannah Arendt, this is the distinguishing mark of totalitarian systems (Arendt, 1951, p. 419).

The literary pogrom is planned without Don Quixote's knowledge, behind closed doors, and while he is sleeping. Conversely, the knight, whose decisions are categorical, always acts alone. He makes his attacks in the open, by surprise and without accomplices. Later, Sancho would often complain about having to take part in totally unplanned actions.

Cervantes was literally thrown into slavery for five years. As punishment for his four attempted escapes, he was within an inch of impalement, the stake, drowning, the mutilations and floggings that killed his companions. Today, it is said that tortures inflicted on slaves around the Mediterranean can be compared to gulags where the captives died of hunger, of poverty and of exhaustion (Davis, 2004). But Cervantes is not attempting to paint horrors for voyeuristic readers. Like many others, he experienced agony that brought him to the brink of unconsciousness, and he thought he was about to die on many occasions; still, what interests him is not to inspire fascination, but to show how to recover and go on living.

His solution always involves escaping from grim worlds. He is familiar enough with poverty and marginality not to glorify them, and to praise the merits of creative survival. As Maurice Molho writes in his Preface to *Picaresque Novels* (Molho, 1968, pp. LXIV & LXXXII), "Turning away from the stifling atmosphere and the stench of latrines of the slums of picaresque novels, Cervantes prefers the fresh air on the rider's face, and the scent of the outdoors, or that of basil planted in an old, cracked pot, placed in the middle of a well-swept courtyard." Thus, the stifling atmosphere of the book-burning turns to mockery. Not the hilarity of the torturer, but the gaiety of the clown, who "takes ownership of the contempt the world shows him", to thumb his nose at too much seriousness.

Cervantian laughter does not delight in righteous indignation, and does not succumb to self-pity. Leaving behind the status of victim, which he knew only too well, he goes on the offensive and uses the fire lit by the arsonists to shed light on what he has to say. Instead of naively condemning the violence that produced it, Cervantes uses the devastating weapon of comic force to rekindle the inspiration that brought into being his first plays and pastoral romances.

Pastoral romances

In the midst of the book-burning Cervantes enters the scene unexpectedly as an author, to save from the flames, in extremis, his favourite books and, above all, his own works. As a result, he saves the famous *Amadis of Gaul* (1508), as well as *Tirante el Blanco* (1490), which is to the curate's liking because in it "knights eat and sleep, and die in their beds, and make their wills before dying [...]" (De Cervantes, 2013, p. 37). Other books are saved as well: Ariosto's *Orlando Furioso* (1532), *Diana* by the Portuguese poet Montemayor (1559), the first pastoral novel published in Castilian Spanish; but above all and most importantly, *La Galatea*, presented as the work of a man who "has had more experience in reverses than in verses" (De Cervantes, 2013, p. 39). Quite a recommendation! With the *Galate*, other works, written by friends cited in the pastoral romance twenty years earlier, were also preserved from the flames.

But twenty years is a long time. Between 1584, when *La Galatea* was published, until the First Part of *Don Quixote* was published in 1605, that is, from the time Cervantes was thirty-seven until he was fifty-eight, no other works were published. Books tossed out the window—they might well have been Cervantes' perception of the works he was prevented from writing during this time. He might have asked himself for what strange reason he had left his pastoral work unfinished. But he returned to it, in a roundabout way, when he wrote the episode of the shepherdess Marcela (De Cervantes, 2013, pp. 64–75), and throughout the novel, until the end of the Second Part.

Towards the end of his adventures, no longer in the grip of delusion, Don Quixote is tempted by the pastoral life, presenting it to Sancho in parodic terms: "[...] and I under the name of the shepherd Quixotise and thou as the shepherd Panzino, we will roam the woods and groves and meadows singing songs here, lamenting in elegies there [...]. Nickolas the barber may call himself Niculoso [...]" (De Cervantes, 2013, p. 791). This is why his niece, who knows him well, expresses the fear, early in the First Part of the Book, that "it would be no wonder if, after being cured of his chivalry disorder, my uncle took a fancy to turn shepherd or, what would be still worse, [turns] poet, which they say is an incurable and infectious malady" (De Cervantes, 2013, p. 37).

Actually, *Don Quixote* describes a series of pastoral adventures with disastrous outcomes, be it Grisostomo's suicide in Chapter XII, or Leandra's ruin in Chapter LI. In fact, the *Galate* had not ended well either. Instead of putting an end to the soldier's troubles, it brought them back.

The romance of the pastoral world seems tied to war. It appears as a breath of fresh air after the fires of hell. When Cervantes returned from war, he constructed the plot of the *Galate* around the threat menacing the shepherdess: that of being abducted by a Portuguese poet. Indeed, the Portuguese poet Camoens (1525–1580) died in poverty at the same period. This, despite the fact that he had saved *Os Lusiades*, a masterpiece of Portuguese literature, during a shipwreck off the coast of *Goa* in 1561, by jumping into the sea holding his manuscript above the water, while his ship was sinking with everyone aboard. Maimed like Cervantes, blinded in one eye in a battle in Morocco, he too was imprisoned several times, and was able to live in exile for over fifteen years, five of which he spent in Macao as "custodian for the property of the dead and absent". *Os Luisiades* was published in 1572, the year which followed the battle of Lepanto, but Camoens did not live to enjoy his fame.

Like Don Quixote, waking to find that his books have been destroyed, the Portuguese poet must have felt that his own work was out of his reach.

Cognitive dissonance

The Cervantian analysis of genocidal logic presents the destruction of all books of chivalry as a must, even though some books escape this faith. When such pseudo-scientific causalist reasoning is pushed to the limits of brutality, we have seen it invoke historic materialism or eugenics to justify the elimination of millions of people, "showing [no] mercy to any of them; [for] they have every one of them done mischief." The same rule applies to the psychiatric confinement of political opponents accused of having "lost their minds" under the influence of suspicious books. In both cases, the same determinism condemns, generation after generation, those who do not have the right ideas; or impel children to inform on their parents, just like Don Quixote's niece delivers her uncle to the authorities: "the curate asked the niece for the keys of the room where the books, the authors of all the mischief, were, and right willingly she gave them. They all went in [...]" (De Cervantes, 2013, p. 34).

However, the profanation of the enchanted space of books does not go undetected by the seismograph of Don Quixote's dreams. What was plotted and carried out there while he slept was perceived. His violent awakening registers subliminally the theft in progress of hundreds of his big books, and their incineration. "At this instant Don Quixote began shouting out, 'Here, here, valiant knights! Here is need for you to put forth the might of your strong arms, for they of the Court are gaining the mastery in the tourney!'" (De Cervantes, 2013, p. 40).

Indeed, the main signifiers of disaster are designated: the "arms" and "the Court". The books were passed from hand to hand, from arm to arm, to be thrown into the courtyard, where the tourney ended in their cremation. The infamy is perceived through the dream, so close to delusion in this instance. The sleeper is prevented from acting by physical incapacity; usually, it is the dream, the guardian of sleep, which filters the unconscious traumatic material.

But when the signifiers are unable to filter the magnitude of the catastrophe taking place at that very moment, the physical incapacity is cancelled and replaced with a literal demonstration. "When they reached Don Quixote he was already out of bed, and was still shouting and raving, and slashing and cutting all around, as wide awake as if he had never slept. They closed with him and by force got him back to bed [...]" (De Cervantes, 2013, p. 40). A perfect illustration of the paradigm reformulated by Wittgenstein after the traumas of the First World War: "Whereof one cannot speak, thereof one [cannot help showing the unsayable]." The somnambulistic enactment shows the battle the hero has to fight against the people in the courtyard (below), and poetically transposes to Charlemagne's Court—where Archibishop Turpin is the equivalent of the curate—the truth which the inquisitional court refuses to tell him.

Thus, Don Quixote's action will take place a little later, when none of the four accomplices is willing to admit the offence. Certain that they were acting with good reason, they plotted in secret for his good, and avoided participating in the fight he calls for to restore his rights. Once again, this indifference devoid of feeling reveals perversion. No abuser ever wants to admit his wrongdoings, except when faking compassion linked with compliance to orders, and with condescendence towards the victim. "'Hush, gossip', said the curate, '[...]; for the present let your worship have a care of your health, for it seems to me that you are over fatigued, if not badly wounded'."

Chronically resistant to pity, Don Quixote replies: "Wounded, no, but bruised and battered no doubt [...]. For the present let them bring something to eat, [...] and leave it to me to avenge myself" (De Cervantes, 2013, p. 40). He eats and falls asleep again at once. His vengeance, *nemesis* in Greek, and his anger, *menis*, will draw their mad energy, *mania*, from the betrayal of those closest to him, which is clearly revealed in this passage.

"Que todo lo cura, todo es locura"

The causalist mechanism of totalitarian systems maintains itself, secretly, through systematic denial of the truth. "One of the remedies that the curate and the barber immediately applied to their friend's disorder was to wall up and plaster the room where the books were, so that when he got up he should not find them (possibly the cause being removed the effect might cease), and they might say that a magician had carried them off, room and all: and this was done with all despatch" (De Cervantes, 2013, p. 41).

This describes the experiential construction of PTSD (post traumatic stress disorder) through the assertion of an official, adulterated version that Hannah Arendt calls "fictitious" (Arendt, 1951, p. 91).

A pasteboard world is constructed in haste, to throw doubt on true impressions. This is the birth of the enchanter, who will gain respectability a little later under the guise of Descartes' Evil Genius. First encountered in *Discourse on Method* in 1637 (Descartes, 2003), he had been created by the philosopher fifteen years earlier, while he fought in the Thirty-Year War, and had a vision on Saint Martin's Eve, in a stove-heated room in Ulm, the winter quarters of the army.

Clearly a collaborator, the housekeeper follows the party line: "Two days later Don Quixote got up, and the first thing he did was to go and look at this books, and not finding the room where he had left it, [...] after a good while he asked the housekeeper where about was the room that held his books." In effect, all these books exist even more vividly in the present now that they have been subjected to purging and destruction.

As Don Quixote knew, it was useless to insist. "The housekeeper, who had been already well instructed in what she was to answer, said: 'What room or what nothing is it that your worship is looking for? There are neither room nor books in this house now, for the devil himself has carried all away'" (De Cervantes, 2013, p. 41).

The niece pushed the masquerade even further: "It was not the devil, but a magician who came on a cloud one night [...], from a serpent that he rode he entered the room, and [...] he made off, flying through the roof, and left the house full of smoke; and when we went to see what he had done we saw neither book nor room."

For the time being, Don Quixote is completely alone. But he confirms the medieval definition of folly: "more a cure than a destiny", with a possibility of recovery. *Que todo lo cura, todo es locura.*

Madness can heal, provided it is received by another, but not any other. Happily, Sancho Panza is here just in time. Now, Don Quixote has only to call "enchanter" the agent of betrayal acting on those closest to him who block access to the archives of memory, and there you have it!

There is only one thing left to do: set out on another adventure. Don Quixote needs fifteen days to prepare his second sally. Determined to be successful this time, he follows to the letter the advice of the first innkeeper: he sells a few acres of land to get some money, acquires some shirts and summons Sancho, whom he hires as his esquire, promising to make him governor of an island, provided he brings with him a well-filled pouch and can get himself a mount.

This time, with Sancho mounted on his ass, the troupe of Quixotic transference is duly complete.

CHAPTER FIVE

Second sally towards the psychotherapy of trauma

Jenin returns

How can a vanished subject be made to rise from the ashes? Cervantes' answer is clear. Madness is a social link that allows the return and revival of erased events, of occupations that have disappeared, of people ostracised by scoundrels. Accompanied by his cortege, Don Quixote takes on the endlessly renewed task of uncovering defeat, loss of face, slaps in the face, all the while placing himself at risk of disappearing.

Through disfigurements and transfigurations, the emergence of madness where least expected is an anti-mechanical device that slips away lightly, sight unseen, free of the burden of psychiatric and psychoanalytic books. Through chance encounters with *kledones*, it re-establishes broken social links where the arbitrary rule of brutes, the trickery of knaves and the slogans of fanatics hold sway. Provided, of course, that it is not alone, but finds its *therapon*, in the guise of one we now call an analyst.

In the course of his analysis, Jenin admitted that his major symptom is that he is out of date. His lifestyle is old-fashioned. He renovates the apartments of other patients free of charge. He likes to work in silence since he is not talkative by nature, does not like to hurry and prefers not to rush his clients. During one of these renovation projects, he encountered a most unusual situation.

A woman had painted her entire kitchen with horizontal black and yellow stripes, in wasp hues, covering the walls, the telephone, the refrigerator, the stove, the door. The part-time, temporary nurse at the clinic, one of the few people he trusted, had asked him to help.

While trying to scrape off the paint with great difficulty to get to the surface underneath, he became curious about something. How was it that the beautiful ceramic dishes displayed above the sideboard had escaped the black and yellow hurricane? A week passed before he brought up the question. Very surprised, the woman told him that no one had asked her about this before, since her doctor and the team of caregivers saw her solely as a patient. And she proceeded to tell him the following story:

> Her father was a talented ceramist. He had worked for prominent people, whose names even Jenin recognised. To be precise, this man was her stepfather; she had never known her real father. She loved her stepfather very much. But he had refused to teach her his craft, because toiling in his little workshop had never provided an adequate living. He had not been forced to burn the furniture to heat the house, like Bernard Palissy, whose story he had told her, but he had ended up taking another job: he had become a bus driver.

After a few weeks, the woman's apartment had been restored to its original state, except for the door, which had been broken down; six months earlier, firemen had forced it open to put out the fire she had caused by falling asleep while smoking. Her drug treatment was incredibly heavy. As for him, he now had a home, which was a big improvement after the shelters and shady hotels which had been his usual lot. The ground was no longer shifting under his feet. In his home, he restored, sanded and polished the real oak floor he had found under the rotting linoleum. But he remained just as terrified whenever he found himself in the presence of more than two people.

While he and the woman worked together, they talked about the First World War. The woman's stepfather had been enrolled very early as a boy soldier. Now, there were three people who had not known their fathers: the ceramist, the woman and him. He told her about the grandfather who was amputated in 1914, and whom he had not known. She then recounted an amusing story about the ceramist, so amusing that it still made him laugh as he was telling it to me.

Try to imagine a bus driver who deviates from the official bus route to follow a funeral procession, because he considers that the deceased is too alone on his way to his final resting place. This bus driver also stopped the bus to let in stray cats, dogs, and people. It was as if he continued to take care of the wartime dead and wounded, my patient remarked. As for the woman, she had started to cook again—healthy cuisine, no less—using an electric steam cooker, since she no longer had access to gas for safety reasons.

Third traumatic revival: windmills

In the stifling summer heat of the La Mancha plain, more mirages will spring up. Don Quixote pounces upon them to force them to name themselves, to commend his exploits to Dulcinea and, aided by Sancho, to rouse the good people from the torpour that blinds them: "[…] they sallied forth unseen by anybody from the village one night, and made such good way in the course of it that by daylight they held themselves safe from discovery, even should search be made for them" (De Cervantes, 2013, p. 42).

Surrealist giants are superimposed on the reality of thirty or forty windmills—the traveller still catches glimpses of them today on the windy hilltops of La Mancha. At the time, these figures were new shapes on the horizon, a technical innovation which must have seemed as strange then as are strange to us now the windmill farms emerging on the Danish and Dutch coasts, and on the hills of Europe. "Surreal" is a word created by Apollinaire in 1917, to describe his play *The Breasts of Tiresias* (Apollinaire, 1964, pp. 55–91), staged one year after its author suffered a head wound at the front, in March 1916, and underwent trepanation at the Val-de-Grâce hospital. Cervantes is familiar with such matters, and so is his son. "Hush, friend Sancho, […] the fortunes of war more than any other are liable to frequent fluctuations" (De Cervantes, 2013, p. 45).

The paradigm of the quest returns once more, unchanged.

1. The sight of a "surviving" form, springing up in the sphere of the chivalric quest. The existence of this form is asserted despite reality, for which Sancho continues to vouch. "What giants? […] did I not tell

your worship to mind what you were about [...]?" (De Cervantes, 2013, pp. 44–45). Quixotic certainty is founded on the confidence gained on paternal battlefields, transmitted wordlessly through the cracks of unhealed injuries. Don Quixote's mission is to identify and inscribe these silent shapes, and to defy them in order to make them speak.

In the same way, when madness is suddenly present in an analysis, the analyst would do well to ask himself if he is not playing the role of certain giants faced by who knows which ancestor, in unequal combat.

2. Immediacy of a challenge requiring great courage, which these patients never lack: "Fly not, cowards and vile beings, for a single knight attacks you" (De Cervantes, 2013, p. 44). The hero then goes into action, to force the shape to speak: "'[...] and if thou art afraid, [Sancho], away with thee out of this and betake thyself to prayer while I engage them in fierce and unequal combat.' So saying, he gave the spur to his steed Rocinante" (De Cervantes, 2013, p. 44). Contrary to the four characters who plotted together to drive him mad, Don Quixote Furioso always attacks all enemies alone, with the speed required in combat.

3. *Kledon*: the breeze that happens to spring up and set the sails of the windmills in motion—just like the swineherd who played his horn at the first inn—triggers the attack on giants, which sends Don Quixote flying through the air and then rolling on the ground, after Rocinante's collapse. The hero does not hear Sancho's cries. Has he gone berserk, like soldiers who lose all awareness of their surroundings, run amok "bare shirt", without armour, taking on the whole world, feeling invincible?

Just like Achilles, haunted by the desire to avenge Patroclus' death, attacks Hector, both godlike and animal-like, according to Homer (Homer, 1924), Don Quixote exceeds the bounds of the human realm. Here, the comical device of mechanical windmills superimposed on living beings refers to the loss of boundaries, during battle, between the spheres of the animal and the superhuman domains. The giants are the phantoms of the wars fought by his father, and the blades propelled by the wind maybe reviving the sails of the battleships on which so many of Cervantes' companions perished.

Sancho as therapist

After the adventure of the windmills, Sancho takes up the role of thera-pist, which consists, first, of examining the injuries, straightening out the warrior's disjointed body and speaking to him. He also voices, in his place, the hunger, fatigue, and pain which Don Quixote is unable to express. Doing so, he serves as his mirror after all mirrors have been broken on the battlefield.

This same misadventure of broken mirrors is no doubt the lot of babies described as very quiet, since their cries meet with the indiffer-ence of parents preoccupied with other things. Later, they will be balls of rage and sadness ready to explode.

"It will be Chernobyl!" one of these old children told me. When one of their nephews died at birth, his wife had suggested that they say nothing to their own child. Instantly, he saw himself at the age of his son, when the death of his father was hidden from him by his family, because, of course, a child does not see anything and is unaware.

Insomniac and anorexic, Don Quixote "lay awake [all that night] thinking of his lady Dulcinea [… and] did not care to break his fast, for […] he confined himself to savory recollections for nourishment" (De Cervantes, 2013, p. 4). He forbade Sancho to ever take up his sword to defend him, to the relief of his peace-loving squire, who was "no friend to mixing in strife and quarrels". But wishing to ward off adversity does not necessarily put an end to it. On the contrary, mis-fortune can be paradoxically exacerbated and can spring up when least expected, just when peace is being declared.

Fourth traumatic revival: dromaderies and sunshades

A second caravan bursts onto the chivalresque scene. Fantastical sun-shades, and dromaderies with them, appear on the horizon. Traumatic revival is played out once again, in the same sequence as before.

1. Advent and acknowledgement of a surreal shape, even more oriental looking, perhaps resembling the caravans seen by Cervantes while he was making his unsuccessful attempt to escape in the direction of Oran. Thus, sunshades and dromaderies frame the carrying off, by magicians, of a princess Don Quixote will rescue, as befits surrealist

logic. This surviving shape creates a new form of language making it possible to inscribe, this time, the episode of Cervantes' recapture.

The traumatic scenario bursts through the reality of a procession of two friars mounted on tall mules, followed by the coach of a lady, not travelling with them, but attended by men on horseback and by two muleteers on foot. Sancho argues in support of reality: "This will be worse than the windmills. Look, señor; those are friars of St. Benedict [...] I tell you to mind well what you are about and don't let the devil mislead you" (De Cervantes, 2013, p. 47).

Here again, an essential distinction is made. Yes, Don Quixote is possessed, but not by the agency invoked by Sancho. The malevolent being has not lodged itself in his synapses, but resides in the target of his action, be it political police or ruthless hostage-takers. Don Quixote's certainty is unshakeable. "I have told thee already, Sancho, that on the subject of adventures thou knowest little. What I say is the truth, as thou shalt see presently" (De Cervantes, 2013, p. 47). What is at stake is to establish a truth that was denied.

2. Immediacy of taking action: the hero seeks confrontation. "So saying, he advanced and posted himself in the middle of the road along which the friars were coming: 'Devilish and unnatural beings, release instantly the highborn princesses whom you are carrying off by force' [...]" (De Cervantes, 2013, p. 47). The friars protest, explaining who they are. But at this toll booth between two worlds, no fare is adequate. The pirates who kidnapped Cervantes, and the henchmen who recaptured him, sprang up like real devils, but Don Quixote remained steadfast: "'No soft words with me, for I know you, lying rabble,' and without waiting for a reply he spurred Rocinante and with leveled lance charged the first friar with such fury and determination [...]" (De Cervantes, 2013, p. 47).

The friars ride away as fast as they can. Sancho dismounts and tries to take the spoils of the battle, while Don Quixote attempts to inscribe the capture of his hostages by persuading the lady in the coach to apprise Dulcinea, in El Toboso, of this foiled hostage-taking and of the name of her rescuer. A hot-headed Biscayan squire (that is to say, Basque) spurs Don Quixote into action again by challenging him to a duel. The swashbuckling scenes are presented with the precision worthy of a modern film director, frame by frame and then speeded up, by the fencing master, Cervantes, for whom the martial arts had been more than a recreational activity.

3. *Kledon*. Here, the Fates arrange for part of the story to be lost. The hero's action is partly suspended. Immobilised in a freeze frame, Don Quixote remains fixed, with lifted sword facing the Biscayan, in a suspended scene where two enemies are ready to split each other in half: "But it spoils all, that at this point and crisis the author of the history leaves the battle impending, giving as excuse that he could find nothing more written about these achievements of Don Quixote than what has been already set forth" (De Cervantes, 2013, p. 49).

4. *Expectancy*. This is Salmon's third principle. Crucial in the psychoanalysis of madness and of traumas, it designates the refusal of despair. "It is true that the second author of this work was unwilling to believe that a history so curious could have been allowed to fall under the sentence of oblivion [...]; and this being his persuasion, he did not despair of finding the conclusion of this pleasant history." This history is the one that the tenacious children of veterans insist on writing with their analysts at a later time.

Surviving forms

Thus, the manuscript becomes one of the characters, and the writing that research may uncover becomes the object of the quest. The author must also make a second narrative sally in order to seize what Proust will eventually call, at the end of his own quest in *Time Regained*, "a fragment of time in the pure state". Like Aby Warburg (1866–1929), his contemporary, Marcel Proust (1871–1922), is a war baby, born during the Franco-Prussian War of 1870. He also speaks of the surviving forms Warburg calls *nachleben*, of the rebirth of "[the] being which had been reborn in me when with a sudden shudder of happiness I had heard the noise that was common to the spoon touching the plate and the hammer striking the wheel, or had felt, beneath my feet, the unevenness that was common to the paving-stones of the Guermantes courtyard and to those of the baptistery of St. Mark's" (Proust, 1993, pp. 264–267). These surviving forms act on all the senses. "But let a noise or a scent, once heard or once smelt, be heard or smelt again in the present and at the same time in the past, real without being actual, ideal without being abstract, and immediately the permanent and habitually concealed essence of things is liberated and our true self, which seemed—had perhaps for long years seemed—to be dead but was not altogether dead, is awakened and reanimated [...]. A minute freed from the order of time has re-created in us, to feel it, the man freed from the order of time."

Don Quixote's madness is an exploit, as is Aby Warburg's madness, an exploit which can vanquish living death. The latter's lecture on serpent ritual (Warburg, 1923) succeeded in awakening his psyche "which had long seemed dead, by freeing it from the order of time" and by connecting cultures threatened with disappearance, from Ancient Greece to the Pueblo Indians.

But Don Quixote pays a price for engaging in this combat. No sooner is time found than it is lost again, pushing the hero, like the narrator of *In Search of Lost Time*, to widen the realm of writing and of the quest, until it reaches the panoramic proportions of a ghostly world war, described in the adventure of the goatherds.

The period of twenty years when Cervantes did not publish, while he pursued his professional wanderings through the Spanish countryside, was so much wasted time that he could have spent writing. Very often he must have experienced the torments of losing his manuscripts, of lacking inspiration, of having to interrupt the thread of the plots he was constructing and, above all, the difficulty of sustaining his desire to write in the midst of the vicissitudes of his work as commissary agent, an occupation diametrically opposed to that of a writer.

The passage of time allows the maturing of the epic tale that the Hellenist scholar Gregory Nagy defines as the story of old veterans transmitted to the children of old veterans. "[…] The children turn its leaves, the young people read it, the grown men understand it, the old folk praise it" (De Cervantes, 2013, p. 418), says Samson Carrasco at the start of the second novel, when he describes to the two heroes the reception given to the First Part of their adventures.

Gregory Nagy also points out that the epic tale is transmitted to those concerned, with little variation, from generation to generation, from bard to bard, troubadour to troubadour, most of them warriors like the knight, their heirs, and at last down to us.

This sustained survival through the centuries is made possible by the fact that the poet, moved by a demonic power, brings the battles of the past into the present. Having been given this "time regained", he himself becomes the subject of the *epos*, the one Proust calls "the man freed from the order of time".

"The alder king": Erlkönig (Von Goethe, 1882, p. 99)

Just like in an analysis, when a foreign language is heard, a language believed to have been banished forever, an opening appears, an author seems to emerge unexpectedly on the other side of the border.

One day, an analyst came to see me, saying that he was suddenly in the grip of such intense death anxiety that he was considering giving up his practice. His name, obviously from Eastern France, sounded Germanic. The night following his visit I dreamed, with great clarity, of one of the only lines of poetry that I knew in German, from Goethe's *Erlkönig*:

> *Wer reitet so spät durch Nacht und Wind?*
> Who rides so late through the night and wind?

I told him about this verse of which I dreamed and gave him this approximate translation, adding that I did not speak German. With "The alder king", the foreign language burst into my office, bringing back from the dead the "against-our-will" of his family, who had fought on the German side, whose names he knew, but who were making their spectral entrance among us for the first time. During a previous analysis, no interest had been taken in these events.

Three authors, three phases in the analysis

The same sudden intrusion, which provokes a *"casus belli"* in the analysis, allows the emergence of a third author in Chapter IX.

First, an anonymous author wrote the First Part, left "in suspense" in the middle of the duel with the Biscayan.

The second author is the narrator, Cervantes, who cannot resist saying "I" to convey his "pleasure derived from having read such a small portion", and to assert his conviction that the knight's story must exist somewhere (De Cervantes, 2013, p. 50).

This is how he saves his son *in extremis*, once again thanks to the god of Chance, appearing in the shape of a young boy, an ally of the terrible god of Time, "the devourer and destroyer of all things", who had left "such a gallant tale [...] maimed and mutilated" (De Cervantes, 2013, p. 50). Thus, Cervantes identifies with his tale, since the strapping youth he had been became maimed and mutilated at twenty-four.

Time seems to have devoured the story and its author, leaving them both maimed. Therefore, a third author is needed to help them both to extricate themselves from these dire straits.

The fact is that the malignancy of catastrophic eras devours and consumes all such tales. Yet, erased from memory, they remain inscribed on stumps of stories passed down to descendants. But these maimed forms do not stay static. They are saturated with the energy acquired from catastrophe, and inspire a burning desire to find the traces of their survival.

They lead to the moleskin notebooks or to the old diaries resold at the flea market, which await a meeting with their narrators when least expected.

As is the case in every analysis of madness and trauma, the original inscription has always been lost. It is found by chance, at a later time, reactivated by a second trauma. There remains, as an original trace, a first truncated part that sets transference in motion, and can possibly act as a sparking wick for going into action.

In the same way, at twenty, Bion (Bion, 1991) lost the war diary destined for his parents, where he recorded, day after day, his campaigns as an officer in the Tank Corps during the First World War. After the war he rewrote it, word for word, with the precision of traumatic memory, carefully reproducing the maps, the landscapes and the tanks drawn the first time. This, then, is the "pure time" brought back by the third author.

Indeed, the third author of the truth of the subject, "whose mother is history" (De Cervantes, 2013, p. 52), says Cervantes, emerges just when everything seems lost. As is often the case in the analysis of trauma, scraps of wastepaper are tossed into our office when the story can no longer be told. In order to pull them out of the wastepaper basket of History, the analyst must assert, even in all unlikelihood, that it is impossible for the rest of these documents to have disappeared completely.

Cervantes, the one-handed veteran, cannot bear for History to remain mutilated. Therefore, he passes on to his son his passion for seeking what was discarded, and his fervent desire to inscribe it. But in the meanwhile, the hero and his suite become the rhythm and the music of the epic tale, punctuating the account of real syncopes followed by resurrections, in each ensuing battle, in which "the common sensation had for a moment grappled, like a wrestler, with the present scene". This common sensation is the very site where surviving elements of madness are linked together to become reason, as Socrates says in the Theaetetus. It is a sensation of disappearance.

In search of the lost son

As Chapter VIII ends and Chapter IX begins, we witness the distress of the author in the face of the disappearance of his character with all his cortege. Cervantes has indeed lost his son in the folds of time. Therefore, he springs back into action, acknowledging his fondness for reading the least scrap of paper he happens upon.

It is this passion that leads Chance to take the shape of a boy who had come to the flea market of Toledo "to sell some pamphlets and old papers", in which his son was hiding. "[...] as I am fond of reading even the very scraps of paper in the streets, led by this natural bent of mine I took up one of the pamphlets the boy had for sale, and saw that it was in characters which I recognised as Arabic" (De Cervantes, 2013, p. 51). Moreover, chance favours Cervantes once again with providential intervention in the form of a Morisco who "opened it in the middle and after reading a little in it began to laugh" (De Cervantes, 2013, p. 51).

Cervantes' strange son is suddenly rediscovered in the "Arabic characters" that provoke bursts of laughter from the reader, who is highly amused by an insignificant detail in the text. Dulcinea has just stepped on stage, making an equivocal entrance, since the text describes her as having "the best hand of any woman in all La Mancha for salting pigs". Thus, the story takes up the thread that tied the prostitutes to the swineherd at the first inn.

Indeed, it is urgent to resume the tale and avoid being trampled by the pigs. Thus, the narrator exercises "great caution to hide the joy [he] felt when the title of the book reached [his] ears, and snatching it from the silk mercer, [he] bought all the papers [...] from the boy for half a *real*; and if [the boy] had known how eager [the narrator] was for them, he might have safely calculated on making more than six *reals* by the bargain" (De Cervantes, 2013, pp. 51–52). Then he sequesters the Morisco in his house for a month and a half, for fear of letting him get away, and pays him to translate the entire text.

Now, the story can continue thanks to the third author, the historian Cid Hamet Ben Engeli, whose name in Arabic is, it seems, equivalent to that of Cervantes. According to Jean Cassou, Engeli means "son of the cerf", alias Cervantes; Canavaggio claims that the name means "son of the Scripture", a nickname given to Cervantes in prison, if we rely on the recently uncovered testimony of those who were his companions in captivity (Canavaggio, 1991).

The ensuing adventures will proceed, in any case, from this place that cannot be forgotten, and from the suspense in which texts and people become lost, only to be reunited, sometimes without knowing each other, through the foreign language of trauma. For Cervantes, this language is that of the bagnios of Algiers, at once foreclosed and unforgettable, in which his survival took shape. It is the only language that can set in motion, in the present, the string of revivals that were to rush forth after the story was interrupted by a lapse of memory.

Towards history, "mother of the truth"

Being a good son and truly crazy, Don Quixote travelled in a fugue-like state to a hellish place, sent there by his father, who had not published anything in many years. However, when one approaches fifty, such events tend to resurface. The Second Part of the first *Don Quixote* describes the difficulty of making a story out of them. When the narrator finds his son again, he does not recognise him, and he no longer understands the language of his adventures. Therefore, he must return to the other side of the Mediterranean, where he had been kept waiting for five years by the repeated failure of the negotiations regarding his ransom, only to find his life hanging by a thread which his son is trying to weave above the void.

Thus, he encounters the history of his son in the language of the enemy. As a result, insults will rain, echoing the trash talk addressed by athletes to the opposing team, before the battle. He calls the Arab historian, later described as a learned, "that dog of a Moor", just as the Moor Hadji Morato will speak of "these dogs [the Christians], our natural enemies" (De Cervantes, 2013, p. 313), in the tale of the captive, when he curses the slave who takes his daughter away.

Still, the tone of defiance throughout the novel is undeniably an antidote to depression. Defiance implies a form of respect of the adversary, to whom Cervantes later pays homage: "[…] besides which, Cide Hamete Benengeli was a historian of great research and accuracy in all things, as is very evident since he would not pass over in silence those that have been already mentioned, however trifling and insignificant they might be" (De Cervantes, 2013, p. 92).

At this moment of interruption in the manuscript, Cervantes must find his son. He must return to the very place where a stain was inflicted on the glory of Lepante, and entrust the story to an Arab historian who will be held to account for his own faults. "If against the present [history] any objection can be captained on the score of its truth, it can only be that its author was an Arab, as lying is a very common propensity with those of that nation" (De Cervantes, 2013, p. 52).

For indeed, what is at stake is the historical truth. Not long after the battle between Don Quixote and the Biscayan, whose only witness keeping a cool head was his mule, "which, unable to execute any sort of manoeuvre [...], dead tired and never meant for this kind of game, could not stir a step"—Cervantes rises above the "it is not my fault", so often heard in political speeches and on children's playgrounds, by a proclamation of faith in the work of historians, who must "be exact, truthful, and wholly free from passion, and neither interest nor fear, hatred nor love, should make them swerve from the path of truth, whose mother is history, rival of time, storehouse of deeds, witness for the past, example and counsel for the present, and warning for the future".

This litany elevates History to the position of another Dulcinea, mother of the truth, starting off the Second Part of the first Don Quixote with a pastoral romance.

Vitek's name reappears

After the loss of the Spanish manuscript and the discovery of the Arabic text that made it possible for the bloody combat with the Biscayan to be continued, the adventures unfold at a slower pace and even stop altogether. Just as I was about to go over this part of the narrative, which had been missing from my comic book, a name re-emerged suddenly, a name I thought had been banished for good, along with the man who bore it.

Vitek's name did indeed appear at the end of an alphabetical list of the fallen, figuring instead of an Index at the end of the book mentioned by one of my patients. The book in question was Madeleine Fourcade's *L'Arche de Noé, Réseau Alliance 1940–1945* (Fourcade, 1968, p. 643). The names listed were those of the fallen members of the network she directed during the Second World War, to provide information to the British.

The book came out in 1968 and did not sell well. The times were not propitious. Obviously, this network which included many women had neglected to take adequate measures to ensure the future marketing of its memory. Forty years went by before I finally opened this book, starting at the end as is my habit; and there, to my astonishment, was the name of the man in the blue uniform!

Vitek, then, had been a member of the Alliance network. When I showed my father this name in the book, he finally agreed to speak, sixty-five years later, to say that Vitek and his taller companion, whose name he could not remember, had been members of a different organisation. They came to the cooperative to send out messages on camouflaged radios.

In the passage where Cervantes comes upon his son after discovering the name of Dulcinea in an Arabic text that he has to have translated, the theme discussed is disappearance. But the reappearance of Vitek's name, written plainly in black and white despite all attempts to erase it, made me pay particular attention to the scene where Cervantes forgets his distress when he hears Dulcinea's name read by the Morisco. Indeed, in the Second Part of *Don Quixote* Cervantes takes the time to reflect on the figure of the Lady as the guarantor of inscriptions. What does he mean by that?

The common fruit of combined toil

Don Quixote almost disappeared, like all those who do not find their place after a war. But instead, Cervantes' robust son embodies regeneration in a world where sense is lost. Therefore, Don Quixote has to re-establish the most basic social relations, to create a kind of communal pastoral life whose praises he sang to the goatherds he encountered. To this day, in the Alps, the cheese originating from herds grazing together in mountain pastures is called "the common fruit".

Don Quixote calls his duty of regeneration after catastrophes "the science, even the religion of knights-errant". After having tested Sancho's skills as a therapist in the First Part, the Second Part is dedicated to the shepherdess Marcela.

Let us go back to the freeze frame at the end of the First Part, in which Don Quixote, brandishing his sword, faces the Basque squire. When the images are set in motion again, the clash is terrible: the fiery Biscayan's sword strikes the knight on the shoulder, carrying away half of his ear. Filled with rage, the Manchegan grasped his sword more firmly with both hands and "came down on the Biscayan with such fury that [...] he began to bleed from nose, mouth, and ears" (De Cervantes, 2013, p. 53). There follow the pleas of the "terrified and disconsolate" lady in the coach—understandably distraught—who begs for her squire's life and promises to say anything the knight wishes to Dulcinea, whoever she might be.

The debriefing of the battle took place in "a wood that was hard by" (De Cervantes, 2013, p. 54), a traditional site of enchantments, where time usually stops and where, as a result, the psychotherapy of madness can be carried out. Once again, Don Quixote's analysis with Sancho reveals the outcome of combat: a severed ear, some lint, white ointment, and Balm of Fierabras that might mend the knight's helmet, so shattered that "he was like to lose his senses" (De Cervantes, 2013, p. 56).

Then, several centuries ahead of time, Don Quixote formulates Harry Stack Sullivan's postulate, "We are all much more human than otherwise" (Sullivan, 1974), explaining that knights-errant "could not do without eating and performing all the other natural functions, because, in fact, they were men like ourselves [...]" (De Cervantes, 2013, p. 57).

The need for nourishment also includes the urge to speak, to narrate, as we see in the exchange with the goatherds. According to Walter Benjamin (Felman, 2002, p. 26), war does not put an end to stories and to storytelling; it merely makes those who know nothing about war deaf to them. To illustrate, I came across another diary written in a magnificent style at the front, during the First World War, by a Jew of the Parisian bourgeoisie. He finally spoke of it to his granddaughter, when the latter found it by chance in a drawer, where contempt had relegated it.

While he was a simple soldier among other infantrymen, men with whom he would not ordinarily have shared such intimacy, he wrote down their stories in the trenches near Reims, to record not only the horrors, but also some marvellous dawns. For instance, there was the unhoped-for welcome given to them by an old woman, after so many doors had remained closed, and the laughter during the meals she prepared by killing her emaciated chickens, when she entertained them with stories of her wild youth. The diary describes these moments like commencements of the world. Considered reactionary by his children, the manuscript recording this grandfather's war memories was published by his granddaughter long after her own mother and grandmother had been assassinated in Auschwitz.

The goatherds as therapists

At the foot of the mountain, goatherds welcomed the two heroes, nearly dead of exhaustion and hunger. After sharing a meal and spending a peaceful night with the goatherds, they would all attend the burial of Grisostomo, a wealthy youth who had returned to the pastoral life, and had taken his own life for the sake of a shepherdess.

Don Quixote forces Sancho to sit down beside him, "that thou be one with me" (De Cervantes, 2013, p. 58), as he says, and delivers a lengthy speech as he contemplates a handful of acorns. While "stowing away pieces as big as one's fist", he meditated on the golden age when animals spoke, when there were "sturdy oaks [...], clear streams [and ...] busy and sagacious bees [and] their republic" (De Cervantes, 2013, p. 59). "'Happy the age, happy the time, to which the ancients gave the name of golden', he exclaimed. '[...] they know not the two words *"mine"* and *"thine"*, [...]. Then all was peace, all friendship, all concord."'

This idyllic time is contrasted with the harsh century, his and ours, where "fraud [and] deceit" reign. In the golden age, "arbitrary law had not yet established itself in the mind of the judge. [...] Maidens [...] wandered at will alone and unattended, without fear of insult from lawlessness or libertine assault [...]. But now in this hateful age of ours not one is safe" (De Cervantes, 2013, p. 59).

The goatherds did not expect such a harangue, and stared dumbfounded. But instead of sniggering or listening in contemptuous silence to this language of another age, they offered a ballad of their own in return. Thus, the goatherd Antonio responded to Don Quixote's discourse, although he did not understand most of it, while another goatherd tended to his thorn ear by applying poultice of rosemary, chewed and mixed with salt, which brought him immediate relief.

Despite this, being hypersensitive to linguistic traumas, the knight could not refrain from arguing about signifiers and tried to impose the correct usage of Spanish. But very soon he accepted the slips that create a "confusion of words", and gave up trying to stem the goatherds' loquacity. When the goatherd Pedro tells the story of the enamoured youth, embellishing his narration with the phrase "though you should live *more years than Sarna*", Don Quixote corrects him, advising: "Say Sarah". Pedro responds, without missing a beat: "Sarna lives long enough, and if, señor, you must go finding fault at every step, we shall not make an end of it this twelvemonth" (De Cervantes, 2013, pp. 65–66). After this, the rest of Chapter XII can be dedicated to informing the knight of the most recent local dramas.

Do you want to see his act?

By contrast, Señor Vivaldo, encountered in Chapter XIII, on the way to the burial of Grisostomo, clearly considers Don Quixote "out of his senses" and intends to amuse himself at his expense. A master of banter and sarcasm, Vivaldo personifies "this hateful age [of] fraud, deceit [and] malice". Instead of engaging light-heartedly with the knight, like the goatherds or the damsels at the first inn, he makes fun of him "in order to beguile the journey", with a treachery which will reach a peak of cruelty in the second novel, at the castle of a ducal couple.

Vivaldo's attitude reflects the typical duplicity shown to those who are out of their senses. In asylums like the one in Toledo, in the second novel, a game is played that could be called: "Do you want to see his act?" At the deftly delivered incitement of a caretaker, the madman performs his act, justifying his confinement.

In one of these places where time stands still—where we began to work in the seventies and where the "inmates" taught us to be analysts—a tall, pale gentleman treated us graciously, as if we were his colleagues from the School of Social Sciences, since he was conducting research in "ideopathology" with a certain Paolo Herzog in Paris.

Another patient, diagnosed as a schizophrenic in her youth, when she must have been very beautiful, would stare at us in silence, her motionless eyes rimmed with deep circles, before going back to speaking to the walls. She had been taken to Sainte-Anne, the psychiatric hospital in Paris where whole busloads of people went to be lobotomised, until not so long ago.

Thirty years later, scientific progress has succeeded in doing even better by disconnecting synapses and speech at the same time.

Presentation of the patient

Vivaldo was of the old school, which considers madness amusing and relishes its inanities, which reinforce one's feeling of superiority.

"Vivaldo [asked] Don Quixote what was the reason that led him to go armed in that fashion in a country so peaceful. To which Don Quixote replied, "The pursuit of my calling does not allow or permit me to go in any other fashion" (De Cervantes, 2013, pp. 69–70). The diagnosis quickly followed: "The instant they heard this all set him down as mad, and the better to settle the point and discover what kind of madness his was [...]."

In that earlier era, curiosity about madness and the madman gave the latter the chance to react, and sometimes even to give his psychiatrist a taste of his own medicine. Research was not limited to the study of countless lineages of mice driven mad by genetic modification, but showed an interest in words: "Vivaldo proceeded to ask him what knights-errant meant."

The catch when using this old method is that the object of the research may not be fully consenting. Don Quixote has noticed the covert unkind allusion, and his reply shows that he is not fooled: "[...] and so I go through these solitudes and wilds seeking adventures [...] in aid of the weak and needy" (De Cervantes, 2013, p. 70).

Here, we are attending a case presentation, like those made by the alienists of the last century, and even by some present-day psychiatrists. Vivaldo hunts down neologisms and plays at being naïve in order to identify delusion: "[...] in order to beguile the short journey, which they said was required to reach the mountain, [he] sought to give him an opportunity of going on with his absurdities." Hypocritical questioning of the patient in a clinical setting is commonplace. "It seems to me, Señor Knight-errant, that your worship has made choice of one of the most austere professions in the world."

Don Quixote has caught the double meaning intended to amuse the audience, but instead of taking a defensive stance, he describes in all sincerity his impossible mission which consists of making war visible in peacetime. To perfidious innuendos he opposes the blood and sweat of warriors. "And as the business of war [...] cannot be conducted without exceeding great sweat, toil, and exertion, [...] I would merely infer from what I endure myself that [...] it cost them dear in the matter of blood and sweat" (De Cervantes, 2013, p. 71). Here, Don Quixote is doubtless bearing witness to Cervantes' wars, and to wars of all kinds.

For instance, when we spoke of Don Quixote and of the Cervantian analysis of madness at a seminar in Brazil, an analyst objected, saying that psychosis had only to do with psychic structure. Another maintained that it was caused by social inequity. Of course, Europe had suffered two world-wars, but that was not the case for Brazil, where the problems had to do with poverty, violence, racism, and street children. At that point, Marcio Pinheiro—who died in 2015—an analyst working with madness and trauma, seized the microphone in Quixotic fashion, to remind us that the war conducted by narcotic traffic lords is endemic, and that to deny this in the name of an anti-historical principle is part of a psychological war strategy particularly well served by denial.

In Cervantes' novel, a veritable psychological war is engaged between Vivaldo and Don Quixote, who sees through him. Underhandedly, the affable inquisitor baits the hook of witchcraft: "[…] knights-errant […] commend themselves to their ladies with as much devotion as if these were their gods, a thing that seems to me to savour somewhat of heathenism." Don Quixote is not daunted and ends up revealing Dulcinea's name, after relentless questioning. And yet, no overt attack takes place in the course of this exchange. Don Quixote is saving his energy for much more worthy combats.

"Sancho Panza alone thought that what his master said was the truth, knowing who he was and having known him from birth" (De Cervantes, 2013, p. 73). Today, the details of the patient's life "from birth" are often considered unimportant in the overall psychiatric picture of his personality, as evidenced by the following story told by a young medical student.

When he was invited to attend the presentation of a psychiatric case, with some of his fellow students, they were surprised to discover that they had difficulty distinguishing the psychiatrist from her "patient" at first. The former wore no white coat and the latter recited the manual with impressive mastery. When it was the student's turn to ask questions, he enquired naively: "But what exactly happened to you?" The answer could be assessed on a scale of pain, from bearable to excruciating. Finding herself pregnant at seventeen, the patient had given birth alone to a stillborn baby. She was hospitalised in a suicidal state, and had since been suffering from a bipolar disorder, with alternating states of joy and enthusiasm followed by such deep depression that she preferred swallowing her medication and collapsing on her sofa like a larva, like her stillborn baby. But why should anyone take an interest in stories that are so demoralising, the student concluded ironically.

Once again, Cervantes answers this question in his own way.

A change of paradigm

In fact, the Second Part of Don Quixote deals with suicide. Did Cervantes plan to die? He does not say. But the idea of suicide is familiar to those who have already died at the site of traumas. According to Benedetti (Benedetti, 1998, p. 65), the subject who has withdrawn from life in order to survive may paradoxically attempt to gain control of an event that was endured passively by taking his own life.

The sudden hiatus that occurs when the manuscript is lost could stand for Cervantes' long absence from the literary scene following his *La Galate*. Could Dulcinea also stand for poetic writing which, by remaining out of his reach, might have given rise to suicidal thoughts? In any case, she refuses the complicity requested of her, and lets her position be voiced by the shepherdess Marcela, whose discourse is clearly antisuicidal. In fact, it still constitutes a masterly lesson today, in this era of legal and illegal drug abuse.

At the age of fifty-five, his only fortune consisting of writings that despair had relegated to the thrash bin, Cervantes decides to dedicate his life to writing again, and to condemn self-destruction. And yet, when he starts to write again, the tone of the Author's Preface in Volume I of *Don Quixote* is not optimistic. He doubts himself and his son: "[...] what, then, could this sterile, ill-tilled wit of mine beget but the story of a dry, shriveled, whimsical offspring [...]" (De Cervantes, 2013, p. 3). Above all, he is afraid inspiration will fail him. His state of mind illustrates the classical posture of melancholy: "[...] not knowing what to write [...], with the paper before me, a pen in my ear, my elbow on the desk, and my cheek in my hand [...]" (De Cervantes, 2013, p. 3), as he confesses to a friend, admitting his lack of self-confidence.

As he starts to write the Second Part, after the manuscript has been found, Cervantes seems melancholy again, since he brings his son back from the land of the Maures only to have him witness—albeit in an idyllic setting—the burial of a young man who took his own life. A strange idea! What does the Golden Age have to do with death?

In fact, the son seems to have been begotten above all to cure his father of the dark moods that would later be called romantic "spleen", and have now become the universal depression so profitable to the pharmaceuticals market. Today, the friend Cervantes mentions in The Author's Pages would have handed him some pills to calm his fears about public opinion: "For how could you expect me not to feel uneasy about what the ancient lawgiver they call the Public will say when it sees me, after slumbering so many years in the silence of oblivion, coming out now with all my years upon my back?" (De Cervantes, 2013, p. 4).

In any case, it appears that the transmission of the gene of Cervantian incarceration, from father to son at least as far back as Cervantes' grandfather—all of them imprisoned for the same financial reasons—has produced this old writer who considers himself a failure. The disparagement of the work he has just written is not motivated solely by his diffidence: "a book as dry as a rush, devoid of invention, meagre in style, poor in thoughts, wholly wanting in learning and wisdom, without [...] annotations at the end" (De Cervantes, 2013, p. 4).

As little inclined to use learned references as Wittgenstein, who invoked the same arguments, Cervantes is "by nature shy about hunting for authors to say what I myself can say without them". He apologises for his lack of academic training, and for not supplying the usual footnotes. Hearing this, the friend in the Preface, in true Sancho style, reassures him. In order to "sweep away all [his] difficulties, and supply all those deficiencies, which check and discourage [him]" (De Cervantes, 2013, p. 5), he suggests that Cervantes introduce quotations here and there throughout his text, to prove himself a man of erudition, as a schoolboy might do in a dissertation.

But above all, his friend recommends that he strive "that in reading your story the melancholy may be moved to laughter, and the merry made merrier still, that the simple shall not be wearied" (De Cervantes, 2013, p. 7). The possibility of comic overtones in the book will depend on "the destruction of that ill-founded edifice of the books of chivalry, hated by some and praised by many more". The remedy has finally been found, in Rabelaisian tradition, to cure Cervantes of the melancholia which his earlier works had not sufficed to heal.

Now, Cervantes will use the ambivalence of the ideals of chivalry which had plunged him in the chaotic universe of war and slavery to direct the comical force against the conceit of public opinion. Thus, he begins writing the Second Part of *Don Quixote* in the same melancholic tone that pervades his *Galate*. Let us go back to the fifth book of the pastoral romance, left unfinished, and find the passage where Cervantes, barely disguised as Lauso, admits in his song, sung in a "no well-measured voice", that he is in the throes of despair (De Cervantes, 2008, p. 218).

> Where is the soul which I once called mine?
>
> But where do I all exist?
> Whence come I and where go?
> Fortunately myself I yet do know.
> I may be what I was,
> Yet never have been who I truly am.
> No understanding do I understand [...]
> In this confusion blind [...]
> In this myself die I see
> In this extraordinary agony [...]
> Pen, tongue, will,
> In this inflexible reason me confirm. (De Cervantes, 2008, p. 218)

Lauso's woeful sonnet is followed by the narration of a naval battle and a hostage-taking, which involved the loss of his self. "Pressed by the memory of my misadventures, [...] I actually lost my sensation in a paroxysm, which left me in an unconscious state." In truth, *La Galatea* is anything but an idyllic narrative. It starts with a murder and is devoted in large part to treason, suicide, raids of Turkish pirates off the coast of Spain, rapes, massacres, and the capture of slaves. What pen, what tongue can be trusted to speak of the "extraordinary agony [when] perdition is certain"? In "Fear of breakdown", Winnicott (Winnicott, 1974, pp. 103–107) describes what he calls "primitive agony" that immobilises the subject, "who no longer knows who he is", in a past-present time experience.

This therapy, "Pen, tongue, will", consists of funnelling through the filter of words the deathly energy of a subject who has stared death in the face, one who might say "myself die I see". Here, the therapy is entrusted to the character of Galatea.

Galatea is a Nereid in Theocritus, and later in Ovid; she spurns the advances of the sadistic monster Polyphemus. Cervantes chooses Galatea to personify freedom. While the other shepherdesses fall prey, one by one, to jealousy, betrayal or submission, his Galatea refuses to submit to an arranged marriage with a Portuguese shepherd. She is "one of the few" described by La Boétie as those who "feel the weight of the yoke and cannot restrain themselves from attempting to shake it off: [...] who never become tamed under subjection ... Even if liberty had entirely perished from the earth, such men would invent it. These are the ones who, having good minds of their own, have further trained them by study and learning. For them slavery has no satisfaction, no matter how well disguised" (La Boétie, 1942).

Like Cervantes, Galatea is among those who resist political blackmail. Yet, the pastoral romance is left unfinished, despite Cervantes' repeated promise, in the text, to continue the story. His therapeutic device probably fell short of exploring traumatic revivals that cannot be encompassed in the pastoral form. He needed the brutality of the second trauma, in a Seville prison in 1592, where he might have feared going mad, to imagine the possibility of entrusting to Don Quixote the extravagant mission of lifting his distress. Even so, he did not disavow his eldest daughter, Galate.

Now, the pastoral romance becomes integrated into the Second Part of *Don Quixote*, in a context where "melancholy [is] moved to laughter", as Cervantes' friend advised. For, in fact, in peacetime the enemy is not the Turkish army, but the depressing "perversion of a hateful age", which forces the minds of former warriors and captives to break with reason.

La razon

Razon means "the right word". *La Galatea* lent itself to onomastic analysis, where names must adjust to an unnamed reality—the Greek word *arariskô*, meaning "to adjust", also resonates with Ares, the god of war. In fact, the tradition of the *locus amoenus* (pleasant place) in the pastoral poem corresponds to the need for creating new names, a need felt by warrior poets or those returning from wars: those whose works Cervantes saved from the book burning of Don Quixote's library.

Indeed, many authors of pastoral novels were men of war. In 1607, when Cervantes published *Don Quixote*, the French writer Honoré d'Urfé, later killed while fighting the Genovese army, published his bestseller, *Astrea*, in which he invented the map of Tendre, on the shores of the Lignon. Undoubtedly, the popular success of these pastoral works, entire passages of which were recited by heart, was due to a search for meaningful poetic invention in a time of war and slaughter, plagues, hostage-taking and corruption.

However, the Cervantian pastoral is insufficient, as are the eighty shepherds and shepherdesses who are "not content with lamenting, singing and bewailing", but engage in *razonar* (De Cervantes, 2008), which serves to find the right word to describe bewildering sensations. Lauso, alias Cervantes, puts this therapy to use in order to shake off his lethargy by freeing himself forever from the tyranny of love:

> Fickle Love, disdain thy chains
> Broke, and to my memory
> Hath restored the liberty
> Born from absence of thy pains. (De Cervantes, 2008)

But he does not tell us what he intends to do once he is freed of the numbness induced by the painful diversion of his fantasies. In fact, it would take fifteen years for the surviving image of a knight-errant to visit him and shake him up, in his prison cell.

An antisuicidal bomb

Some time had to pass before Cervantes would come back to his literary endeavours, and free himself, through laughter, of the tyranny of traumatic memory.

Piercing the screen of fantasy, the image of the Lady, alternately ideal and disidealised, disappears, like the shepherdess Marcela does somewhere in the mountains. She backs away from passion-driven conflicts between the shepherds, leaving behind only the trace of her name.

In *La Galatea*, the plot proceeds from the curiosity to hear the stories of others. But the narratives started by each shepherd in turn, interrupted and taken up again as new characters are introduced, do not suffice to create the emphasis needed by the veteran who returns to his homeland. For him, the tale to be told does not consist of a simple narrative addressed to a benevolent listener, nor merely of signifiers to be articulated. In truth, the new inscription must be accomplished by bringing into the present unformulated stories and foreclosed events that burst forth in delusional episodes. Long after writing his pastoral romance and his early plays about life in Algiers, Cervantes gives free rein to the genius of the theatre of fools and jesters travelling on the roads of Europe with the jugglers.

One of the functions of this theatre in France, performed like mock trials, was to drag tyrants on the stage in order to judge them, revealing the hypocrisies of the era. Thus, the shepherdess Marcela condemns the tyranny of suicide, at the burial of the one who killed himself for her. Far from giving in to the blackmail of death and to the pressure of well-meaning sentiments, she lays bare the cruel harassment hidden behind the absolute power of suffering, in whose name all must be forgiven.

The shepherdess Marcela defends her freedom

As we saw, the shepherdess Marcela—Galate's double—refuses all guilt. Through her, Cervantes expresses his opinion about Grysostomo's suicide. He attributes the responsibility clearly, without feigned compassion. The shepherdess has not enticed or deceived anyone. If Grysostomo wanted to cast aspersions on her character by making her appear to be responsible for his death, he has no one to blame but himself. But she had nothing to do with his decision to abandon his place in society, nor with a strategy of love aiming to subject her to his will. She cannot be manipulated, and defends her freedom fiercely.

Between the almost Druidic burial of Grysostomo at the foot of the mountain, in chapter XIII, and the next body carried to its tomb in Chapter XIX, Cervantes opens an enchanted space that will be filled gradually with successive visions making it possible to show, but also to filter, experiences saturated with the energy of traumas.

The first filter is presented in Marcela's uncompromising discourse. She delivers her verdict unequivocally, at the burial of the shepherd who wanted to force her to love him. Thus, the position of the Lady becomes clearly established. Before new adventures begin, she dissociates herself from the grim rhetoric of Grysostomo's posthumous writings, and refuses to bear the torture inflicted by sinister pronouncements like: "Thou whose injustice hath supplied the cause, that makes me quit the weary life I loathe [...]" (De Cervantes, 2013, p. 78). The young girl says "no" to the loathing of life.

This beautiful, tough orphan girl declares herself unmoved by the type of seduction in which Celestina delighted, and which served as a means of inciting young people to suicide. Marcela states firmly that she is not susceptible to falling prey to guilt-producing discourses. The accusation of homicide made by the man who killed himself for her does not affect her. She responds to it by invoking the motto of the Lady with the Unicorn: "After my own desire". She defends herself by declaring: "I have, as you know, wealth of my own, and I covet not that of others; my taste is for freedom, and I have no relish for constraint; I neither love nor hate anyone; I do not deceive this one or court that, or trifle with one or play with another. [...] my desires are bounded by these mountains" (De Cervantes, 2013, p. 81).

Having perhaps suffered as an orphan, she knows the value of life, and her words echo those of Plato's *Phaedrus* on the subject of refusing one's favours to one who is not loved (Plato, 2003). "Those whom I have inspired with love by letting them see me, I have by words undeceived [...]. He was persistent in spite of warning, he despaired without being hated [...]. [...] let not him call me cruel or homicide to whom I make no promise, upon whom I practice no deception" (De Cervantes, 2013, p. 81).

It would be hard to find a clearer definition of the given word. She remains unaffected by blackmail, but does not preach: "I was born free, and that I might live in freedom I chose the solitude of the fields" (De Cervantes, 2013, p. 80). And that is that. She has spoken. Like a divinity of the land, she disappears into the space of wilderness where she is safe from attempts at violating her soul by proxy through another's suicide.

As Vivaldo suspected, the shepherdess is very much like a pagan goddess. Like a fairy, she returns to the space of the marvel. "With these words, and not waiting to hear a reply, she turned and passed into the thickest part of a wood that was hard by, leaving all who were there lost in admiration as much of her good sense as of her beauty" (De Cervantes, 2013, p. 81).

The case has been heard: Marcela refuses to participate in a discourse of death disguised as a utopian quest, and takes a stand against the political strategy of guilt-making. Don Quixote supports her resistance against suicidal forces. "Let no one, whatever his rank or condition, dare to follow the beautiful Marcela, under pain of incurring my fierce indignation. She has shown by clear and satisfactory arguments that little or no fault is to be found with her for the death of Grisostomo."

CHAPTER SIX

Widening of the field of war and beyond

Fifth traumatic revival: the Yanguesan shepherds

Cervantes takes care to warn the reader not to fall prey to the confusion between the field of war and that of torture.

The sudden turn from pastoral romance to a beating takes place in a grassy glade used as a pasture, where a drove of young mares is feeding. Once again, Rocinante initiates the transference. "Sancho had not thought it worthwhile to hobble Rocinante, feeling sure, from what he knew of his staidness and freedom from incontinence, that all the mares in Cordoba pastures would not lead him into an impropriety" (De Cervantes, 2013, p. 84).

But still waters run deep, as the saying goes. The old horse, no doubt inspired, like his master, by Marcela's discourse, and feeling rejuvenated at the sight of the winsome ponies, "without asking leave of his master, got up a briskish little trot and hastened to make known his wishes to them" (De Cervantes, 2013, p. 84). But the young damsels took fright at the sight of his sizeable member and sent him packing. They "received him with their heels and teeth to such effect that they soon broke his girths". Thus, he was left naked and without a saddle. So far so good, the fillies were able to defend themselves.

But this undisguised desire awakened other desires in the muleteers. Roused from their midday rest, they gave Rocinante a fierce beating for the attempted rape and battery of their mares. And before long they would subject the horse's master and his squire to the same punishment. In the meantime, Don Quixote, who witnesses the injustice to which his equestrian partner is subjected, goes berserk: "[…] he drew his sword and attacked the Yanguesans and excited and impelled by the example of his master, Sancho did the same." The confrontation between plural bodies is disproportionate: two against twenty, according to Sancho. But Don Quixote declares, undaunted: "I count for a hundred."

For the first time, the scene exceeds the bounds of an ordinary brawl and moves towards the *Massen Psychologie* (group psychology) discussed by Freud (Freud, 1921c, pp. 103–114). Now there is bloodshed—"Don Quixote […] laid open a great portion of [the] shoulder" of one of the muleteers—and what takes place is a lynching. After being savagely thrashed, the threesome is left lying in a heap. "[…] fate willed it that [Don Quixote] should fall at the feet of Rocinante, who had not yet risen; whereby it may be seen how furiously stakes can pound in angry boorish hands" (De Cervantes, 2013, p. 85).

The assailants hasten to take off, "seeing the mischief they had done", having acted worse than animals, since their own ponies restrained themselves in time. These outraged fillies defending their honour were not out to kill, despite their hysterical reaction to what they perceived to be a bawdy satyr. On such occasions, a youth movement can quickly degenerate into a manhunt.

The third part of Volume I introduces the reader to more dangerous enemies, ordinary men hard to imagine as criminals. They constitute the mob described by Hannah Arendt, an impersonal, uninhibited, and undifferentiated mass of all ages, both sexes and all social classes.

Here, Cervantes makes another important distinction: that between the unleashed plural body of survivors—even when it faces overwhelming adversaries—and the monstrosity of a collective body which, moved by pure brutality, "driving the two men into the middle […] began to lay on with [the] great zeal and energy of about twenty stakes held by forty hands" (De Cervantes, 2013, p. 85). The anonymous, inhuman mob pounded its victims without saying a word.

But a question remains. It is clear that Don Quixote started the fight. He is the one at fault. What is the distinction between a scene of sadism and a scene of traumatic revival? In effect, the Yanguesans defend the honour of their Galician fillies, and are carried away by their zeal. Who can blame them? We might have done the same thing, as "reasonable" people often say.

Here Cervantes points out a detail that constitutes the difference between the knave and the knight. This detail has to do with the unconscious, which suddenly moves the horse's phallus. Rocinante's erection is not premeditated, but occurs spontaneously and surprises everyone. However, the muleteers give it an entirely different interpretation, transforming "a briskish little trot" quickly stopped by a few kicks into full-fledged molestation.

This politically flawless trick consists of accusing the victims of the wrongs to which they were subjected. Accused of attacking the *habeas corpus* of his young colleagues, Rocinante, usually so staid and continent, cannot understand that he is accused of rape, and could in no way have foreseen that he would incite such a paroxysm of cruelty.

While in slavery, Cervantes must have experienced or witnessed on more than one occasion the reign of arbitrary rule, to be expected in lawless realms. When the relentless logic of the scapegoat—be it goat or horse—holds sway, there is no point arguing or becoming indignant. Awakened from their rest or their apathy, sleeping henchmen always find a reason to get excited. But suffering in silence is not an option either. So what is there to do? After the distressing experience of being treated like crap, therapy is needed to heal the physical and psychic trauma.

Don Quixote as therapon

We have already reviewed the stages of Cervantian analytic sessions, which offer invaluable lessons.

Proximity makes it possible to construct a mirror, as a first step, when waking from a coma after loss of face. Don Quixote and Sancho are on the ground, but call to each other and receive an answer. Suffering the same anguish, they "come to" and find themselves in a strange world. One regains consciousness, but consciousness of what?

The weakness and apparent passivity of this state is akin to that of the new-born who calls for his mother, like so many dying men on battlefields, or like victims of attacks. Sancho calls for his master "[in] a weak and doleful voice: 'Señor Don Quixote, ah, Señor Don Quixote!'", who answers: "'What would thou, brother Sancho?' [...] in the same feeble, doleful tone" (De Cervantes, 2013, p. 85). During the First World War, millions of dying soldiers were calling "mommy". My grandfather continued to hear these calls for years afterwards.

In Japanese, *amae* designates dependence on a primary maternal agency—which Cervantes can confirm from first-hand experience. The regressive moment when one comes back to one's senses after fainting or being in a coma is not to be attributed to some neuronal malfunction. Japanese psychiatrist Takeo Doi (Doi, 1973) discovered this concept, translated as "dependence" in English. According to Doi, the value of this concept, particularly well suited to the context of madness, is underestimated by Western theories, which tend to disqualify dependence and stigmatise lack of autonomy, symbiosis and passivity.

In fact, it is precisely because he engages in *amae* with Sancho, that once they have voiced their woes Don Quixote is able to assume his responsibilities once again. "I take all the blame upon myself, for I had no business to put hand to sword against men who were not dubbed knights like myself [...]". Having said this, he is able to rise from his position of defeat and to imagine a different future. The hierarchy between him and his squire is re-established, allowing Sancho to express his political convictions. "Señor, I am a man of peace, meek and quiet [...] and I can put up with any insults [...], whether they have been, are or shall be offered me [...] by high or low, noble or commoner" (De Cervantes, 2013, p. 86).

Undeniably, the hero barely escapes with his life. Don Quixote admits it and can even say: "I would lay me down here to die of pure vexation" (De Cervantes, 2013, p. 87). What is the use of living when the assassins think so little of your life? But in order not to let himself die, Don Quixote consoles and bolsters his squire. Forward psychiatry, his frontline psychotherapy, solicits hope for the future. "[...] there is no recollection that time does not put an end to, and no pain that death does not remove. [...] Pluck strength out of weakness. [...] Fortune always leaves a door open in adversity" (De Cervantes, 2013, p. 88). Expectancy. The old soldier says: "When things go wrong, they are just about to go well."

For the moment, the only member of the troupe who escaped unscathed, the only one not mentioned so far, is the donkey. "What I wonder at is that my beast should have come off scot-free where we come out scotched." Thus, the donkey takes the lead, for in the case of a plural body of survivors, this place is variously assigned, depending on changing priorities. Don Quixote is demoted from his position as *therapon*, becoming a sort of sack of manure slung across the pack-saddle.

Sixth traumatic revival: the inn as a brothel

This scene shows that mistreatment does not automatically provoke violent retribution, as is commonly claimed, but can sharpen therapeutic and poetic faculties. To describe his unfortunate position, Don Quixote turns to mythology, comparing himself to Silenus mounted on his ass, in Dionysian processions. He closes the episode with an epic pronouncement: "Wounds received in battle confer honour instead of taking it away", a statement Cervantes repeats, speaking in his own name, in The Author's Preface of The Second Part.

Don Quixote and Sancho finally arrive at an inn described as a "ladies' domain" (De Pizan, 2000), reminiscent of Pizan's "city of ladies". There, three women are entrusted with looking after travellers: the innkeeper's wife, his daughter and the servant lass Maritornes; all of them tend the two wounded guests as best they can.

But soon something goes wrong. The servant lass is about to succumb to the "unholy" desires of a rich muleteer stopping at the inn while on a business trip. She has given him her word to sleep with him as soon as the two new guests were going to be asleep in the same room. It was out of the question for her to betray her promise, for she was of Asturian descent and "plumed herself greatly on being a lady" (De Cervantes, 2013, p. 92). All Asturians claim to be connected by blood to the best families of the province, as we will learn in The Second Part from Doña Rodriguez (De Cervantes, 2013, p. 676). For this reason, Maritornes "never made promises [...] without fulfilling them, even though she made them in a forest and without any witness present" (De Cervantes, 2013, p. 92).

This time, Don Quixote's work will consist of reinstating the given word which has been violated through twisted promises, by using the upheaval he will cause at the inn to defend the honour of this woman of easy virtue. Transformed into a Mary Magdalene, she will in turn become a therapist, to help Sancho recover from the humiliating game in which he is treated like "a dog at Shrovetide" (De Cervantes, 2013, p. 101).

Maritornes is clearly the agency which reorients prostitutive social relations in a therapeutic direction. These are, after all, the two oldest professions known to man. But how does Maritornes go from one to the other, from money earned by selling herself to money spent for Sancho, who will be made the plaything of scoundrels, and treated no better than she had been? How does she change from the "strumpet", to whom the innkeeper calls out: "Where art thou, strumpet? Of course this is some of thy work" (De Cervantes, 2013, p. 94), turning from Maritornes, whose name has become a common noun, into the soft-hearted servant reminiscent of the kind damsels at the first inn?

This time, Cervantes will show that the indispensable feminine agency without which the knight cannot carry out his deeds is not always a daughter of the gentry, like Marcela. In the person of Maritornes, the Lady is liberated of image politics—which will be so skilfully exploited by the Duchess in The Second Part of the novel. Here, she reveals her hidden serpentine nature when, like Melusine on Saturday evenings, she turns into a river mermaid. A "lass with a broad face, flat poll, and snub nose, blind of one eye and not very sound in the other" (De Cervantes, 2013, p. 90), she brings to mind the two-faced figure of the Lady, whose nature is double, one less and the other more than human, as befits intermediary creatures living between our world and the wild world of enchantment.

An unstable figure of border zones and brothels, she will spin like a ball of yarn between two different discourses that clash violently. Don Quixote's crazy quest, in the course of which "when one thing is looked for another thing is found" (De Cervantes, 2013, p. 91), comes in conflict again with mercantile discourse, held here by the innkeeper and the muleteer—in its most basic sense, in which everything can be bought and sold, while skimping on the merchandise and on the quality of services. "The hard, narrow, wretched, rickety bed [...] and a blanket that looked as if it was of threadbare canvas rather than of wool" (De Cervantes, 2013, p. 92), and the sex trade that went with them, were no doubt familiar to Cervantes from the years when he travelled through the Spanish countryside as a commissary agent.

So far, all is well, all is as it should be, all is quiet: "the inn was all in silence" (De Cervantes, 2013, p. 92). The stillness waits only for the advent of the erotic object in the darkness that has fallen over the ordinary affairs and desires of men. The story could have followed its course, recounted with the precision of Cide Hamete Benengeli, a true micro historian, "to some degree a relation of [the muleteer]; [a man] of great research and accuracy in all things". Thus, all would be well if

Don Quixote did not wreak havoc once again, while half sleep. "[…] his eyes as wide open as a hare's", all his senses alert, as can be expected after a close brush with death.

Topsy-turvy Maritornes

This impressive energy, never dormant, was to precipitate the most unlikely event: the metamorphosis of Maritornes who, thanks to Don Quixote, will turn into a thing sublime. The protocol never varies.

In the dark garret, the glimpse of a furtive form is followed by the knight's resolve to take up the challenge, and then by an immediate assault in which a plural body will be formed again, with Sancho. Don Quixote seizes the wench, who is searching for the muleteer "with noiseless and cautious steps", in the obscurity of the silent garret. The knight's seismograph detects the approach of this venial quest. As a result, the lass loses her status as the muleteer's object and, held tightly by the knight, she changes instantly into a surviving form of the ladies of yore—"But where are the snows of yesteryear?" (Villon, 1904) who breathed life into worn-out, exhausted poet-soldiers.

Unbeknownst to her, Don Quixote ascribes all the qualities of a princess of the castle to Maritornes. All his senses awakened, his touch changes into silk "her smock, […] although it was of sackcloth", and transforms her coarse hair into "threads of the brightest gold". His eyes change the glass beads on her wrists into precious pearls, and his nose draws in a sweet aromatic fragrance, when in truth "her breath […] no doubt smelled of yesterday's stale salad, […] that would have made any but a carrier vomit" (De Cervantes, 2013, p. 93).

When such ghostly forms emerge—*nachleben* from the afterlife of antiquity, as Aby Warburg called them—their demonic nature is usually accompanied by pure frenzy. Hubris transforms the run-of-the-mill desires of the muleteer into a scene worthy of a Buster Keaton movie. Propelled onto the centre of the stage, like a ferret running in the woods, Maritornes dashes from place to place, passing from hand to hand, "crouching, [making] a ball of herself", terrified. But, like a live coin, she escapes from the muleteer's purse, transforming the Spanish inn into a den of chaos.

At this point, a free-for-all breaks out, like those which would later become a cinematic tradition. Bodies are pummelled and pounded, in a scrimmage the son of the barber-surgeon describes with clinical precision, sparing the reader no detail. Laid upon by the muleteer who "mounted on his ribs and with his feet trampled all over them at a pace rather smarter than a trot" (De Cervantes, 2013, p. 94), attacked by a heraldic and invisible figure whose "hand attached to some arm of some huge giant [...] planted such a cuff on my jaws that I have them all bathed in blood" (De Cervantes, 2013, p. 96), Don Quixote accelerated this furious chain-reaction.

Sancho endured "the heaviest whacks in all [his] life", delivered by more than four hundred Moors, so that the beating inflicted by the Yanguesans seemed "cakes and fancy bread" in comparison. And the wildfire spread from one person to another, "as the saying is, cat to rat, rat to rope". Here, the role of the *deus ex machina* is played by an archer of the municipal police, member of a Holy Brotherhood of military peacekeepers. As for Don Quixote, he remained "stretched senseless on his back upon his broken-down bed, [and] did not move or stir" (De Cervantes, 2013, p. 95).

Placing his life at risk, the knight enacts paradoxically, lest the merchants forget, what a righter-of-wrongs like him forces them to remember: not to confuse the trading of goods with the trafficking of human beings. "Shut the inn gate; see that no one goes out; they have killed a man here!" The cry of the cuadrillero sent everyone back to his quarters: the innkeeper to his room, the carrier to the packsaddles that make a comfortable bed, and the servant lass to her crib.

Now, Maritornes, a girl of modest extraction, has been freed, like Galate, of the Cyclopes and of masculine harassment. Don Quixote draws no benefit from his chivalrous action. He departs from the inn without paying, leaving behind the less than glorious image of a beaten and sorry-looking man.

This meeting of two worlds that are not meant to meet—the prosaic world of those who visit prostitutes, and the world of the former captive who dreams of escaping from a sordid reality—produces an explosive combination once again. A great expenditure of energy has forced Don Quixote to exhaust himself beyond reason. Clearly, he is acting in a parallel world where slavery, sexual or not, is no more acceptable than Cervante's slavery in the bagnios of Algiers. One day, in a hospital, a young woman who, thanks to her delusion, had been able to break a contract forcing her into prostitution, told me: "Infamy introduces a vacuum where thought used to be, but we, the mad, are armed to the teeth."

From house of ill repute to field hospital

When madness emerges, the sessions start to resemble each other.

There is *amae* upon awakening from a swoon. The maternal link is evoked by the chirping of birds fallen from the nest, "in the same tone of voice in which [Don Quixote] had called to his squire the day before [...], 'Sancho my friend, art thou asleep? Sleepest thou, friend Sancho?'" The unbearable repetition that discourages advocates of short-term therapy and of lasting progress always goes back to an initial loss of consciousness, and aims at reviving thinking, which in this instance is inseparable from healing.

Succor for a wounded heart is first provided by reassuring words that have less to do with analytic technique than with the art of living. Don Quixote reiterates this to Sancho, who has become as reluctant as an analyst discouraged by successive crises. Despite all the work you have already done, you have to start over. "At any rate, I have more confidence in thy affection and good nature" (De Cervantes, 2013, p. 96). Medication can also be used when needed. "I will now make the precious balm with which we shall cure ourselves in the twinkling of an eye" (De Cervantes, 2013, p. 97).

The second step, which consists in a confession, is often avoided by analysts concerned with their reputation. Don Quixote speaks openly: "This that I am about to tell thee thou must swear to keep secret until after my death." The avowal of a secret in such circumstances—in this case, having held in one's arms the damsel of the castle—was a custom in American Indian warrior societies, in which young men confided such secrets to each other before going on the warpath. Anthropologist Edward Sapir describes this custom among the members of the Crazy Dog Society (Sullivan, 1974, p. 227). Their unfailing loyalty is guaranteed by such avowals to each other. Sancho promises to keep the secret, but reluctantly, saying: "I hate keeping things long, and I don't want them to grow rotten with me from overkeeping" (De Cervantes, 2013, p. 96).

As we might expect, the confession precedes the moment when the archer, returning with a light, is rebuked by Don Quixote for his bad manners and breaks his oil lamp over the knight's head, delivering a formidable blow endured by the hero with the exceptional forbearance of the moonstruck. But unlike the muleteers, the municipal official provokes first-aid intervention. A goatherd's remedy, made of vinegar, wine, oil, salt, and rosemary is boiled for a good while by Sancho, with many *paternosters* and signs of the cross.

Medicinal molecules, as is well known, can be unpredictable, sometimes producing opposite effects on similar symptoms. Some patients are left exhausted, while others are cured of their anguish. To illustrate, we have the clinical description of the effects of the draught concocted by Sancho. Don Quixote experienced spasms, vomiting, and profuse sweating, after which he was covered up and left to sleep for three hours, and awoke cured. The concoction had the opposite effect on Sancho. He too was seized with sweats, retchings, and faintness, "[discharging] both ways" and convulsing, until in the end he was "left so weak and exhausted that he could not stand" (De Cervantes, 2013, p. 99).

Sancho is traumatised by the betrayal of his high command

In an analysis, clashes are sometimes produced when the analyst leaves his patient in the lurch, as will be the case for Sancho. Suddenly, Don Quixote, relieved and well, takes his departure, deaf to the demands of the innkeeper, who wants payment for their stay at the inn, while the knight invokes the exemption due to warriors. Like many traumatised veterans, he feels that he has paid enough. Unconsciously, he hands Sancho over to the innkeeper as a hostage who falls victim to the ensuing cruelty, suffering the same fate as Andrés.

Here, a vertical space opens. The squire is projected into it, like a ball, from a blanket held by nine merchants, "lively fellows, tender-hearted, fond of a joke, and playful" (De Cervantes, 2013, p. 100), rascals using their occupations as a "cover". This trauma was to become an indelible memory for Sancho. Afterwards, he would remind his master of it often, although the event endowed him with Quixotic endurance.

Now, the therapeutic function is taken over by Maritornes. Removed from the unacknowledged play of desire in which she had been thrust, she acquires the status of subject, chooses to take Sancho's side and pays with her own money for the right to have her say. Like a good Samaritan, she comforts him with "a jug of water which, […] that it might be all the cooler she fetched […] from the well" (De Cervantes, 2013, p. 101); and when he asked for wine, she brought it "with right good will, and paid for it with her own money".

Indeed, psychic structure is not fixed, but is made of changing relations, as shown by Quixotic transference, creating places to which no one is assigned permanently. For a brief moment which seems an eternity to Sancho, Don Quixote occupies the place of the indifferent bystander, an accomplice of his persecutors. Maritornes takes the place of therapist normally held by Sancho. She gives him her consideration, while the crafty merchants are busy assessing the value of all things. Don Quixote and his procession, like the practice of psychoanalysis today, are worth nothing. "[There] were fellows who would not have cared two farthings for [him], even had he been really one of the knights-errant of the Round Table" (De Cervantes, 2013, p. 102).

The young girl in black

I once met a young girl who embodied this lack of worth. She had just been released from a psychiatric hospital, where she was taken after a suicide attempt. Pale and expressionless, she told me everything was wrong with her. She had no plans, no future, she lived from day to day, there was no work she could do well. She had a simple job, that she got as a favour, she said, but even there she was hopeless. She was impolite, never said hello, and did not want to know anyone. Indeed, she spoke in a plaintive, monotonous voice, wincing when I tried to make her smile. She hadn't come to see me on her own, but only because her physician had convinced her to do so. She was not taking her antidepressants, there was nothing she wanted, she had no self-confidence at all. Even as a child in school, she was bored and never knew what to do. Of course, she got this from her family: her mother was sick, her father silent, obsessive, and unable to communicate with anyone, not even his wife.

- Since when?
- Ever since I was born, during the Algerian war. He was among the last to be drafted.
- Did he serve in the war?

For the first time, she looked at me, surprised, and nodded her head, as if the answer was obvious. After a few sessions, I started to ask myself if she was not enacting, twenty years later, the worthlessness of the battles in which her father fought, when he himself was twenty.

- Like many others, he probably had no one to speak to …
- Oh, no! There was the Association of Veterans of the Algerian War, the annual banquet, the family trips to Thoiry and Versailles, the Christmas party for the children.

What impresses her is how well I remember what she told me two weeks ago. Not her. She has no memory, she remembers nothing. I advance a hypothesis:

– I remember because we are talking about it together. In my family, we also avoided the subject of past wars. You are the living memory of your father's feeling of worthlessness, of no longer belonging and of no longer remembering anything.

In the months that followed, I continued in this vein, to my own surprise. I wondered if it was because I was reading *Don Quixote* at the time, but I did not speak of this to my patient. Little by little, she became more animated; bits of colour started to appear in what she wore. Then she decided to return to her native town, where she would feel less isolated than in Paris.

After this, I saw her only once. She rang my doorbell one day, out of the blue. Since I was with a patient just then, I saw her in my waiting room, thinking she was there because of a relapse. But I was wrong: back in Paris for a brief visit, she had dropped by to thank me and bring me an art book describing an enchanting garden. She left without saying anything more, smiling mysteriously like a maiden from the Medieval Romance of the Rose. Much later, her physician told me that she was married and had children.

Seventh traumatic revival: a hallucinated battlefield

Once outside the tavern, veritable cavern whose *chiaroscuro* summons the spectral shadows of yore, the field can widen enough to accommodate the vision of a great battle. Don Quixote is once more in possession of his entire team: Rocinante has recovered from the fall occasioned by his earthly appetites, and Sancho, mounted on his ass, is glad to leave without paying. Still, Don Quixote had to boost his squire's morale, for Sancho was "so limp and faint that he could not urge on his beast" (De Cervantes, 2013, p. 103). Perplexed by his master's abandonment when he was being tossed in the air, he is confused and discouraged, and wants to go back home and tend to his own affairs.

To dissuade him, Don Quixote relegates the merchants to a secondary position, and emphasises the art of the warrior, saying: "[…] what greater pleasure can there be in the world, or what delight can equal that of [...] triumphing over one's enemy?" (De Cervantes, 2013, p. 104). To provide support for his arguments, all he has to do is conjure up the combat zone, using a method he has mastered perfectly. What is urgent now for Don Quixote is to introduce Sancho to the world of combat.

Their peaceful conversation is interrupted by a *kledon* sent by the gods, in the form of clouds of dust. Always ready for battle, Don Quixote seizes upon the phenomenon to stage a battle, like in a movie, "seeing in his imagination what he did not see and what did not exist" (De Cervantes, 2013, p. 105). In the same way, Aby Warburg conducted the First World War on his own, from the library in his home. He called the incandescence of such visions *pathosformel*.

Surviving forms appear in the guise of what the Surrealists call *"hazard objectif"* considered as a chance-appointed event. On a precise day, at a precise hour, the Quixotic troupe meets a cloud of dust on the plain; this encounter will produce nothing less than a world war. On the Russian front, Wittgenstein wrote: "There are, indeed, things that cannot be put into words. They make themselves manifest. They are what is mystical" (Wittgenstein, 2001).

Don Quixote accomplishes such an epiphany to the letter. "This is the day, Sancho, on which will be seen [...], shall be displayed the might of my arm, and on which I shall do deeds that shall remain written in the book of fame [...]" (De Cervantes, 2013, p. 104). The vision is not a static hallucination, but rather a psychodynamic scene in which the true feat is to bring into the present events not witnessed, and then inscribe them in the past. This will be the aim of the Discourse on Arms and Letters, in Chapter XXXVIII, followed by the captive's discourse, the true reason for the mad passion to write, despite any discouragement. For Cervantes, the course of fame will, indeed, be changed.

To achieve this, he first lets his son open the way through his visions. A faithful projectionist of his father's wars, Don Quixote sees "a vast army composed of various and countless nations". When Sancho points out that, in fact, there are only two, "Don Quixote turned to look" and, like in the Bible, "found that it was true".

For once, the reader is given the facts before the protagonists. The whirlwind illusion is produced by "two great droves of sheep coming along the same road in opposite directions" (De Cervantes, 2013, p. 105). But knowing the end of the story, or the end of a movie, doesn't prevent the reader or the spectator from being drawn into the plot of such a super production. From his panoramic vantage point, Don Quixote contemplates, like a general through his spy-glass, nothing less than a Jihad or one of the Crusades, depending on your allegiance: "Alifanfaron [against] Pentapolin of the Bare Arm."

Now the aerial reconnaissance mission can start to identify, in the thick of battle, the heraldic symbolism of shields, devices, and mottoes on both sides, and the origin of the squadrons. On one side, the armies of the Trapobana in South-East Asia, of the Numidians of Tunisia, those of the three Arabias, the Parthians from Iraq and Jordan, the Persians and the Medes of Iran, the Scythians of Turkey, as well as Libyans and Ethiopians. Facing them, could be seen "all [the nations] Europe includes and contains: Spain and France, Portugal, Italy, and many others. The list resembles that of participants to a United Nations Assembly meeting. "Good God! What a number of countries and nations he named! Giving to each its proper attributes with marvellous readiness; brimful and saturated with what he had read in his lying books" (De Cervantes, 2013, p. 107).

Yet the books in question include Homer and Virgil, and other more recent tales whose content allows Cervantes to portray the state of the modern world. He leaves it to Don Quixote to create the clamour made by the neighing of steeds, the sound of drums and bugles which, mixed with the bleating of sheep and with Sancho's cries produce the explosive fury of combat. "The fear thou art in, Sancho, prevents thee from seeing or hearing correctly, for one of the effects of fear is to derange the senses and make things appear different from what they are; if thou art in such fear, withdraw to one side [...]" (De Cervantes, 2013, p. 107). Sancho's fear is that of all those who have known combat. How often have I heard: "You want to know what war is? It is being scared to death."

The speed of the assault overcomes the terror. "[...] and so saying he gave Rocinante the spur, and putting the lance in rest, shot down the slope like a thunderbolt." Like a bolt of war-crazed lightning, he dashed into the enemy camp "with much spirit and intrepidity", unaware of pain, fortified by adrenaline, endorphins, and other profound changes in body biochemistry, which caused him to remain deaf to Sancho's cries: "Come back, Señor [...], come back!" Nor did he feel the "stones as big as one's fist [that] began to salute his ears", propelled by slings. Here, the madness of war is brought in full view. "Watching the crazy feats his master was performing, Sancho [was] tearing his beard and cursing the hour and the occasion when fortune had made him acquainted with him" (De Cervantes, 2013, p. 108).

Cervantes' genius consists of giving the word "folly" its literal sense here. He does not say: "God, what a beautiful thing, war!", but does not discredit the experience of those who fought, like he did. On the contrary, he testifies to the difficulty of simply surviving such frightful chaos. Cervantes' clinical account is precise, as usual: injured ribs, smashed teeth, two crushed fingers. Don Quixote imagined himself slain, as did the shepherds who "came up, and felt sure they had killed him; [...] they collected their flock together, took up the dead beasts [...], and made off [...]" Fortunately, his death was only apparent. Sancho found him "in very bad case, though not unconscious". This is an improvement over the previous episode.

Analytic use of the mirror in the context of trauma

Don Quixote swallowed his rosemary balm in one gulp, and proceeded to check if the plural body was still in working order. Rocinante had not been spooked by the panic and "had never stirred from his master's side—so loyal and well-behaved was he" (De Cervantes, 2013, p. 109). Sancho examined his master's injuries: "[He] came so close that he almost put his eyes into his mouth." But the clinical signs were confusing and what he thought to be brain haemorrhage due to trauma was in fact a spurt of vomit "discharged [...] with more force than a musket, and full into the beard of the compassionate squire". Sancho "perceived the colour, taste, and smell" of rosemary, but despite his efforts to remain objective, "he was taken with such a loathing that his stomach turned, and he vomited up his inside over his very master".

The limits of their bodies become diffuse, inside and outside are confused, and both men are left in a sorry state, since the innkeeper has confiscated their provisions in payment of what they owe him for their stay. The betrayal of the Service Corps leaves them no choice but to sink into the apathy of castoff victims.

All they can do now is provide ordinary maternal care for each other, like infantrymen in the trenches. Face to face, mirroring each other, they strike the classic pose of melancholy, hand to the cheek, when all hope is gone, when the fighting has lost all meaning, and most importantly when there is nothing left to eat. Don Quixote sees Sancho "leaning over his ass with his hand to his cheek, like one in deep dejection". As for him, he holds his cheek for reasons more physical than metaphysical: "[He] now rose, and put his left hand to his mouth to keep his teeth from falling out altogether [...]".

Becoming an antidepressant for his *therapon*, he pays Sancho back for his ministrations by providing talk therapy, while extracting him from the pool of collective vomit. His discourse recommends excellence—*aristeia* in Greek. "Bear in mind, Sancho, that one man is no more than another, unless he does more than another." This bit of wisdom is coupled with the wheel of fortune symbolised by the rosettes decorating furniture in Brittany and Savoy, and by cathedral transcept rose windows. "All these tempests that fall upon us are signs that fair weather is coming shortly, and that things will go well with us, for it is impossible for good or evil to last for ever."

Don Quixote has taken charge of the therapy, now based on an organic diet, a little less vegetarian than that recommended by Dioscorides, the Greek herbalist of the second century BC. Acorns, herbs and roots can be accompanied by worms, flies and tadpoles. "Nevertheless, [my good] Sancho, mount thy beast and come along with me, for God, who provides for all things, will not fail us (more especially when we are so active in his service)" (De Cervantes, 2013, p. 109).

Et exaltavit humiles! (God exalted the lowly) This motto of the Medieval Feast of Fools might be encouraging, but it doesn't put bread on the table. So it is that the Spartan fare proposed by Sancho sounds mouthwatering to Don Quixote, making him dream of proteins and slow sugars. He would gladly eat a quarter of bread, or even "a loaf and a couple of pilchards' heads, [rather] than all the herbs described by Dioscorides, even with Doctor Laguna's notes" (De Cervantes, 2013, p. 109) he says, referring to the famous Spanish humanist physician who died in 1560.

But in order to chew, one needs teeth, and Don Quixote, who was so proud of his sound teeth, feels pain in his jaw where several teeth are now missing. A great misfortune for one who could say, in that era: "[...] never in my life have I had tooth or grinder drawn, nor has any fallen out or been destroyed by any decay or abscess". As a form of self-therapy, Don Quixote sings his favourite song on Arms and Letters: "The lance has never blunted the pen, nor the pen the lance", which brings him to conclude that knights-errant have nothing to envy the graduates of the University of Paris.

But all this did not stop the pain in Don Quixote's jaw from becoming excruciating. Wittgenstein once said: "I cannot choose the mouth with which I say 'I have toothache'" (Wittgenstein, 2011), and so the task fell to Sancho to count the knight's teeth, both top and bottom, and to announce his sad findings: "in this lower side your worship has no more than two grinders and a half, and in the upper neither a half nor any at all", although previously even the knight's back teeth had been "all whole and quite sound". Once his losses are articulated by his alter ego, Don Quixote allows himself to express regret at not having lost an arm instead, "for [...] a mouth without teeth is like a mill without a millstone, and a tooth is much more to be prized than a diamond" (De Cervantes, 2013, p. 110). The talking cure stumbles along and Sancho does his best "to amuse and divert him by talk of some kind", but it is clear that a drastic change has taken place.

Having himself become a useless windmill after the loss of the treasures held in his mouth, Don Quixote is shaky, no longer quite himself. He feels his appearance is in ruins. Now, he is able to join his father's dead companions, to visit them on the other side of the mirror, in the place of dread.

The solider at the Boston train station

One day, immersed in a book as usual, I waited at South Station in Boston for the Amtrak express train that would take me to Penn Station in New York. I looked forward to the trip, since the train travelled along the Atlantic coast, passing through the picturesque port of Mystic. But I was distracted from my reading by a monotonous voice speaking rather loudly.

The voice belonged to a burly young man who sat on the edge of his chair, talking and talking, his upper body, his neck and his head stiff, slightly bent forward. I noticed that he was not looking at anyone and was projecting his words straight ahead, although an older couple was seated at his table. I assumed that they were his parents. The woman was slim and wore a beige raincoat and a hat that put one in mind of the Puritans of New England. The man, immersed in his newspaper, was wearing a dark blue cap.

I told myself that he must have some score to settle with them, and went back to my book. But the voice went on, without inflection, giving no sign that it might stop. I looked over again, intrigued by the strange scene, and tried to listen.

I heard place names: Tikrit, Baghdad,—names often repeated on the news about the war in Iraq, which had been going on for a year. I could not make out what it was all about, but I heard several times that "we" should have done this or that. I quickly concluded that the young man was crazy and that his parents were no doubt taking him back to his institution, after some kind of leave.

That is when the little lady started to talk to him, so softly that I could not hear her. He had finally stopped talking, but remained stiff. Then the older man lifted his eyes from his paper and said out loud, very distinctly: "I was made deaf in combat too."

The young man stood up at once and went to get his canvas camouflage jacket, which he had left at another table. I understood that he had just come back from Iraq, that these people were not his parents and that he had gone to sit at their table for a simple reason that soon became evident. As the young man was returning to their table, the older man leaned over to pick up his paper that had fallen, and I could read the words "US Navy" on the front of his cap. This had been the reason, *razon*, which had brought the young soldier to their table, to confess that he had lost his reason.

When he sat down again, his posture had changed. He was relaxed, sitting with one hand to his cheek, smiling at them while with his other hand, which was all black, he was showing them maps and other battle sites that I could not see. Now, the three people around the little table were talking as if they knew each other. I eventually heard that the older man had fought in the Pacific.

Soon the loudspeakers announced that it was time to board my train; the scene at the station, lengthy and brief at once, reminded me of a playlet by Cervantes, "The Vigilant Sentinel" (De Cervantes, 1991). The hero is a soldier who carries his only prized possessions around his neck, in a cylinder containing his rolled up service record. The young man in Boston had also rummaged through his bag at length, before waving stamped and sealed documents that he proudly showed the older couple, to prove that he had fought in a certain place, on a certain date.

When I boarded the Amtrak (*âmes-track*, to my French ear) train, this scene was engraved on my mind as if I had actually travelled on the footsteps of the Dead Souls to whom this young veteran was lending his voice.

Eighth traumatic revival: the myth of Er

In Plato's *Republic* (Plato, 2007a), a soldier named Er is left for dead on the battlefield. But he cannot have access to metapsychosis, since he is not altogether dead. His soul cannot be given a new life and undergo transmigration, allowing it to forget everything about this world. Instead, Er returns to earth in an intermediate state: although he has not forgotten anything, he is unable to say that he is returning from the world of the dead. The mythical traumatised soldier, Er, like the soldier at South Station, is no longer completely of our world, and departs at times to visit the places where he has left his friends.

Don Quixote is now in a similar situation, face to face with a dead body which travels, under cover of night, to its grave, in an intermediate state, in which the corpse is between two deaths: biological death and its symbolic inscription. The deceased is physically dead, but has not yet taken his place among the dead through the ritual of burial. Historically, this account could correspond to the transfer of the body of St. John of the Cross, in May 1593, from Upper Andalusia to Segovia, in Castilla, at the time when Cervantes was travelling through these provinces. The late hour, the solitary place, the strange procession, are conducive to spectral apparitions.

It was in similar circumstances that Ronsard, who had set out one evening to visit his mistress across the Loir, had a terrifying encounter with the retinue of the King of the Dead, Herlat. Goethe's *Erlkönig*, the Alder King, who led the furious armies of deceased young warriors killed in combat, would also become Harlequin, the character of *Commedia dell'arte* who wears a black leather mask. As for Ronsard, he unsheathes his sword and furiously draws figures of the cross in the air, until the sinister apparition dissolves. Then, losing no more time, he writes *Les Daimons* (De Ronsard, 2002, p. 144) in 1555.

The encounter with spectres emerging from the furious battle in the previous chapter occurs as a natural consequence of combat. Moving lights appear and fill the space, making "Don Quixote's hair [stand] on end" and causing Sancho "to shake like a man dosed with mercury" (De Cervantes, 2013, p. 112). This glimpse into the beyond causes the plural body to close ranks and reaffirm the oath of feudal loyalty. "Be they phantoms ever so much, I will not permit them to touch a thread of thy garments." But Sancho doubts that phantoms are subject to such a law. "And if they enchant and cripple you as they did the last time?"

Indeed, "this strange spectacle they set themselves to observe closely" was composed of "moving lighted torches carried by men in long shirts, terrifying white shapes like those that made their appearance in 1829 during the War of the Demoiselles of Ariege" (Sahlins, 1994). "[...] they muttered to themselves in a low plaintive tone; [...] behind them there came a litter covered over with black and followed by mounted figures in mourning". This time, the scene before them was not a hallucination. "[...] all Sancho's resolution had now broken down", but Don Quixote used the encounter to enter into a dialogue with the errant souls, since his imagination "immediately conjured up all this to him vividly as one of the adventures of his books" (De Cervantes, 2013, p. 112).

Clearly, no effort must be spared in the attempt to establish a dialogue with the plaintive whispers or monotonous monologues whose strangeness had struck me when I was listening to the young girl in black and the young man at the Boston train station.

Thus, Don Quixote was not content to remain paralysed with fear, but initiated contact. Laying his lance in rest, fixing himself firmly in his saddle, "with gallant spirit and bearing", he demanded an explanation. His demeanour contrasts sharply with the sinister atmosphere, and proves once again that breaking away from depression takes not only courage, but intelligence as well. Determined not to be intimidated or duped, he wants to be informed. "[...] whosoever ye may be, [...] render me account of who ye are, whence ye come, where ye go, what it is ye carry upon that bier, for, to judge by appearances, either ye have done some wrong or some wrong has been done to you, and it is fitting and necessary that I should know."

The first hypothesis seemed to be confirmed when the *encamisado* to whom he addressed these words ignored Don Quixote's proposal "and spurring his mule he moved on", thereby exposing himself to the threat of the attack announced by the knight in his second declaration: "Halt, and be more mannerly, and render an account of what I have asked of you; else, take my defiance to combat, all of you."

The man's mule, showing more good sense than the rider, reared up and sent him to the ground. There followed the inevitable chaotic scene worthy of a silent film, in which Rocinante swept down on these timid people like a horse from the Apocalypse, "as if wings had that instant grown upon [him], so lightly and proudly did he bear himself". The funeral procession now turned into a carnival scene in which the *encamisados* "set off at a run across the plain with their lighted torches, looking exactly like maskers running on some gala or festive night" (De Cervantes, 2013, p. 113).

Here the inversion ritual comes into play. The world is literally upside down—a world in which Don Quixote appears to the mourners to be the "Daimon" of a band of spirits, "a devil from hell come to carry away the dead body they had in the litter". Their impression is, in fact, not far off the mark. The knight and his troupe are headed for the depths of hell, which will be enacted in the next scene. As for Sancho, he sees with his own eyes that "this master of mine is as bold and valiant as he says he is". The spoils of war that fell to them in the form of provender are all the proof he needs.

A second inversion occurs in the language of the mourner thrown off his mule, when he speaks of his broken leg: "[...] from straight you have made me crooked [...]; and the height of misadventure it was to fall in with you who go in search of adventures" (De Cervantes, 2013, p. 114). The important thing is that he converses with Don Quixote, who can then attempt to undo the wrong he has done, and help "to remove the bachelor from under the mule". The knight also asks him to beg pardon of his companions, for the wrong he has done them.

A good session at last

The episode ends with the second baptism of the one who was born again, after looking death in the face in battle. Instead of the name Don Quixote had given to himself, he is now called by Sancho the "Knight of the Rueful Countenance". Entrusted with the safekeeping of his master's symbolic identity, the squire takes the place of "the sage whose duty it will be to write the history of [the knight's] achievements". Enthusiastic, Don Quixote means "to have a very rueful countenance painted on my shield" (De Cervantes, 2013, p. 115).

This is when Cervantes demonstrates, in three rapid steps, what a name truly is, with at most Saussurian and Wittgensteinian rigour.

First, Sancho intends the name to represent its meaning literally, making it simply a label of what it signifies, and making the name simply the translation of the image painted on the shield. In short, he takes the signifier for the signified: "There is no occasion, señor, for wasting time or money on making that countenance, for all that need be done is for your worship to show your own [...] to those who look at you, [...] for I assure you, señor[...], hunger and the loss of your grinders have given you such an ill-formed face that, [...] the rueful picture may be very well spared" (De Cervantes, 2013, p. 116).

Don Quixote's reaction—the second step—is to laugh at Sancho's pleasantry. By doing so, he denies that this name fits his countenance perfectly, and by maintaining that someone else "thought it proper that I should take [this] name", he attests that the name is a signifier, springing from the ominous space in which a spectre between two deaths is left to wander.

The third step consists of inscribing the name of the Knight of the Rueful Countenance for posterity.

In a single page, Cervantes brings together all the components of the birth of language and of the new names given in battle. Nicknames given during wars, so greatly cherished by soldiers, are often sobriquets, such as Corporal Trim, the nickname given to Captain Toby's orderly, whose real name is James Butler, and who is another Sancho Panza for Uncle Toby, Tristam Shandy's uncle (Sterne, 1999), a genuine Don Quixote in Laurence Sterne's novel. In most cases, the nickname refers to a defect, a whim, a peculiarity or a distinctive trait, just as family names used to do. The perceived insult is sanctioned by a burst of laughter, in the tradition of ritual pleasantries—farces, comedies, *kyôgens*—, without which tragedies or Noh theatre would be incomplete.

Sancho the trickster holds up a mirror to Don Quixote, who has not looked at himself in a mirror since the stoning episode involving the shepherds. A burst of laughter suffices to change the image into a signifier. As a result, the knight can have engraved, under the rueful countenance virtually painted on his shield, "This is not a rueful countenance", imitating Magritte's famous "This is not a pipe", written under his painting of a pipe.

The salient conclusion of this adventure is neatly captured in the phrase "the dead to the grave and the living to the loaf". This saying closes the episode, accomplishing a kind of exchange, like the ritual for changelings (Schmitt, 1983), in which the baby was given back to his mother after being rebaptised in a nearby river. But in Cervantes' tale the ritual cannot be completed for lack of an essential element.

At this turning point in his life, Don Quixote is truly about to be reborn. But when the crucial moment comes, water is lacking. The two companions only realise this after feasting, as is customary for carrying out a ceremony: they enjoy all sorts of cold meat taken from the *encamisados*, in a wide valley, "stretched upon the green grass, with hunger for sauce". In this idyllic décor, perfect for coming back to life, "another piece of ill luck befell them, which Sancho held the worst of all, and that was that they had no wine to drink, nor even water to moisten their lips" (De Cervantes, 2013, p. 116).

So it came about that the search for water led them into the beyond, in the course of a night of penance in which they were almost dead to the world.

Ninth traumatic revival: Nekyia

Nekyia is the journey to the realm of death, a voyage Ulysses, Theseus, Eneus, and many others made to visit their dead companions.

Before setting out, the tavern, where worlds intersect, allows for a change of scale. The usual points of reference gradually become unrecognisable. Proximity becomes intrusion and even foul-smelling promiscuity. Immediacy of action is paralysed. As for expectancy, it limits itself to waiting for an improbable dawn in the gloom of a never-ending night. Here, like in Descartes' nightmares, the world beyond is made manifest through wind and sinister sounds. In Brittany, such signs announce the arrival of Ankou, the Graveyard Watcher.

Having set out to look for water at Sancho's prompting, since "this grass is a proof that there must be hard by some spring or brook to give it moisture", they are stopped by a formidable phenomenon of cognitive dissonance which confuses sensory analysis and hinders thinking. The pleasure of hearing water "that seems as though it were precipitating and dashing itself down from [...] lofty mountains" is mixed with the fear instilled by "incessant hammering that wounds and pains [their] ears" (De Cervantes, 2013, p. 118): "strokes which resounded with a regular beat", coupled with "a certain rattling of iron and chains", created the paradoxical signals of terror which Gregory Bateson calls a double bind.

This contradiction which reason cannot resolve requires a supernatural interpretation. The hammering comes from an inferno, and the slightest breeze becomes a brush with the souls of the damned. "[...] leaves stirred by a gentle breeze made a low ominous sound; so that, what with the solitude, the place, the darkness, the noise of water, and the rustling of leaves, everything inspired awe and dread" (De Cervantes, 2013, p. 117).

But dread, of course, prevents action. When Don Quixote attempts to lunge against the unnamable, he is literally impeded by the halter Sancho has covertly tied around Rocinante's legs. For the first time, the possibility of a final separation is discussed. "Wait for me here three days and no more, and if in that time I do not return, thou should return to our village, and thence [...] thou wilt go to El Toboso, where thou shalt say to my incomparable lady Dulcinea that her captive knight hath died [...]."

In these sinister circumstances, Sancho has taken the lead, justifying his actions by constant laments, "weeping in the most pathetic way", by attempted blackmail—"I shall yield my soul up to anyone that will take it", and by reference to the sacrifices he has consented to make: "I left home and wife and children to come and serve your worship, trusting to do better and not worse; but as covetousness bursts the bag, it has rent my hopes asunder [...]" (De Cervantes, 2013, p. 118).

The plural body now takes the shape of a freakish monster, created by the squire to resist the clamorous Leviathan which remains nameless and shapeless. His head leaning against his master's thigh, while the latter remains mounted on Rocinante, unable to advance, Sancho stays glued to his master, immobilised by fear which results in farts and diarrhea, causing Sancho to be fettered in his turn by his own breeches lying around his ankles.

Tell me a story

Talk therapy is intimately related to the art of storytelling, from which psychoanalysis clearly takes its roots. But analysts sometimes forget that *Oedipus Rex* is not the only myth it can enlist in the service of patients. Indeed, the art of storytelling is the analytic art *par excellence*, provided certain conditions of the oral tradition are met, as Cervantes teaches us.

What better time for storytelling than the dark, terrifying hours of the night? Sancho offers to serve as narrator. "I will amuse your worship by telling stories from this till daylight, unless indeed you like to dismount and lie down to sleep a little [...]" (De Cervantes, 2013, p. 119). But this second option is unacceptable to Don Quixote in a situation of mortal danger. "What art thou talking about dismounting or sleeping for? [...] Sleep thou who art born to sleep [...]" (De Cervantes, 2013, p. 119). Hypervigilant and therefore insomniac, Don Quixote chooses the first option and asks his *therapon* to "tell some story to amuse him". He has no inkling of the complexity of the device he has requested, nor of the obligations he has accepted.

To produce the desired effect, "the storyteller must be the story" while he is telling it: "You are the music while the music plays." This is why Sancho starts by saying: "I will strive to tell a story [the telling of] which, if I can manage to relate it, nobody [must interfere] with [...]." The beginning and end of the story delimit a space outside of ordinary time, through ritual phrases that serve as conjuring formulas to open and close the magic space where the monsters will be killed, or tamed, in the narrative. The start of the story is formal. "[...] here I begin. What was, was; and may the good that is to come be for all, and the evil for him who goes to look for it—your worship must know that the beginning the old folk used to put to their tales was not just as each one pleased; it was a maxim of Cato Zonzorino" (De Cervantes, 2013, p. 120).

Sancho's confusion (when naming the Roman statesman Censorino) shows that the boundaries between learned literature and oral tradition are not so rigid. But this diversion is also Sancho's first mistake. By doing what he advises others not to do, he interrupts his own tale to insert a cautionary adage, obviously intended for Don Quixote: "the evil for him who goes to look for it". After this, the spell is broken. The narration becomes didactic and boring, specifying that "this means that".

Exasperated, Don Quixote remains aloof, displaying his usual critical acuity: "If that is the way thou tellest thy tale, Sancho, repeating twice all thou hast to say, thou wilt not have done these two days; go straight on with it, and tell it like a reasonable man, or else say nothing" (De Cervantes, 2013, p. 120).

There is no justification for desecrating a story with endless watchwords. Sancho's attempt to invoke tradition is of no avail: "Tales are always told in my country in the way I am telling this, and I cannot tell it in any other, nor is it right of your worship to ask me to make new customs" (De Cervantes, 2013, p. 120). But he becomes mixed up about ancient and modern styles, and ends up following Don Quixote's advice to the letter. Thus, his tale is reduced to the adventures of a fairly hysterical shepherdess who "[...] when she found herself spurned by Lope, was immediately smitten with love for him, though she had never loved him before" (De Cervantes, 2013, p. 121), and to the obsessive counting of Lope's goats carried across the river, at which point the count curtails the story. "Let your worship keep count of the goats the fisherman is taking across, for if one escapes the memory there will be an end of the story, and it will be impossible to tell another word of it" (Cervantes, 2013, p. 121). The same is true when the obsession with accounting keeps count of the number, duration, price, and even absence of analytic sessions, putting an end to inspiration.

Oscillating transference

Don Quixote cares nothing about quantity. It is not in his nature to pay attention to instructions, and he quickly tires of this useless occupation. When Sancho asks him "How many have gone across so far?", he answers curtly, "How the devil do I know? Take it for granted he brought them all across." He makes his decisions freely, influenced by no one: "I will act as I think most consistent with my character." When, speaking of Sancho's tale, Don Quixote exclaims: "Let it end where it will, well and good" (De Cervantes, 2013, p. 122), he transforms, like in an analysis, the technical error in the count into a new opening onto the unknown.

But the cathartic effect has taken the form of a purge, and the discharge from Sancho's lower quarters is a veritable intestinal fiasco. Don Quixote comes to the rescue of his nose "by compressing it between his fingers, saying in a rather snuffling tone, 'Sancho, it strikes me thou art in great fear'" (De Cervantes, 2013, p. 123). Through this psychosomatic interpretation, the knight resumes his therapeutic position and reinstates the proper limits. "Then go back three or four [paces], my friend", said Don Quixote, all the time with his fingers to his nose, "and for the future pay more attention to thy person and to what thou owest to mine; for it is my great familiarity with thee that has bred this contempt".

Now the transference is re-established with the required distance, as it ought to be after critical moments when both patient and analyst have been entangled in the frenzy of a crisis. Following the panic of an interval of rather intense closeness in which analyst and patient learn too much about each other, dawn breaks over the horizon. A new day provides a fresh start. "It makes it worse to stir [these matters], friend Sancho."

At last, daylight reveals the demons of the night to have been nothing more than water mills this time, driving fulling hammers for wool cloth! The two men are speechless. "When Don Quixote perceived what it was, he was struck dumb and rigid from head to foot" (De Cervantes, 2013, p. 124). Now that the infernal mystery is solved, mortification follows. But Sancho's prodigious peals of laughter soon come to the rescue. The flow of the water revives the flow of words that had been arrested by the counting in the tale.

Here, folly, from the Latin *follis*, meaning bellows—bursts the ominous illusion, after the explosions of gas and wind, giving rise to such fits of laughter that now the heroes might die of it, instead of dying of fear. "Don Quixote glanced at Sancho and saw him with his cheeks puffed out and his mouth full of laughter, and evidently ready to explode with it, and in spite of his vexation he could not help laughing at the sight of him; and when Sancho saw his master begin he let go so heartily that he had to hold his sides with both hands to keep himself from bursting with laughter. Four times he stopped, and as many times did his laughter break out afresh with the same violence as at first [...]"

The clinical description shows the therapeutic effect of laughter, as Rabelais asserted, and of madness, considered in his time "more a cure than a destiny", a way to subvert the tyranny of melancholia and give birth to life on the edge of deathly tension, as Sancho's posture illustrates.

The rapid oscillations of transference, inevitable in such situations, eventually taper down. The squire is called to order by his master, who thinks the pleasantry has lasted long enough. "Well, then, if you are joking I am not" (De Cervantes, 2013, p. 12). Still, he invokes the unconscious to resolve the standoff: "our first movements are not in our own control" (De Cervantes, 2013, p. 12).

Now, the analysis can take a more traditional course. The roles are reestablished: "[...] bear in mind, that thou curb and restrain thy loquacity in my company [...]; and in fact I feel it to be a great fault of thine and of mine." The proper distance is also recreated through the question of payment of the fees. "In these wretched times of ours", Sancho is mentioned in Don Quixote's will. In exchange, having resumed his role as therapist, Sancho promises: "I will not open my lips henceforward to make light of anything of your worship's [...]" (De Cervantes, 2013, p. 126). Analytic silence returns, confirming by contrast that critical moments require atypical techniques. Sancho is sure to keep this in mind, and might even make a comeback someday as Papageno, with a lock on his mouth.

Tenth traumatic revival: Cervantes' childhood

As the Quixotic troupe rides away from the fulling hammers, it starts to rain. The reader can only trust the knight when he says, "Where one door shuts, another opens" (De Cervantes, 2013, p. 127). This time, the opening of the surreal space is not brought about by a gust of wind, or by some gallant desire exhibited by Rocinante, any more than by a cloud of dust, a procession of lights or a great hammering. Like in a cumulative song or riddle—"The twelve days of christmas", for instance—we can't help enumerating and remembering the triggers which provoke the onset of each successive storm. Now the greyness of the rain is chased away by a new flash of light appearing on the path Rocinante and Sancho's ass are following of their own initiative. It was "[…] a man on horseback [who] wore on his head something that shone like gold". All that glitters is not gold, but the object sparkled on every side, suggesting its multiple functionality.

The aperture suddenly narrows the view of the space of war, to focus in on a particular object. Given where they have arrived now, Don Quixote and Sancho cannot go beyond the beyond. But strangely, this glittering object arouses in Don Quixote the desire to possess it, despite the fact that he is not normally given to greed. But it is a helmet, and he wants a helmet. For the first time, the image fits quite well with a Lacanian object of desire, instead of being a trigger to fight against it. Thus, the analysis has entered a second, more classical phase.

This desire for a helmet corresponds to a very practical need that the hero will end up confessing. He must replace the one the Biscayan destroyed in Chapter IX, for the lack of it caused him to lose consciousness on two occasions, along with almost all his teeth. He seizes it quickly, not overly concerned with its true nature, as he admits to Sancho: "[…] this [helmet] is like a barber's basin as thou sayest" (De Cervantes, 2013, p. 129). But he makes a virtue of necessity: "I will set it to rights at the first village where there is a blacksmith." Still, the object's utility does not diminish its value as a surviving image.

The glow on the head is gold. It is a ready-made solution to the inadequacy of Cervantes' equipment, which serves as a reminder of the negligence of Army Services responsible for the outfitting of soldiers. "In 1939, we went into battle wearing puttees and carrying Chassepot rifles from the last war, that were bigger than we were", the old soldier keeps saying, still in disbelief. After the war, families keep the bullet-pierced helmet that failed to save the life of a brother, a father, a fiancé.

For the knight, the problem is how to hold the surviving image in place. The indentation in the barber's basin, to make it fit against the client's neck, causes our hero to have trouble fitting it on his head: "[He] immediately put it on his head, turning it around, now this way, now that […]." This basin, used to protect an itinerant barber's new hat from the rain, springs straight up from Cervantes' childhood, as the sign and work tool of his father, Rodrigo. An itinerant barber for nearly fifteen years, Rodrigo too first took his family to Andalusia after his imprisonment for unpaid debts in Valladolid, in the same prison where his own father, the licentiate Juan Cervantes, Miguel's grandfather, had been held for the same reason. Don Quixote's "father" was to be taken there as well in 1605, six months before *Don Quixote* was published, long after his imprisonment in Sevilla, where he was remanded in custody when a man was murdered in front of his house.

Miguel was five years old when his destitute father was jailed. The boy already stuttered. At that age, he may have played at being a knight, placing a barber's basin on his head, as Don Quixote, heir to the family history, was to do later. It is no wonder, then, that upon emerging from hell this forefather crosses his path wearing a golden crown. And now that he himself has acquired his war name, it is important to him to wear the symbolic headpiece gained as spoils of war, through the recognition of a familiar object.

"God is always in the details", where the fantastic and the real dwell side by side. Nowhere is this more true than in battles and trenches, where ridiculous appearance is not deadly, or in any case less so than bullets, shrapnel and fragmentation bombs: "[...] in the meantime I will wear it as well as I can, for something is better than nothing; all the more as it will be quite enough to protect me from any chance blow of a stone."

Don Quixote goes into action to seize the sacred object. "At Rocinante's top speed he bore down upon him with the pike pointed low", shouting the ritual injunction authorised by superhuman laws. "Defend thyself, miserable being, or yield me of thine own accord that which is so reasonably my due." What is Don Quixote's due, and rightfully, for he has earned it in the previous episodes, is nothing less than the symbol of the name of the father, that he will don for posterity.

Transfigured by this supernatural energy, Don Quixote takes on, once again, the demeanour of a "daimon", in the eyes of "the barber, who without any expectation or apprehension of it saw this apparition coming down upon him, had no other way of saving himself from the stroke of the lance but to let himself fall off his ass; and no sooner had he touched the ground than he sprung up more nimbly than a deer [...]. He left the basin on the ground, with which Don Quixote contented himself, saying that the pagan had shown his discretion". Ever since his encounter with the corpse being carried to his grave, Don Quixote has acted as a revolving door between the here and the beyond, and gives the impression of a terrifying ghost.

Nobel prize-winning mathematician John Nash (Nasar, 2011) and art historian Aby Warburg also gave the impression of being phantoms. At Princeton, Nash was nicknamed "the ghost". In Kreuzlingen, at the Binswanger clinic, Aby Warburg roamed "like a phantom among ghosts" (Binswanger and Warburg, 2007), at the start of the 1920s, shouting that all Jews would be exterminated—just before Hitler wrote *Mein Kamph* in prison.

The vital need to speak

No one is immune to denial, since it is so tempting to say "Goodbye to all that" (Graves, 1958), as Robert Graves wrote after World War I. Sancho has also fallen victim to his master's negation of the terrible trick played on him when he was tossed in the blanket. Don Quixote's disloyalty is precisely what makes the tormenting episode unforgettable. Contrary to his habit, the knight forgives himself for this attitude, while minimising and ridiculing his squire's trauma. This reaction is common among veterans who denigrate their sons who go off to fight the next war. Often, there is a tone of scorn like that found in his master's admonishment: "But know that it is the part of noble and generous hearts not to attach importance to trifles. What lame leg hast thou got by it, what broken rib, what cracked head, that thou canst not forget the jest. For jest and sport it was, properly regarded" (De Cervantes, 2013, p. 129).

But Don Quixote soon abandons the role of tormentor, since Sancho objects: "Let it pass for a jest as it cannot be revenged in earnest, but I know [...] it will never be rubbed out of my memory any more than off my shoulders" (De Cervantes, 2013, p. 130). The master does not insist, and grants his squire the compensation he is requesting: the barber's abandoned pack-saddle, with its brand new trappings.

Having been recognised as the bearer of traumatic memory, Sancho responds forcefully, taking his task seriously and defending the vital need to speak: "Señor, would your worship give me leave to speak a little to you? For since you laid that hard injunction of silence on me several things have gone to rot in my stomach, and I have now just one on the tip of my tongue that I don't want to be spoiled" (De Cervantes, 2013, pp. 130–131).

It would be hard to express more clearly the Freudian idea of *das Ding*, which spoils and becomes rotten when it cannot be put into words. As he continues to speak, the squire becomes the advocate of the history of simple people, generally overshadowed by that of heroes. "I make bold to say that, if it be the practice in chivalry to write the achievements of squires, I think mine must not be left out" (De Cervantes, 2013, p. 131). In other words, madness and trauma affect all social classes with the same *hidalguia*, and their deeds deserve the same nobility.

The conquest of the signifier of the name of the father, and of the honour associated with it, logically leads to a discussion of lineage. Whoever one's father, a distinction remains to be made between imaginative lineages that allow one to acquire name and fame by achieving great deeds "in some kingdom [...] not likely to be on the map" (De Cervantes, 2013, p. 133), and social hierarchies which constantly compare those who "were what they no longer are, and the others [who] are what they formerly were not" (De Cervantes, 2013, p. 134). And finally, the best of all is an aristocratic status won at the point of a sword, or sometimes at the tip of a pen, "and mean be who thinks himself mean" (De Cervantes, 2013, p. 134).

One last episode of traumatic revival of Cervantes' wars takes place to test the quality of this aristocracy, in an encounter with galley-convicts.

Eleventh traumatic revival: the galley slaves, a vision of the father in chains

Knighted for a second time, Don Quixote is ready for an ethical war, different from that of the herds of sheep, which smacked of the Crusades, in clear contrast with the one being waged by Spain at the same period in the Americas, where Indians were being exterminated. This is why the historian Cide Hamete uses contradictory adjectives to relate this history, which is at once "most grave, high-sounding, minute, delightful and original" (De Cervantes, 2013, p. 136). In fact, the delightful empathy in the episode will soon be transformed into the most grave event of a second intifada.

Seeing "company along the road [...] some dozen men on foot strung together by the neck, like beads, on a great iron chain, and all with manacles on their hands" can only mean having to free them of their chains at once, in the mind of the captive's son. Taken to the bagnios of Algiers in chains, Cervantes spent five years there, the equivalent of the sentence of each of these men, except the one sentenced to ten years.

The first liberation is that of speech. As is his habit, Don Quixote addressed the guards directly, wanting "to know from each [convict] the reason of his misfortune" (De Cervantes, 2013, p.136). The guard on horseback grants permission for a debriefing: "Come and ask themselves." All the convicts, with one exception, are glad to oblige. Each one's story reveals excessive sentences for minor acts of delinquency, received primarily because the accused did not have the money to bribe notaries or attorneys: the theft of a basket of linen, horse theft denounced by accomplices, an accusation of sorcery involving an old man, and lastly a charge of making several girls pregnant, brought against a student who "was a great talker and a very elegant Latin scholar" (De Cervantes, 2013, p.139).

All these offhanded judicial decisions give Cervantes the opportunity to praise freedom of thought: "[…] there are no sorceries in the world that can compel the will […], for our will is free" (De Cervantes, 2013, p. 139). Once this is established, the rest of the episode reveals the sophism that would automatically link liberation with freedom, and literature with freedom of speech.

The quarrel of the rogues

Not all of the captives defend freedom of speech, as we see when Don Quixote attempts to question the last thief, a "master thief of extra measure" (De Cervantes, 2013, p. 140), who refuses to answer his questions, telling him: "You are becoming tiresome with all this inquisitiveness about the lives of others." He says his name is Ginés de Pasamonte, whose life is written by these fingers".

Cervantes speaks out virulently against a literature which sticks too closely to reality, placing the reader at the mercy of criminals. Pasamonte, who is proud to be a crook, is also a successful author. He is glad to return to the galleys to have the time to write his next best-seller, since the Spanish, unlike the Turks, as he says, do not go out to sea during the winter. "I know by this time what the biscuit and courbash are like, and it is no great grievance to me to go back to them, for there

I shall have time to finish my book." But in the name of literature, true mistress of his heart, Cervantes condemns books intended to fascinate the impressionable reader. In a tear-jerking tone, Pasamonte adds: "Misfortune always persecutes good wit" (De Cervantes, 2013, p. 141). This time, it is Dulcinea herself who takes the initiative in wreaking havoc; she takes the lead in the adventure, after Don Quixote, Rocinante, the ass and Sancho.

The *casus belli* creates a confrontation between the professional knave and the knight. At first, the thieves are in support of the two leaders who defend the just cause of their liberation. Don Quixote has called them "dear brethren", in his magnificent indictment against torture and captivity. "[…] it is not fitting that honest men should be the instruments of punishment to others, they being therein no way concerned." As always, "acting on the word", Don Quixote fell upon the guard "so suddenly that without giving him time to defend himself he brought him to the ground" (De Cervantes, 2013, p. 142).

This is where Dulcinea interferes, when Don Quixote invokes her, asking the convicts to pay her their respects. "I desire […] that, laden with that chain which I have taken off your necks, ye at once set out and […] present yourselves before the lady Dulcinea" (De Cervantes, 2013, p. 143). The mere mention of this name and of its function causes the little group "collected around him" to draw back. Pasamonte "made answer for all", explaining the incompatibility of his request with their own perspective: "to ask this of us is like asking pears of the elm trees" (De Cervantes, 2013, p. 143).

In effect, Pasamonte speaks of their inability to express gratitude, not so much to their benefactor, as to the symbolic agency in whose name he is acting—the beautiful "Lady Without Mercy". This Lady is not so much concerned with their fate, but demands a tribute of words, as we shall see later, at the end of the novel, in the legend of "The Lake of Bubbling Pitch" (De Cervantes, 2013, p. 373).

The encounter of these two heterogeneous social links—one based on the giving of one's word, the other on accumulation and predation—has an explosive effect. Don Quixote insults Pasamonte, hitting below the belt this time, calling him "Don son of a bitch, Don Ginesillo de Paropillo", which means "winged penis". "[…] you will have to go yourself alone, with your tail between your legs and the whole chain on your back" (De Cervantes, 2013, p. 373). Ready to attack, Dulcinea has sent her knight to take down the inflated phallus of the Egocrat incapable of gratitude. This also serves to show the limitations of humanitarian policies applied to "winged penises".

The ringleader drops his mask right away: "Pasamonte, who was anything but meek (being by this time thoroughly convinced that Don Quixote was not quite right in his head as he had committed such a vagary as to set them free), [...] gave the wink to his companions." And stones began to rain down on Don Quixote at such a rate "that he was quite unable to protect himself with his buckler".

Having woven the collective body into a gang of malefactors, Pasamonte pulls the strings. Is it not the case that one of them is a "canary" who did not have "spirit enough to say nay; for, say they, *'nay'* has no more letters in it than *'yea'*"? As for the student who was a "great talker", he attacks the knight with the greatest enthusiasm, confirming Hannah Arendt's observation on the alliance between the mob and the elite, in a pre-totalitarian period (Arendt, 1951). "[...] the student pounced upon him, snatched the basin from his head, and with it struck three or four blows on his shoulders, and as many more on the ground, knocking it almost to pieces." Prefiguring the graduate Samson Carrasco, the intellectual reveals his limited understanding of the intelligence of madness.

The incomparable quartet is left defeated, except the thoughtful ass. Shaking his long ears, resembling a dunce cap or a fool's cap with bells, he is the only witness left standing after an act of resistance carried out on Dulcinea's behalf. To reflect on the small difference between madness and perversion, Don Quixote retreats into the mountains, out of reach of the vulgarity of boors: "*Odi profanum vulgus et arceo*" (I hate the profane mob and keep them at a distance) (Horace, 2002, p. 11), says Horace. From this retreat, he withdraws even further into the wilderness of the Sierra Morena.

For Don Quixote, the exhausting work of bringing to light and narrating his father's traumatic revivals is now almost finished.

CHAPTER SEVEN

Don Quixote becomes a psychoanalyst in the Sierra Morena

Don Quixote goes underground

The mountain, which in France has always offered refuge from persecution to Jews, Vaudians and members of the Underground, is also, for the Plains Indians, the summit where one climbs naked, in a Star Quilt, to carry out the ritual of Vision Quest. The Sierra Morena provides such a place of refuge to Don Quixote, a place where he can build new stores of energy. Sent into hiding in the Maquis by Lady Dulcinea who has just caused the retreat of petty thieves, an informer and a pimp incited by a scoundrel, Don Quixote has escaped from the movement of liberation he himself set in motion.

An unexpected wild card, the agency of the Lady, has cropped up like Mother Folly. Protecting the insane, her henchmen, she incites them to rise to the necessary heights without which the vividness of speech is reduced to mere slogans. Don Quixote confirms Lacan's aphorism, "despite the work of analysis, once a scoundrel, always a scoundrel", but he formulates it differently: "I have always heard it said, Sancho, that to do good to boors is to throw water into the sea. But […] it is only to […] take warning for the future" (De Cervantes, 2013, p. 145). To this,

his squire replies that Don Quixote will always be Don Quixote: "Your worship will take warning as much as I am a Turk."

For the first time, the talking cure with Sancho takes a different turn, and Don Quixote finally hears what his squire is saying. "Thou art a coward by nature, Sancho, but lest thou shouldst say I am obstinate, and that I never do as thou dost advise, this once I will take thy advice, and withdraw out of reach of that fury thou so dreadest".

An analyst without qualities

But as soon as Sancho earns a place of authority, he loses all self-assurance. His ass was stolen by the infamous Ginés de Pasamonte. Deprived of his agent of transference, he voices a lament as doleful as a funeral oration: "O son of my bowels, [...] my children's plaything, my wife's joy, the envy of my neighbors, relief of my burdens, and lastly half supporter of myself [...]" (De Cervantes, 2013, p. 146). It is small comfort that Don Quixote promises to give him three of his own ass colts; the injury has been inflicted, the wound is gaping. And to make matters worse, the place is sinister.

At the time, the mountains were not an idyllic site for an enjoyable vacation. Until barely a century ago, when the British made Chamonix fashionable as a mountain resort, the air at high altitudes and the majesty of lofty peaks held no attraction for tourists. In fact, three centuries after Don Quixote's time, the mountains were still thought to offer nothing but rugged and retired spots, "never trodden except by [...] wolves and other wild beasts". Even in the Sierra Morena, the only climber at ease on those heights, who fascinated those who saw him by the agility with which he sprang from rock to rock, was a man out of his mind.

As Don Quixote and Sancho advance on the solitary trail, there is nothing to attract their attention except an abandoned suitcase; a godsend for the despoiled travellers, it contains half-rotten objects and a richly bound notebook—in the tradition of the moleskin notebooks of veterans and of the manuscript found earlier by the narrator in Toledo. But this is not all. After discovering fine linen and gold crowns in the suitcase, Sancho finally feels rewarded for his previous hardships—"the blanket flights, balm vomits, stake benedictions, carriers' fisticuffs, the missing *alforjas*, stolen coat, and all the hunger, thirst and weariness he had endured in the service of his good master"

(De Cervantes, 2013, p. 149)—which he enumerates like items in a cumulative song.

Now, Sancho's distress over losing his donkey recedes, replaced by the mystery which launches the quest once again. The mystery deepens. An anonymous poem in the notebook creates suspense, in its last lines: "I only know it is my fate to die" (De Cervantes, 2013, p. 148)—and triggers instantly the therapeutic move to which the poem incites:

> "To him who knows not whence his malady
> A miracle alone a cure can give."

This is enough for Don Quixote to get on his hobby horse and set out to perform miracles, in pursuit of what Bion called "thoughts without a thinker" (Bion, 1997). In the absence of a thinker to think these thoughts, a poet is needed to give resonance to the anonymous poem. Don Quixote proves to be this poet, to Sancho's great surprise: "Then your worship understands rhyming too?"

Emerging as the official analyst of the stranger lost in the mountains, Don Quixote presents several characteristics which impel us to compare this psychoanalysis of madness and trauma with the work of knights-errant.

An interest in stories that interest no one

The leitmotiv of the discourse on Arms and Letters—commenced as early as the pastoral gathering of the first goatherds, and soon to be expanded in Chapter XXXVII—returns like a refrain, to give voice to the poem found in the mud. "[…] I would have thee know, Sancho, that all or most of the knights-errant in days of yore were great troubadours and great musicians."

On the back of the page, they find the text of a letter with no address, like the ones found in the pockets of young men killed in battle. The semantic field encompasses war and treason. "Peace be with thee who has sent war to me" (De Cervantes, 2013, p. 149). This sender of war is called ungrateful and accused of making "false promise". The tone of the letter calls up the spectre of suicide once again. But contrary to Grisostomo, the unfortunate poet seems to have endured actual mistreatment. "[…] thou hast rejected me for one more wealthy, but not more worthy."

The missive ends here. Finding no other clues as to the identity of the poet, Don Quixote determines to give free rein to his horse. "[…] he saw nothing else for it but to push on, taking whatever road Rocinante chose—which was where he could make his way" (De Cervantes, 2013, p. 149).

Rocinante's free associations foster Don Quixote's transference directed towards the stranger. The anonymous letter must find its sender, and Don Quixote does not intend to give up the quest. He "made up his mind to go in search of him, even though he should have to wander a year in those mountains".

Stories fallen in the mud, that no one wants to pick up, are the stuff that can create an analyst for those who have known repeated hospitalisations and have defeated all attempts at treatment. Such an analyst precedes the patient, through his interest in what happened to him, sparked by his own experience.

As Dori Laub (Laub, 1992, pp. 57–74) points out, based on his experience at Yale with the Fortunoff Video Archives Testimonies of the Holocaust, the analyst cannot expect a request from one who has dropped out of the ranks of humanity long ago. But he must expect the question "Who are you?" addressed to him personally. He adds that at first the analyst precedes the patient, through his interest in what happened to him, sparked by his own experience.

This is the position in which Don Quixote finds himself. Having learned from his adventures and from his analysis with Sancho, he lets his imagination wonder, at the rhythm of Rocinante's gait, asking himself who might be the author of such a desperate letter, and wishing to meet him. When the stranger finally appears, he is greeted by his potential analyst's daydreams, triggered by what he has heard about him.

This nonsensical apparition—a man who has broken away from any sense—is seen from below "on the summit of a height that rose before their eyes". Don Quixote is "very anxious to find out who the owner of the valise could be". As sure-footed as a chamois, the stranger "went springing from rock to rock and from tussock to tussock with marvelous agility". His decision to retreat from humanity was evidenced by his nudity, and his hairy, animal-like appearance. A veritable yeti, "he was unclad, with a thick black beard, long tangled hair, and bare legs and feet, his thighs were covered by breeches apparently of tawny velvet but so ragged that they showed his skin in several places. He was bareheaded".

"Imponderable evidence" (Wittgenstein, 2010, pp. 358–360)

At the end of the *Philosophical Investigations*, Wittgenstein introduces the question of the genuineness of the expression of a fact or a feeling, and the criteria which distinguish what is genuine from what is feigned. He describes as "imponderable" the evidence involved in this investigation. Madness has a special talent for such investigation. Having been tricked by a betrayal of good faith, the madman gives endless tests which no pretence can pass. These tests, which cannot be graded, are highly reliable and are based, the philosopher tells us, on "subtleties of glance, of gesture, of tone", on the capacity resumed in the phrase "to have a flair" for something. He adds that this capacity cannot be taught in training courses, but can only be acquired through experience. Quixotic transference relies on precisely such infinitesimally subtle evidence.

Don Quixote registers details in the twinkling of an eye, with the speed characteristic of the martial arts. "[...] notwithstanding the swiftness with which he passed as has been described, the knight [...] observed and noted all these trifles." This acute sense of observation also pertains to the wild man.

Before the face-to-face encounter, which Don Quixote is determined to have "though he should have to wander a year in those mountains", it is crucial for him to look and listen carefully in order to recognise the booby traps he will encounter in the course of the adventure on which he embarks. This is why Sancho is asked to do reconnaissance on foot. "So come on now behind me slowly as well as thou canst, and make lanterns of thine eyes; let us make the circuit of this ridge; perhaps we shall light upon this man that we saw, who no doubt is no other than the owner of what we found."

One does not choose the mouth which says: I have pain in my soul

Don Quixote is not distracted by the hirsute appearance of the creature springing from rock to rock, or by his ragged condition. He is certain that this is indeed a man, and that he is the "owner" of the things abandoned on the mountain path. The knight wants to return them, in exchange for the story to which they bear testimony.

In fact, the carrion of the mule—immortalised by Daumier's painting—"saddled and bridled, [...] lying in a ravine, dead and half devoured by dogs and pecked by jackdaws" (De Cervantes, 2013, p. 150) illustrates the paradigm formulated by Sancho: "I hate keeping things long, and I don't want them to grow rotten with me from over-keeping." It testifies to that which rots indefinitely for a madman no longer in possession of himself, as long as he remains unable to meet an interlocutor who can challenge his silence.

The field of speech in zones where the dead without graves, as well as the wounded whose stories rot in their stomachs, linger, is opened once again in ritual fashion by the sharp sound of a whistle. An old goatherd appears, surrounded by a great number of goats. But this time the whistle does not trigger any action. Don Quixote's field of research has widened to include another's madness.

To testify to the fact that he has re-entered the course of time, the knight enquires first about the story of the subject. "One does not choose the mouth which says 'I have toothache or a soul ache'"; the discarded objects strewn here and there prompt the memory of the old goatherd.

Don Quixote conducts the enquiry according to the rules. When? "About six months ago" (De Cervantes, 2013, p. 151). Where? "At a shepherd's hut three leagues, perhaps, away from this." Who? "A youth of well-bred appearance and manners, mounted on that same mule [...], and with the same saddlepad and valise [...]." To what purpose? "He asked us what part of this sierra was the most rugged and retired." He was shown a spot with no way out, "for there is no road or path that leads to this spot". And he made for this place at once, "leaving [the goatherds] all charmed". The outcome? He emerged from this wilderness much later, unrecognisable,—as if he had been taken away by fairies, called Fata in Latin, who inhabit the wild space of the marvel, where the words are spoken in the sacred sphere of the *fatum*, or destiny.

MDI or PTSD?

Cervantes provides an accurate psychiatric description of decompensation occurring in bipolar disorder, also called manic-depressive illness or MDI. While in a manic phase, the madman attacks one of the shepherds, delivering blows and kicks, and then turned to the ass with the provisions and "took all the bread and cheese it carried, and having done this made off back again into the sierra with extraordinary swiftness". When he was calm, "he saluted [the shepherds] courteously" and addressed "well-spoken words" to them. The goatherds who went in search of him "found him lodged in the hollow of a large thick cork tree". Then the same circus starts all over again. "He came out to meet us with great gentleness, with his dress now torn and his face so disfigured and burned by the sun, that we hardly recognised him."

Reluctant to say who he is, he makes no revelations, vaguely mentions a penance, begs pardon, and breaks down once again. He then starts to weep so bitterly (De Cervantes, 2013, p. 152) that the goatherds become social workers assisting the homeless man he has become. While eating his bread and cheese, he speaks in such polished language that "rustics as we were […], even to our rusticity his gentle bearing sufficed to make [his breeding] plain". And suddenly, bang!—another fit comes.

The goatherd displays great semantic finesse: "But in the middle of his conversation he stopped and became silent, keeping his eyes fixed upon the ground for some time", while his interlocutors "stood still waiting anxiously". Fascinated, they saw him overwhelmed by a delusional state. As they watched him "staring at the ground with fixed gaze and eyes wide open without moving an eyelid, again closing them, compressing his lips and captaining his eyebrows, [they] could perceive plainly that a fit of madness of some kind had come upon him". Better take cover! "[…] he rose in a fury from the ground where he had thrown himself, and attacked the first he found near him with such rage and fierceness that if we had not dragged him off him, he would have beaten or bitten him to death, all the while exclaiming 'Oh, faithless Fernando!'" (De Cervantes, 2013, p. 152).

MDI or PTSD? If we were asked, like Don Quixote, to express an opinion on this case presentation, we would tend to choose the second option. Our advantage over the goatherd is that we can interpret the breakdown in the light of the ensuing chapters, from the perspective of treason committed by a nobleman who betrayed the feudal oath and abused his best friend and vassal.

In this light, the fit of madness can be seen as an episode of traumatic revival triggered by the kindness of the shepherds. Without knowing it, their solicitude revives the image of the sweet-talking abuser whose words are a perversion of loyalty. But for the moment, the goatherds have run out of patience; their empathy and resourcefulness have reached their limits, and they are thinking of having him locked up, to cure his malady. Several goatherds have decided that, together, they would take him, "whether by force or by his own consent", to a place where he can be treated—as people say euphemistically before bringing about an involuntary commitment—and give notice to his relatives.

This is when Don Quixote intervenes. He takes it upon himself to save the madman from being committed, since he knows exactly what that is like. His own team of caregivers has taught him what "home care" means, and they will continue their insistence on this form of therapy until the end of the novel. Coercion is the next logical step after the failure of the "holding environment" provided in milieu therapy. Still, the knight prefers the improbable tool of transference, because he knows more than the shepherds—despite their pastoral qualities—about acting out, mood swings and personality disorders. And transference experienced by the analyst Don Quixote has become keeps intensifying: "[He was] more eager than ever to discover who the unhappy madman was; and in his heart he resolved, as he had done before, to search for him all over the mountain, not leaving a corner or cave unexamined until he had found him" (De Cervantes, 2013, p. 153).

The narration of the Quixotic transference, proceeding from the analyst, will unfold in several stages that are analysed with great precision.

Immediacy

When you speak of the devil, the devil appears. Thanks to synchronicity, to the "objective chance" of surrealism, to the "horlogism" so dear to Marcel Duchamp, the madman appears just in time, as if to keep a rendezvous. This happens in institutions, where patients often pop up suddenly, like genies out of their medication bottles, right at the moment when the staff is talking about them in a meeting. "But chance arranged matters better than [Don Quixote] expected or hoped, for at that very moment, in a gorge on the mountain that opened where they stood, the youth he wished to find made his appearance, coming along talking to himself [...]."

This monotonous monologue of words catches in his throat, like in a mountain gorge. But the gorge of the Sierra Morena spews out the madman, just as the cry of Mother Folly, at the start of a sottie, initiates the roll call of her fools wearing dunce caps and bells, who will conduct the trial of the abuses of the times through their folly. In the theatre of the Sierra, Fool number one, Cardenio, speaks to himself in jargon, until he engages Fool number two, Don Quixote, the analyst in the indictment of Don Fernando, the tyrant, while Sancho and the goatherds, Fools number three, four, five, six, etc., lend them their support.

Proximity

To the one who has lost all human countenance and whose voice has become "harsh and hoarse", without resonance, strange to his own ears, the sight of Don Quixote is a first reflection of himself, in the same pitiful state.

By taking him in his arms without hesitation, and holding him in his embrace, the knight lets him know that he will be the interlocutor he can count on to reflect on his madness, and the one who will set limits. Contrary to the inexpressive faces called "psychoanalytic" —mimicking, as Max Schur (Schur, 1972) says, Freud's physician, the face of the master who suffered from mouth and jaw cancer during the last twenty years of his life, Don Quixote does not hide his pleasure upon encountering him. "[…] dismounting from Rocinante [he] advanced with well-bred bearing and grace to embrace him, and held him for some time close in his arms as if he had known him for a long time." This greeting in no way resembles psychiatric observation.

The obvious reconnaissance, in the geographical sense, on the part of someone who has lived through the same thing, allows Don Quixote to step unwaveringly into the role of the youth's therapist, the role of his second in combat. They do in fact share a long-standing understanding of regions of catastrophe; this gives their encounter a twin-like quality, reflected in the other meaning of the Greek term *therapon*, that of ritual double.

The mirror effect is emphasised by Cervantes through the name by which he designates the madman. "The Ragged One of the Sorry Countenance" comes face to face with the Knight of the Rueful Countenance. "[…] after submitting to the embrace"—a surprising concession on the part of such a wild being who must be as astonished as the knight— "[he] pushed him back a little and, placing his hands on Don Quixote's shoulders, stood gazing at him as if seeking to see whether he knew him, not less amazed, perhaps, at the sight of the face, figure and armor of Don Quixote than Don Quixote was at the sight of him". This gaze does not reduce the subject to a thing, but creates a haphazard reflection which does not give a hoot about self-image, and can therefore reflect that which mirrors fail to capture.

Here, the question asked is the one Dori Laub (Laub, 1992, pp. 57–74) expects: *Who are you?* Who are you to interfere with what I have become? This glance is one which always scrutinises, even when thrown sideways, judges, evaluates and asks the analyst: why do you do this work?

The answer is not so easy, because it always originates in *La Mancha*, a place "the name of which I have no desire to call to mind". And yet, this is the place towards which madness leads its investigation, a place lying beyond the well-meaning person who held the other in his embrace for a moment. In fact, once the blind spots of the analyst have been exposed, the analysis often breaks down, as we shall see. After this, the work has to start over, but on more solid foundations, based on the discovery and recognition of the therapist's fault, which has been exposed and explored in the first phase of transference, contrary to the totalitarian Other who propelled his prey into madness.

But this is only the beginning, the threshold of the analytic adventure, where the Ragged One tells his story, up to the *casus belli* which sends him into a fit of madness once again. "To be brief, the first to speak after embracing was the Ragged One, and he said what will be told farther on". Don Quixote listened very carefully. "The history relates that it was with the greatest attention Don Quixote listened to the ragged knight of the Sierra" (De Cervantes, 2013, p. 154).

Life expectancy

Through an initial "yes", the knight/analyst declares his commitment to the madman. "[My fate] is to be of service to you, so much so that I had resolved not to quit these mountains until I had found you, and learned of you whether there is any kind of relief to be found for that sorrow under which from the strangeness of your life you seem to labor" (De Cervantes, 2013, p. 154). This promise, to be kept for better or worse—and the worst was yet to come—was sealed with an embrace, which also seals feudal pacts of alliance.

Although the analysis, conducted in traditional manner starting with anamnesis, will be interrupted later, Don Quixote will not give up. He is familiar with the areas of catastrophe and knows how much patience is needed to resist in the face of overwhelming despair. "And if your misfortune should prove to be one of those that refuse admission to any sort of consolation, it was my purpose to join you in lamenting and mourning over it, [...]; for it is still some comfort in misfortune to find one who can feel for it."

This phrase has come to my mind many times, when words were clearly of no avail. The Italian analyst Mario Isotti once said, speaking of a woman patient (Isotti, 1996), that in this case the only possible hope was the match held by the analyst next to the wall of ice which protected her from the violence of the world. He assured her that his intention was not to melt the protective ice by lighting a great fire, but only to show her that he was there. Don Quixote reveals the paradigm of analytic discourse in the making, never ready-made, invented from scratch, aiming for the continuation of speech and alterity in the midst of despair familiar to Cervantes.

Drawing on lessons learned in the previous episodes, the analysis of this madness starts on the spot. Don Quixote asks Cardenio to tell him the reason for his unreason. "I [...] conjure you by whatever you love or have loved best in life, to tell me who you are and the cause that has brought you to live or die in these solitudes like a brute beast, dwelling among them in a manner so foreign to your condition as your garb and appearance show." This entreaty has a psychodynamic foundation. It implies that structurally the madman is not what he appears to be. Don Quixote differentiates clearly between the man to whom he is speaking and the strangeness which has taken hold of him, and he knows too that his interlocutor has retreated very far and remains alert to the danger of any new intrusion.

Cardenio's assessment of Don Quixote as an analyst

It is this vigilance that causes the Ragged One, also called Knight of the Sierra or Knight of the Thicket, to evaluate the genuineness of this new language game. He trusts the "imponderable evidence" described by Wittgenstein: tone of voice, posture, facial expression, and gaze, or feigned interest. "The Knight of the Thicket, hearing him of the Rueful Countenance talk in this strain, did nothing but stare at him, and stare at him again, and again survey him from head to foot."

Putting his curiosity aside for the moment, the Ragged One assesses Don Quixote's ability to deal with people in a state of shock and exhaustion, before asking them any questions. "[...] and when he had thoroughly examined him, he said to him: 'If you have anything to give me to eat, for God's sake give it me, and after I have eaten I will do all you ask [...].' [...]and what they gave him he ate like a half-witted being [...], gorging rather than swallowing; and while he ate neither he nor they who observed him uttered a word" (De Cervantes, 2013, p. 155). A hungry belly has no ears, says the proverb, and a hungry mouth can only say "I am hungry". Any further debriefing must be postponed.

Preliminary assessment

Once he has had his fill, Don Quixote's first patient wishes the analysis to respect established protocol.

The analyst must be someone about whom he knows nothing personal. "Of a surety, señor, whoever you are, for I know you not, I thank you for the proofs of kindness and courtesy you have shown me" (De Cervantes, 2013, p. 154). He even insists on lying down: "[...] he led them to a green plot [... and] stretched himself upon the grass" (De Cervantes, 2013, p. 155). Finally, he asks the analyst to remain silent, so as to respect the fundamental rule and ensure that he will not interfere with the free association and the emergence of unconscious content. "If you wish, sirs, that I should disclose in a few words the surpassing extent of my misfortunes, you must promise not to break the thread of my sad story with any question or other interruption ..." (De Cervantes, 2013, p. 155).

This is where Freud is caught in the act, covertly copying the technique described in this passage of his favourite writer, not noticing that he has overlooked half of the instructions. For, in fact, this prototype of a psychoanalytic process is doomed to fail. This is how it came to be that the analysis of madness was left by the wayside and came to be seen, by many Schools, as a "the deranged relative".

The fact is that standard treatment was invented by Cardenio for the express purpose of botching the job, in order to be done with it as quickly as possible, and "pass briefly over the story of [his] misfortunes". Another more serious reason to be brief had to do with his intuition—justified, of course—that another crisis was impending, which he tried to prevent by reducing the level of stimulation. To this end, the other must be kept at a distance and, most importantly, must not be allowed to rub salt in the bleeding wound of his misfortunes, "for recalling them to memory only serves to add fresh ones".

Ever-present traumatic memory is very different from memories made up of repressed signifiers. From the start, it is clear that the aim of free association and of benevolent listening is not to lift repression. On the contrary, the return of trauma has to be kept at bay, since it is overwhelming.

Happy to see his patient so compliant and ready to cooperate in the analytic process, Don Quixote promises everything and settles into his virtual armchair. There is only one glitch, which the patient is quick to point out: he has not asked for anything. The desire to know belongs to his analyst. "[…] the less you question me the sooner I shall make an end of the recital, though I shall not omit to relate anything of importance in order fully to satisfy your curiosity."

Ouch! This is where we encounter a crucial stumbling block. It is, in fact, out of the question that the analyst should desire in place of the patient. And yet, this principle reveals its limitations in psychiatric hospitals, where the analyst who "waits for a request" may be left waiting for ever. But in our scene in the Sierra Morena, we witness the start of a genuine analysis of madness.

History taking

The madman finally tells the knight his name: Cardenio. He comes from Andalusia, his family is noble, and his dearest wish was to marry Luscinda, a damsel as noble and as rich as himself. The young girl's father agrees, on condition of a delay: the lovers had to part for a time, and their separation, which "added love to love and flame to flame" (De Cervantes, 2013, p. 156), enforced silence on their tongues but not on their quills. Cardenio went off at the bidding of an overlord of his father's, who wished him "to become the companion, not servant, of his eldest son" (De Cervantes, 2013, p. 156). In fact, this Don Fernando, "the duke's second son, a gallant youth, of noble, generous and amorous disposition", will take up all his time and attention.

Seemingly full of charm, this youth had a rather envious character and thought of nothing but obtaining whatever he desired. He seduces Cardenio, will take advantage of Dorotha, "a vassal of his father's, the daughter of wealthy parents", by making false promises of marriage, and finally he falls madly in love with Luscinda, his best friend's fiancée. His scheming to take her away from him created a state of excitement, heightened by the fact that "with young men love is for the most part nothing more than appetite" (De Cervantes, 2013, p. 157). In stark contrast to the desire that gives wings, as it were, to the exchange of letters between the two lovers, Don Fernando is obsessed with envy and the desire to possess that which belongs to another, and succeeds in obtaining it through hypocritical means: "[He] contrived always to read the letters I sent to Luscinda and her answers to me" (De Cervantes, 2013, p. 158).

The vocabulary of courtly love uses terms like "flatterer" and "rough lover" to refer to the great lord who is a villain. In 1623, this character will be represented by Don Juan in *The Trickster of Seville*, written by Tirso de Molina; and later still, in 1685, by Molière's and the Don Juan in The *Fiest with the Statue*. Here, Cervantes compares two kinds of knights, the Quixotic and the Donjuanesque—before this latter term was coined. Both are steadfast adventure seekers and pursue their desires, letting no conventions stand in their way. They are both prompt to take action and they both defy the social order. The only difference is that one keeps his word, while the other violates it for the sole purpose of subjecting another's will to his own.

The cut-away unconscious

Right in the middle of Cardenio's anamnesis, the unconscious enters the scene, on both sides, through a fortuitous blunder. Cardenio's account of Fernando's devious schemes involving Luscinda awakens in him a certain feeling of jealousy. He mentions a particular object in this context, which fills Don Quixote with a certain feeling of chivalry. A book is inserted in the conversation, a very special book that takes the knight back to the loss of his library, which shielded him from the harsh twists of fate. This object is *Amadis of Gaul*, of which Luscinda is very fond and which she asks Cardenio to send her, in one of her letters. As soon as this book is mentioned, the Quixotic transference is ignited and starts to boil.

Interrupting his patient's narrative, unable to check his enthusiasm regarding intelligent women, Don Quixote transgresses the sacred rule of neutrality. "Don Quixote no sooner heard a book of chivalry mentioned, than he said: 'Had your worship told me at the beginning of your story that the Lady Luscinda was fond a books of chivalry, no other laudation would have been requisite to impress upon me the superiority of her understanding'." And, continuing in this vein, he finally offers to give her "more than three hundred books" in his personal library—now no longer in his possession—"which are the delight of my soul and the entertainment of my life;—though it occurs to me that I have not got one of them now [...]" (De Cervantes, 2013, p. 159).

In the wink of an eye, the vector of transference is reversed. Without knowing it, Don Quixote passes on to his patient his trauma resulting from the book burning, for analysis. In an instant, the knight has destroyed the reputation of the profession by presenting an unflattering image of a talkative analyst—such as I myself cannot help being—unable to control the unconscious, or at least to check its impetus.

But the unconscious, taking advantage of the situation, reveals for the first time that Don Quixote was not fooled when his books were destroyed. The cut out unconscious at work while he slept now found a way to call for a witness to the abuse he suffered, in the person of the Ragged One, the patient robbed of what he held most dear, just as the knight had been.

The analyst's blunder, theorised by Winnicott

Fortunately, retrospective praise of such fortuitous blunders has been reported by many analysts of psychotic transference (which may be called Quixotic transference).

Such blunders are remarkable in any analysis of psychosis, although they are always hard to swallow, as Winnicott tells us, referring to one of his patients, in *Playing and Reality* (Winnicott, 1971, pp. 73–75). "I had grown accustomed to a routine of good work, good interpretations, good immediate results, and then destruction and disillusionment that followed each time because of the patient's gradual recognition that something fundamental had remained unchanged; there was this unknown factor which had kept this man working at his own analysis for a quarter of a century", with other analysts before Winnicott. In truth, this man was exploring his analysts' blind spots.

Winnicott goes on to admit to making a remark "that surprised me", since it is more Quixotic than Freudian. Out of the blue, he told this patient: "The mad person is myself". After this statement, incredible on the part of a psychoanalyst, "[the] patient said that he now felt sane in a mad environment." Winnicott then points out the particularities of delusional transference in cases like this: "I found [...] that here is one of those examples of delusional transference that puzzles patients and analyst alike [...]."

Analysing its characteristics, he concludes that one must take the time to step back when an untimely intrusion occurs: "[…] the crux of the problem of management is just here in this interpretation, which I confess I nearly did not allow myself to make." This pause brings back the analytic process to the analyst: "For my part, I have needed to live through a deep personal experience in order to arrive at the understanding I feel I now have reached." The patient's search can now find support in the common quest he conducts with the analyst. In his encounter with the madman of the Sierra Morena, Don Quixote will go through "a deep personal experience". Like Winnicott, he informs Cardenio of it, triggering an explosive fit of rage. But this is precisely the rage the young man—momentarily stunned—had been unable to express when the trauma was inflicted.

Near the end of his life, in his last article entitled "Fear of Breakdown" (Winnicott, 1974), Winnicott elaborates on this difficult process, new for him, but familiar to writers, as he points out. "Naturally, if what I say has truth in it, this will already have been dealt with by the world's poets." Still, he feels he must explain his contentions. He criticises very severely analyses where nothing happens, because "the analyst and the patient are having a good time colluding in a psycho-neurotic analysis" focused on repressed material, "when in fact the illness is psychotic" or of traumatic origin. Here, unconscious content is not that which is repressed; we speak rather of that which is cut out, "not yet experienced".

This is Winnicott's brilliant discovery. This peculiar unconscious has less to do with an actual trauma which "is easier for a person to remember […] than to remember nothing happening when it might have happened". Winnicott designates as "primitive agony"—like the agony of Lauso in *Galate*—the experience of that particular nothing, and points to "this queer kind of truth, that what is not yet experienced did nevertheless happen in the past. […]then the way can only be open for the agony to be experienced in the transference, […] in reaction to the analyst's failures and mistakes."

This inevitable stage of mistakes and failures is often avoided because "All this is very difficult, time-consuming and painful, but it at any rate is not futile". Winnicott tells us that when anamnesis fails, these helpful mistakes are the best part of the analyst's work, as Don Quixote was to discover at his own expense.

In fact, he unwittingly enters the scene of catastrophe and provokes the failure of the analytic pledge. First, he breaches his promise to remain silent. Then, without noticing it, he starts to dream of making gifts to Cardenio's fiancée, in whom he takes an interest very much like that of the "flatterer". Although he is far from being as shameless as a pervert who never admits his faults, his excuses are in vain:

> "[...] pardon me for having broken the promise we made not to interrupt your discourse; for when I hear chivalry or knight-errant mentioned, I can no more help talking about them than the rays of the sun can help giving heat, or those of the moon moisture".
> (De Cervantes, 2013, p. 159)

But it's too late. The analyst's insight into his own unconscious is of no avail; the thread of the narration is broken and cannot be repaired. This heuristic stumbling block, key in the analysis of psychosis, is a real test. Failing it is what brings about genetic or structural determinism, and raises an outcry against anyone who succeeds in overcoming this obstacle, guided by his patient.

Cardenio's traumatic revival

As for Cardenio, he does not give a hoot about the analyst's excuses, for he is now in a trance. "While Don Quixote was saying this, Cardenio allowed his head to fall upon his breast, and seemed plunged in deep thought." But instead of thinking about having his patient committed for his own safety, Don Quixote persists in keeping his promise to be there and remain loyal no matter what. The reader will learn three chapters later (De Cervantes, 2013, p. 180) the truth about Cardenio's primitive agony, suffered when, in Winnicott's words, "nothing [happened] when it might have happened". But this nothing—which testifies to a real event from which the subject exiled himself—has just found a means, through Don Quixote's mistake, to reconnect with the original rage from which Cardenio's psychic and physical exile had cut him off.

Despite Don Quixote's resolve to refrain from interrupting, his phantom books came to Cardenio's rescue. To aid the madman deprived of his story, they lent him their stories, to allow the primitive agony to be experienced in the transference. As a result, the analyst and the patient were able to speak to each other through fiction, and thought became embodied through the characters of *Amadis*, on behalf of Cardenio, who has deserted his body. Freed from Cardenio's rigid interpretation, the fictional characters will take on a life of their own in Don Quixote's imagination, and will be recreated by the knight, who will return this life to his patient. This is how the Ragged One will be brought out of his living hell.

Although a clash is imminent, the subtle metamorphosis being prepared deserves a closer look.

Books speaking as transitional subjects

When Cardenio emerges from deep thought and can speak again, *Amadis* has become the stage on which the trauma can be played out in the present. This scenario depicts a therapist seducing his patient: "I cannot get rid of the idea, nor will anyone in the world remove it, or make me think otherwise—and he would be a blockhead who would hold or believe anything else than that arrant knave Master Elisabad made free with Queen Madasima" (De Cervantes, 2013, p. 159). The tone of defiance is no less impressive than that used by Don Quixote when he throws the gauntlet to some knave encountered in the course of his adventures.

Thus, provocations of this kind are not unfamiliar to him, and he takes up the gauntlet right away, in order to right the wrong inflicted on this other Dulcinea. Without hesitation, he answers insult with insult: "That is not true, by all that's good", said Don Quixote in high wrath, turning upon him angrily, as his way was, "and it is a very great slander, or rather villany. Queen Madasima was a very illustrious lady, and it is not to be supposed that so exalted a princess would have made free with a quack" (De Cervantes, 2013, p. 159). Cardenio has transformed Don Fernando's treachery into the quite common scenario of betrayal of the Hippocratic oath. Faithful to the rules of fiction and of reverie, Don Quixote has unwittingly taken Luscinda's defence.

This scene provides a perfect illustration of the notorious massive transference of which young analyst are taught to be wary, when in fact it would be more useful to them to familiarise themselves with daydreams. Of course, the analyst must proceed with caution.

Aporia, "Kôan"

In fact, the analytic session now takes a turn for the worse. "Cardenio was looking at him steadily." This attentive gaze tries to see beyond appearances, to scrutinise the paradox in the reasoning. Either Don Quixote denies that the knave, Elisabad, carried out his scheme of seduction; or he refuses to believe the madman's interpretation. In either case, Cardenio is betrayed.

In general, this type of aporia is characteristic of such *casus belli*, and yet a solution must be found. Two modes of action are possible: taking time to find a way out through self-analysis, as Winnicott does, or charging ahead as Don Quixote will do, thereby interrupting the analytic process. The patient abandons the work, but may come back later to see if, thanks to other patients, the analyst has learned something in the meantime. Thus, Cardenio will return three chapters later, to take up the thread of his story and to check the results of Don Quixote's training, since the latter has been practicing his skills in the interim.

But for the moment, each crisis begins in the same way: "[…] his mad fit having now come upon him, he had no disposition to go on with his story." Likewise, Don Quixote has no disposition to question himself in any way. "[…] nor would Don Quixote have listened to it, so much had what he had heard about Madasima disgusted him. Strange to say, he stood up for her as if she were in earnest his veritable born lady." Through the intercession of literature, the arena of transference has made possible the emergence of the unspeakable—in this case, Cardenio's cowardice, which prevented him from defending Luscinda.

We might take this opportunity to praise the "catastrophic" analytic technique which encourages analysts to make unhesitating use of their favourite books. The caveats which warn us against intruding into the fragile universe of our patients do not take into account the magnitude of the challenges with which we are presented, in the wild hope that we will rush into battle, armed not so much with psychoanalytic precepts, but above all with our "experience *par excellence* as foremost example" (Wittgenstein, 2014, p. 42), to use Wittgenstein's words.

Of course, this involves no small risk of injury to our image, as Cervantes shows us literally in the passage that follows.

Catharsis achieved through a brawl

True to his nature, Cardenio pummelled and kicked, leaving the knight, his squire and the goatherd sprawling on the prairie, where he had stretched himself upon the grass so peacefully earlier. "Cardenio, then, being, as I said, now mad, when he heard himself given the lie, and called a scoundrel and other insulting names, not relishing the jest, snatched up a stone [...]" and we know the rest. But what is surprising is the outcome of the fight, which calms Cardenio, who "quietly withdrew to his hiding place in the mountain." No doubt delighted to have wreaked havoc once again, he is above all glad to have found someone to talk to, and share stories and blows with. More will be revealed during the second round, when Don Quixote will have made progress by acquiring some experiences that sharpen his abilities. For the first time, Cardenio is able to direct his rage to a kindred spirit, for until now he had turned it against himself. Later, in Chapter XXVII, when he will take up the thread of his story again, he will describe exactly how events unfolded.

His first fit came upon him upon when he heard the announcement of the marriage of Don Fernando to his fiancée. "Now the night of my sorrow set in, the sun of my happiness went down, I felt my eyes bereft of sight, my mind of reason. I could not enter the house, nor was I capable of any movement" (De Cervantes, 2013, p. 188). At first, he tried to remain strong and resist the despair which threatened to annihilate him. "[...] but reflecting how important it was that I should be present at what might take place on the occasion, I nerved myself as best I could and went in [...]; without being seen, I found an opportunity of placing myself in the recess formed by a window of the hall [...]."

It was there that he heard Luscinda's "yes", which caused him to become estranged from himself. The same was true of Luscinda, who fell unconscious in her mother's arms. "Fool that I am! Now that I am far away, and out of danger, I say I should have done what I did not do [...]; in short, as I was then a coward and a fool, little wonder is it if I am now dying shame-stricken, remorseful and mad" (De Cervantes, 2013, p. 189).

Whether he knows it or not, he has just fought the battle he should have fought then, this time against Don Quixote who, through his blunder, has taken the place of the scoundrel. Such incidents, crucial in an analysis, are those in which the analyst's errors put him momentarily in the place of a lawless other who must be brought into the present through transference. It is towards him that can now be directed that which, albeit cut away, did in fact exist. This painful situation that everyone would rather avoid is one in which the analyst will be projected sooner or later. It is up to him to extricate himself from it more or less rapidly.

But first, in the free-for-all that follows, each protagonist blames the other. This is the "defeating process" Martin Cooperman (Cooperman, 1983, pp. 21–28) has identified. Cooperman was an analyst who saw combat in the Pacific and who used psychoanalysis to treat psychosis. The process he describes involves chain reactions which intensify conflicts. Cooperman observed this phenomenon in the series of events that trigger catastrophe in the psychoanalysis of madness or trauma— just like scenes in a Laurel and Hardy movie. "Sancho rose, and with the rage he felt at finding himself so belaboured without deserving it, ran to take vengeance on the goatherd, accusing him of not giving them warning that this man was at times taken with a mad fit." Bad faith triumphs, as it does in institutional quarrels: "[…] the altercation ended in their seizing each other by the beard, and exchanging such fisticuffs that if Don Quixote had not made peace between them, they would have knocked one another to pieces."

But something else is at stake here, and Don Quixote separates them, saying: "I know that he is not to blame for what has happened" (De Cervantes, 2013, p. 160). He reminds them both that the aim of this *casus belli* is the analysis of madness, and not the petty quarrels between caregivers: "With this he pacified them and again asked the goatherd if it would be possible to find Cardenio, as he felt the greatest anxiety to know the end of his story", and to find him, "either in or out of his senses".

Aerial reconnaissance of a radio silence zone

One day, a psychoanalyst came to see me, not really knowing why she was there. Perhaps to go on to something new—writing—she told me. She had heard me mention Cervante's age when he wrote the second part of *Don Quixote*—almost the same age as hers. We established a routine of pleasant regular meetings that went on for one year. Suddenly, she became angry and, without warning, she rebuked me roundly:

– What exactly are we doing? I haven't come here to chat or have a tea party.

In truth, our inoffensive meetings gave me a rest from more "energetic" sessions, like the ones with the patient I saw before her. She had been nauseous for several nights. Naively, I had asked her what she had eaten. Now, she blamed me for my question, as well as for the times I had been late—proof that I treated her casually.

Since her nausea did not trigger any associations, I remembered mine when, as a child, I was about to be reunited with family or, even worse, when on my way to school I had to walk along the gates of a garden where a wolfhound was barking and leaping up against the gate. After a bit of hesitation, I recounted these recollections, all the while thinking, as I always did, that I should have kept quiet. Finally, she smiled and said:

– A German Shepherd.
    I confess that it had not occurred to me to associate the war with this dog, although my memory concerned the period just after the war. Nor had I associated the war with homecomings, when I went back and forth between my grandparents' house and the Alps, while the war was in full swing.
– What about you, where did you go to school?
– In my village, in the North of France, where my family had emigrated from Eastern Europe before the war. It was a one-room school. Because I was easily distracted, I sat in the front, at a desk by myself.

There was a pause, and I saw myself sitting, like her, in the front row, alone, in a one-room school, before I went to the one that forced me to confront the German Shepherd. Although I was too young to go to school, I had done everything possible to be allowed to join the children I could hear at recess shouting in the yard of the elementary school just up the road from my grandmother's house. The teacher had given in and had set up a little table for me, in the front, where I reigned, delighted to be playing at going to school. I was careful not to reveal this whim of my childhood to my patient, and concentrated instead on her story.

– And were you in danger during the war?
– No, I can't think of anything … No, we were evacuated, and then we came back. No, nothing particular happened, the people in the

village did not appear to be anti-Semitic. On the contrary, my family seemed to be well-liked.

But, as the session was about the end, she made a point of telling me that she was still displeased.

Clearly, we had not touched on the "nothing happening". The next time, to my surprise, she arrived smiling. In a dream she had dreamed in English, she had made a slip: "The sky bites me", instead of "The child beats me". In her dream, there was in fact a beaten child, which she associated with Freud's text (Freud, 1955 [1939a], p. 175)—since she knew the analytic literature well, but also with the refugee children at the shelter where she volunteered.

It so happened that I was rereading Jule Roy's *La Vallée heureuse* (Roy, 1946) just then. Roy, who had been a fighter pilot in the Royal Air Force, describes the bombing missions over the Ruhr Basin in which many pilots lost their lives. Another patient, a war child too, was deciphering, with me, the long-neglected notebooks of her father, a French fighter pilot in the RAF. He had gone over to England of his own accord, and had learned to fly other types of planes. The writer Jules Roy had been the bomber on his missions. All this made me say to my patient with the dream of the biting sky:

– It might be that these airplane squadrons leaving to bomb the Ruhr Basin passed above your head, and their roar could make the sky bite.
– It could be, she answered laconically, especially since not far, near Amiens, there were sites used to launch the V-1 s.
– And so?
– And so? No, nothing.

My arms and legs had been itching to move for some time now, despite my conscious effort to be reasonable and not get distracted, since I had a patient sitting before me. But the need to act won out, despite the risk to my reputation. I stood up suddenly, stretched out my arms and enacted for her our favourite game, when we were children in the schoolyard: imitating the sirens, I executed banks, drops and crashes of fighter planes, Spitfires, Stukas and other planes whose names I don't remember. She showed no surprise:
– I played the same game. I did the same things, and still do them, from time to time, in my apartment.

She burst out laughing, and so did I. Then she had a memory of herself in her village. After an action carried out by the Resistance, the Germans had searched all the houses and made all the inhabitants gather on the village square. She was hiding in the hen house with her grandmother, but they were given away by their feet, that could be seen under the door. The Germans used their rifle butts to break the door down. The greatest danger was avoided thanks to the priest, who offered to be taken hostage in their place. I reminded her that the greatest danger continued to exist during the hours of suspense when anything might have happened.

Contrary to my expectations, she did not hold it against me that I had infringed on analytic neutrality with the foolishness of my so-called "private" history, which is, in fact, shared by all war children and those born after all the wars of history, in their sometimes "forbidden" games, as René Clément's film (Clément, 1952) illustrates.

"Nothing is further removed from technical procedure than the spontaneous and involuntary bursting forth from the analyst of echoes originating in similar zones of danger", writes Benedetti (Benedetti, 1998, p. 97). Testifying to their existence, always after some hesitation, produces a literal reflection of the hellish loneliness associated with periods when the social link is broken.

Debriefing: Sancho as supervisor

Don Quixote has now reached the point where he has seen his patient forcibly interrupt the analysis, and can only hope that Cardenio will come back. Therefore, he must get ready for the next meeting by freeing himself from the cognitive and affective distortions which entrap all analysts of madness, so as to extricate Cardenio from the trap that has driven him mad. What he needs is an exercise program that will strengthen his muscles and make him supple.

Strange circumstances, these, where one madness is countered by another or when, as Jean-Max Gaudillière says, "trauma speaks to trauma". There is, however, a dissymmetry, because the previous episodes of the novel have given Don Quixote a head start. He knows that all of occasions in which he took action contributed to create in him a growing desire to know the "reason for the unreason" of hostage-taking, of beatings, of slayings, of book-burnings and of slavery. Or course, the meaning he attributes to this quest is rooted in what he has read in his books of chivalry, but it so happens that their fictional character contributes to discrediting false discourses—*fictitious*, as Hannah Arendt calls them, by overturning *their serious tenor*.

Don Quixote's incorrigible optimism never loses sight of the possibilities of Gay Science (*Gai Savoir*) and of courtly love for the Fine Lady. In the twelfth century, Hildegarde of Bingen called this vitality *viriditas* (Green Flame), the energy of spring, which sycophants try to subjugate by inflicting their lack of humour on youth.

But this stolen vitality can be recovered provided a talking cure can take place, as Cervantes demonstrates episode after episode. This "antidepressant" remedy seems to have gone out of style today, due to the blatant attack carried out by drug merchants of all kinds subject it. But Sancho is old-fashioned. After the blows he just received, he is "dying to have a talk with his master" (De Cervantes, 2013, p. 161) and argues in favour of lifting the injunction which imposes silence.

One after the other, he invokes his usual means of blackmail: the threat of retreating from the frontlines and going home to his wife and children, "with whom [he] can at any rate talk and converse as much as [he likes]"; the risk of dying, for "not [to] speak […] is burying me alive"; rebelling against his master, for "it is a hard case […] to go seeking adventures all one's life and get nothing but kicks and blanketings, brickbats and punches, and with all this to have to sew up one's heart, just as if one were dumb".

Sancho's final argument is a reference to the Golden Age, a subject likely to strike a chord in his master's heart: in that case, I will talk to my horse. "If luck would have it that animals spoke as they did in the days of Guisopete, […] I could talk to Rocinante […] and so put up with my ill-fortune." This reminder of the traumatic theft of his ass wears down Don Quixote's resistance; he lifts the prohibition to speak: "Consider it removed […] while we are wandering in these mountains" (De Cervantes, 2013, p. 161). Thus, during their stay in the Sierra Morena the waste land (Eliot, 2004) of the mountain will echo with healing words.

Now, Sancho starts to speak, in the role of self-appointed supervisor of the analytic session with Cardenio. Sure of himself, he prompts the novice analyst to examine his unconscious blunder, an infringement of the fundamental rule which created the hullabaloo that followed. "[…] what made your worship stand up so for that Queen Majimasa, or whatever her name is […]? For if your worship had let that pass—and you were not a judge in the matter—it is my belief the madman would have gone on with his story, and the blow of the stone, and the kicks, and more than half a dozen cuffs would have been escaped."

Sancho's argument is irrefutable. A licensed supervisor would not have done better, while touching on a sore point of the practice: "[…] whether they misbehaved or not, I come from my vineyard, I know nothing; I am not fond of prying into other men's lives." Who can quarrel with that?

When the name-making tool is broken, the name of the lady remains

But when we are dealing with abuse, should we follow Sancho's advice and listen without judging, without "minding the words of a madman"—playing into the hands of the abuser—or intervene as Don Quixote does, at the risk of being attacked in turn? Moreover, Cardenio is not simply an unfortunate victim, but a formidable challenger as well, forcing Don Quixote into a corner, where he forbids the knight to speak while at the same time provoking him to speak. This is an arduous endeavour, for which Don Quixote decides to train.

His first move is to reaffirm the sovereignty of the Lady. "Against men in their senses or against madmen, every knight-errant is bound to stand up for the honour of women, whoever they may be." For this reason, "a great blasphemy it is to say or imagine that a queen has made free with a surgeon. Cardenio when he said it […] was out of his wits." Once this element of faith is established, the Lady can conduct herself as she pleases in reality, as Sancho is beginning to understand: "Let them look to it; with their bread let them eat it; […] whether they misbehaved or not; […] but who can put gates to the open plain?" (De Cervantes, 2013, p. 162).

Don Quixote does not give a hoot about rumours or the tabloid press. But he is a staunch defender of the integrity of transference. "[…] every knight-errant is bound to stand up for the honour of women whoever they may be, much more for queens of such high degree and dignity as Queen Madasima, for whom I have a particular regard."

It is out of the question for Don Quixote to let the tool of speech be reduced to an instrument of subjection. The matter is clear. The queen's love for her therapist Elisabad, whose "counsel and society […] were a great help and support to her in enduring her afflictions"—is transference love, whose worthiness, like that of the royal patient, must be protected from abuse of power.

Now, the knight focuses his efforts on building the transference linking him with the madman of the Sierre Morena—combat transference, as he has discovered at his own expense. This is why he gives Sancho this advice: "Understand with all thy five senses that everything I have done, am doing, or shall do, is well-founded on reason [...]."

Foundation of the analytic discourse in case of madness

Here, the question of the analyst's desire takes centre stage. We are often asked this question, formulated as simply as Sancho's enquiry when he wants to know why his master had had the strange idea of exercising this occupation. "Señor, is it a good rule of chivalry that we should go astray through these mountains without path or road, looking for a madman who when he is found will perhaps take a fancy to finish what he began [...]?"

Don Quixote's answer is clear. His motivation is not altruistic. "[...] it is not so much the desire of finding that madman [...] as that which I have of performing [...] an achievement [...]." At the risk of advocating chivalresque psychoanalysis, we confirm that this answer is relevant. Linking together, through transference, scattered elements saved from catastrophe, so that a subject exiled from his own history can be reborn, is in fact quite an undertaking, and far from unappealing.

To carry out this deed, Don Quixote intends to call upon his allies from literature, the only ones who can help when all else fails. Cervantes must have had recourse to this helpful resource in captivity, as did Maria Antonia Garcés and many other hostages who have described their experiences.

Thus, the knight will imitate the jesters and fools of yore, practicing their art like a martial art, training, like them, to perform falls and somersaults, dodges, tricks, jumps, and backflips, in order to become Cardenio's equal. "[...] when a painter desires to become famous in his art he endeavors to copy the original of the rarest painters that he knows; and the same rule holds good for all the most important crafts and callings that serve to adorn a state" (De Cervantes, 2013, p. 163). Now, Don Quixote is ready to train alongside masters in poetic jousting like Homer and Virgil, and alongside heroes like Amadis and Orlando, to prepare for the second part of the analysis—in truth a second round, with Cardenio.

This imitation is a form of poetic mimesis, the opposite of forgery. It is carried out through a fusion of identity with the author, not limited to the intellectual level. Just as at the Panathenaic Games, where the bard who recited Homer "was Homer when he said 'I'" (Nagy, 1996), Don Quixote hesitates between being Amadis or Orlando—a choice between the two major styles of madness, schizophrenic or paranoid.

At first, he chooses to alternate between them, opting for one after the other: "[Amadis] when he withdrew, rejected by the Lady Oriana, to do penance upon the Pena Pobre, changing his name into that of Beltenebros"; then "the victim of despair, the madman, the maniac, so as at the same time to imitate the valiant Don Roland". The latter was much more violent, and even went berserk "when […] he had evidence of the fair Angelica having disgraced herself with Medoro and through grief thereat went mad, and plucked up trees, troubled the waters of the clear springs, slew shepherds, destroyed flocks, burned down huts, leveled houses […]" (De Cervantes, 2013, p. 164).

In fact, Don Quixote is preparing to enter the universe of Cardenio, who has been betrayed and scorned by Luscinda, in order to grasp the scope of the event and play his part in it. But the knight is realistic, and must downscale the action planned initially. He gives up the idea of a superproduction in which he would be "cleaving giants asunder, cutting off serpents' heads, slaying dragons, routing armies, destroying fleets, and breaking enchantments", and agrees to resign himself to a more modest scenario, easier to enact and, above all, less energy consuming. "[…] perhaps I shall content myself with the simple imitation of Amadis, who without giving way to any mischievous madness but merely to tears and sorrow, gained as much fame as the most famous."

Alright, economising energy will suffice. More spectacular means are superfluous for his next encounter with Cardenio. But the conscientious knight lets the reader know that madness can only be analysed on its own ground, and by referring to long-established classical methods.

All this implies foregoing causalist reasoning. But Sancho insists on finding a "cause" for madness. "It seems to me that the knights who behaved in this way had provocation and cause for those follies and penances; but what cause had your worship for going mad?"

His mistake is to think than an explanation for madness is enough. If Don Quixote had interpreted Cardenio's madness as stemming from his friend's betrayal, Cardenio would have answered that he knows that already.

Therefore, the knight prefers to examine the resonance in himself with the madness of the other. "[…] that is the beauty of this business of mine; no thanks to a knight-errant for going mad when he has cause; the thing is to turn crazy without any provocation, and let my lady know, if I do this in the dry, what I would do in the moist?" (De Cervantes, 2013, p. 164). "If I do this in cold blood, what might I do in hot blood" is another way of putting it.

In fact, the analyst "turns crazy" in cold blood and in hot blood at once. While he has one foot in the fire of madness, he keeps the other on the ground, to maintain the solid support allowing him to pull the patient out of hell. Without this mimesis, which creates the role of a "passionate witness", to use Dori Laub's term, in a context of trauma, madness is condemned to endless repetition. Thus, Don Quixote continues to consolidate his role, in order to transform Cardenio's fate, which appears set in advance, into a story to be written, a means of foiling destiny. "And so, friend Sancho, waste no time in advising me against so rare, so happy, and so unheard-of an imitation."

The profession of fool

After appointing himself Cardenio's analyst, Don Quixote takes the liberty of practicing the profession of fool, shaming those of us who try to avoid it, intimidated by psychotic transference. But he intends to play this role only briefly, the time it takes to send Dulcinea a letter, delivered by Sancho: "[Sancho] could swear he had left his master mad; and so he will [remain] until his return, which was a quick one."

What exactly is this interval dedicated to the profession of fool? It is the time required to take on the role of jester, heir to pagan rituals, who reveals through a display of gestures that which cannot be said. Condemned by the Church, jesters were authorised to perform during the upside-down time of carnival periods, when their somersaults constituted a concrete illustration of an upside-down world, and tamed the wild thoughts Bion describes (Bion, 1997), acting through the demonic forces "in attendance upon us".

When he takes on the ritual function of fool and poet, for the benefit of the madman of the Sierra Morena, Don Quixote remains realistic. When the world is upside-down, one may invoke local gremlins and write a letter to the Lady beyond the mountain. But in truth, the answer he awaits does not matter at all to Don Quixote. What matters is to recreate over and over a place for the possibility of thought, which might allow the return of speech, whatever its content; "and if it be such [an answer] as my constancy deserves, my insanity and penance will come to an end, and if it to be to the opposite effect, I shall become mad in earnest and, being so, I shall suffer no more" (De Cervantes, 2013, p. 164).

By acting the fool, Don Quixote carefully defines the limits of the ceremonial space where one can invoke a Lady so far-removed that she barely exists, and yet remains the only reference when the ground of speech is compromised. In fact, just as he is about to write the letter, Don Quixote remembers the barber's basin, a heraldic signifier hardly metaphorical, since his grandfather was actually a barber. He remembers too the pitiful state in which it was left. This is why it is urgent to recreate the theoretical and practical agency of the Lady, for himself and for Cardenio, in place of a paternal agency so shattered that it can no longer act as a guarantor in any circumstance.

Supervision of the psychotherapeutic tools

Given Sancho's positivist supervision—of the type "a cat is a cat, not a demonic spirit"—and his insistence that a barber's basin is a barber's basin and not a magic helmet: "[...] anyone that heard your worship calling a barber's basin Mambrino's helmet [would think] that one who says and maintains such things must have his brains addled" (De Cervantes, 2013, p. 165), Don Quixote concludes that Sancho has "the most limited understanding that any squire in the world has or ever had". At this stage in his psychoanalytic training, he gives Sancho a lesson combining Wittgenstein's teaching on the infinity of language games and Winnicott's teaching on the role of illusion in the construction of reality.

This lesson brings to mind Julie Andrew's song in *The Sound of Music* (Wise, 1965) "My favorite things", when she consoles children who have lost their mother, while the annexation of Austria is taking place in the background.

The primary function of these insignificant objects is to remain unnoticed and not arouse envy, any more than do fools or hobby horses in Tristan Shandy. "[…] rare foresight it was in the sage who is on my side to make what is really and truly Mambrino's helmet seem a basin to everybody, for, being held in such estimation as it is, all the world would pursue me to rob me of it; but when they see it is only a barber's basin they do not take the trouble to obtain it, as was plainly shown by him who tried to break it, and left it on the ground without taking it […]" (De Cervantes, 2013, p. 165).

As a transitional object, the barber's basin fills all functions without really having one, unless it be to make reference to Cervantes' father's occupation, when the tool bearing the father's name no longer exists. Wittgenstein has provided directions for use: "When the tool with the name no longer exists" (Wittgenstein, 2009), it suffices to take any tool in the toolbox and agree to give it that name, provided the other consents to the name: "[…] all things belonging to knights-errant seem to be illusions and nonsense and ravings, and to go always by contraries."

Defying mainstream tendencies, Don Quixote goes back to the origin of words to avoid falling prey to fallacious discourses. His theoretical and practical proceedings are presented *ab ovo* and even naked. "I shall have to take of all this armor and remain as naked as I was born." This is how the Festival of the Mad, the Innocent and the Children is brought about, despite the "swarm of enchanters […] that change and alter everything with us".

Dojo

The dawning of this new era requires a ceremonial space, carefully chosen and demarcated, the domain of a local Spirit, where the mountain is no longer terrifying, but enters the sphere of language: Winnicott's "safe space" or Plato's *khôra* in *Timaeus* (Plato, 2007b).

The topography is three-dimensional. The vertical rocks overhanging the mountain face, as if the spirit of the mountain keeps a watchful eye over all that goes on below. This shape "stood like an isolated peak among the others that surrounded it". At a sloping angle, "past [the mountain] base there flowed a gentle brook", through a green meadow dotted with wild flowers and trees. In the horizontal plane of the now clearly demarcated cathartic space, Don Quixote can vaticinate like an oracle. "Upon this place the Knight of the Rueful Countenance fixed his choice for the performance of his penance, and as he beheld it exclaimed in a loud voice as though he were out of his senses [...]." The tone of discourse has changed, and has become playful.

Here, entering the sphere of madness is associated, since the Middle Ages, with fairy creatures, goblins, elves, trolls and korrigans, sources of the first words, *fata* (fates) from times past when animals and trees could speak: "Oh, ye rural deities, whoever ye be that haunt this lone spot, give ear to the complaint of a wretched lover whom long absence and brooding jealousy have driven to bewail his fate among these wilds and complain of the hard heart of that fair and ungrateful one [...]! Oh, ye wood nymphs and dryads, [...] nimble wanton satyrs [...]! Oh, Dulcinea del Toboso [...]" (De Cervantes, 2013, pp. 165–166). All the figures of pastoral mythology are enumerated.

But in truth, who is the "I" speaking here: Don Quixote or Cardenio? No matter, since the fusion of identities continues and, as Wittgenstein would say, one does not choose the mouth which says "I ache" to the fair, ungrateful maid.

In the meanwhile, Sancho has been promoted to a new position. After having acted as supervisor of Cardenio's analysis, he has become a historiographer, Cid Hamet Ben Engeli's rival. "I declare, Sancho, [...] I wish thee to observe in the meantime what I do and say for her sake, that thou mayest be able to tell it" (De Cervantes, 2013, p. 166). Since none of the witnesses sent to Dulcinea ever reached her, the most faithful of faithful servants is entrusted with accomplishing the inscription.

To do justice to this distinguished mission, Sancho asks to be given the reins of the motor of transference, Rocinante—no less—and Don Quixote consents, "giving [the horse] a slap on the croup". This done, the knight had only to perform a few "insanities", on the model of the madness to which Tristan succumbs for Iseult (Bédier, 2011), or that of Amadas for Ydoine (Arthur, 2014). Like them, Don Quixote intends to make a great show of how betrayal drives men mad, by making a display of torn garments and scattered armour, and knocking his head against rocks to receive blows that "must be real, solid and valid, without anything sophisticated or fanciful about them".

But Sancho has no taste for violent displays. "But what more have I to see besides what I have seen?", he protests, for he does not want to be retraumatised for no reason. Therefore, he advises his master to do these things "against something soft", or at least to shorten the duration of the acts of self-punishment to be recounted to Dulcinea. "I beg of you, too, to reckon as past the three days you allowed me for seeing the mad things you do, for I take them as seen already and pronounced upon, and I will tell wonderful stories to my lady; so write the letter and send me off at once, for I long to return and take your worship out of this purgatory where I am leaving you" (De Cervantes, 2013, p. 167). Although he has now been elevated to the status of reporter, the *therapon* in him is still at work, and he worries about the consequences of such hardships on the knight's health. But Don Quixote disagrees: "Rather call it hell, or even worse if there be anything worse."

There follows a theological discussion which we would do well to include in manuals of psychiatry, and even in a dictionary of psychoanalysis: is psychosis hell or purgatory? Can one come out of it?

The question of the existence of a "temporary hell" was a much-debated subject in the twelfth century, Jacques Le Goff tells us in *The Birth of Purgatory* (Le Goff, 1986). This controversy abolished, once more, the barriers the Church had erected between the worlds of the living and the dead, to fight animism. As a result, it became possible again to speak to the wandering souls encountered in dreams. Like in the good old Pagan Era, the river Acheron could be moved (*Acheronta movebo*), without waiting for Freud's intervention ("I shall move Hell").

Thus, the unconscious causes Sancho to make a slip, erring on the side of hope. "For one who is in hell, *nulla est retention*", he says, instead of *redemptio*. Here again, we are given a performative definition of the analysis of madness, in a different form. The formulation "no one is retained" in madness does not presume a structure or illness from which there is no escape; it opens the possibility of a way out. "[I will] take your worship out of this purgatory that seems to be hell but is not, as there is hope of getting out of it." Duly noted.

The agency of the lady, the agency of the letter

The letter is finally written. Paper is scarce, so Cardenio's notebook serves as a palimpsest, reused to write the letter to Dulcinea, as well as the order for payment of three ass colts to Sancho. The question of the signature is negotiated at length. Don Quixote agrees to sign the order of payment of the asses, a legal document, but refuses to sign the letter to Dulcinea. This letter is addressed to the Lady, the one to whom the knight owes his title: to add it explicitly would be redundant.

When Sancho expresses concern about possible falsification of the letter—a strange foreshadowing of the fate of the novel—Don Quixote answers haughtily: "[…] it will be no great matter if it is in some other person's hand, for as well as I recollect Dulcinea can neither read or write, nor in the whole course of her life has she seen handwriting of letter of mine, for my love and hers have been always platonic" (De Cervantes, 2013, p. 168).

The idea of the platonic takes us back to *Phaedrus*, (Plato, 2003) to the procession of winged souls, "psyches" circling around "to on", the Real, on chariots pulled by a pair of horses. After a glimpse at surviving forms, or Ideas, the chariot will inevitably fall when the rebellious dark horse pulls down the soaring white horse. The fall of the knight's Dulcinea, gives her an "altered" aspect, which Sancho will describe with great realism. A merciless dismantling process begins. The form perceived by Don Quixote is, in truth, precisely an "idea"—an ideal form—since it is that of the never-seen, distant Lady, his scrutiny "not going beyond a modest look, and even that so seldom that I can safely swear I have not seen her four times in all these twelve years I have been loving her more than the light of these eyes that the earth will one day devour".

To complete the nomination of the symbolic agency, the latter must fall into a rough corporeal envelope. Beautiful or ugly, the name of the Lady is essential. Sancho delights in dismantling her idealisation. A masculine figure, "she can fling a crowbar as well as the lustiest lad in all the town. Giver of all good! But she is a brave lass, and a right and stout one". And vociferous: "What sting she has and what a voice!" Not shy either, "and the best of her is that she is not a bit prudish, for she has plenty of affability, and jokes with everybody, and has a grin and a jest for everything". This uncourtly portrait includes activities unbecoming to a high-born maiden: combing flax, threshing wheat, as well as basking in the sun, since "going about the fields always, and the sun and the air spoil women's looks greatly" (De Cervantes, 2013, p. 169).

This heated exchange leads Don Quixote to formulate a definition worthy of Wittgenstein. Mainspring of the knight's word play, the Lady is what his language makes of her. "I picture her in my imagination as I would have her to be, as well in beauty as in condition." Thus, having regained her place in the dream world—the "World of the Dreaming" of Australian aborigines—she cannot be subjected to sociological investigation. "[…] and as to her pedigree it is very little matter, for no one will examine into it for the purpose of conferring any order upon her […]; and let each say what he will" (De Cervantes, 2013, pp. 169–170).

Although she inspires troubadours, the Lady is not a sexual object. "It is not to be supposed that all those poets who sang the praises of ladies under the fancy names they give them, has any such mistresses." To prove his point, Don Quixote makes reference to the star system of his era: "The Phillises, […] the Dianas, the Galateas", the equivalent of our Dianas and Marilyns, "that the books, the ballads, the barber shops […] are full of". He even relates a bawdy moral tale on the subject, to show that he is not prudish either.

The tale concerns a clever widow, "free and easy", "independent and rich", taken to task by the superior of a lay-brother in a teaching community, who proffers "brotherly remonstrance", expressing consternation at her infatuation with a coarse, stupid lay-brother, when in his community there were so many intellectuals, "masters, graduates […] among whom [she] might choose as if they were a lot of pears […]".

The young woman replies, unabashed: "My dear sir, you are very much mistaken, and your ideas are very old-fashioned, if you think that I have made a bad choice in So-and-so, fool as he seems; because for all I want with him, he knows as much and more philosophy than Aristotle." Just as cleverly, Don Quixote points out (demonstrating that he knows no less about sexual desire than Freud and Lacan put together): "In the same way, Sancho, for all I want with Dulcinea del Toboso she is just as good as the most exalted princess on earth." In the Sierra Morena, the function of the Lady is to be the instance to whom thoughts are addressed, when thinking has become impossible, as it has for Cardenio.

As for the letter itself, addressed by Don Quixote to his "dear enemy", it is written in the style of negative mysticism. "The pierced by the point of absence, the wounded to the heart's core, sends thee, Dulcinea del Toboso, the health that he himself enjoys not" (De Cervantes, 2013, p. 170). Thus, the letter carves out a space both theoretical and concrete, in which poetic signifiers can resonate—without which neither literature, nor analysis, nor any social link would be possible. This being so, the "fair ingrate [who] despises [Don Quixote], [whose] worth is not for [him], [whose] scorn is [his] affliction", is not, despite all appearances, a totalitarian tyrant. Her indifference is that of a dimension imposed by mathematical logic and as unalterable as the paradigm of worth.

The document "done in the heart of the Sierra Morena, the twenty-seventh of August of this present year" (De Cervantes, 2013, p. 171), is legitimated by the knight's signature. The mountain has given birth to the fundamental element of the social link, in the form of a letter attesting to the name of the knight. Reduced to a mere flourish, the signature is enough to certify the bequest of the asses: as soon as the knight's niece will see it, she will honour it without question.

But in the general confusion illustrated by Cardenio's madness, the remedy needed to rebuild good faith cannot be applied solely in the abstract. A body is needed for speech to be possible. Brought into play in a ritual theatre which is not content with pure signifiers, Don Quixote's body enacts a language which links the gesture to the word.

The paradigm of ceremonial man

So there we are. To put an end to the bedlam caused by traumatic revivals, a sacrificial ritual must be accomplished: "At any rate, Sancho", said Don Quixote, "I should like—and there is reason for it—I should like thee, I say, to see me stripped to the skin and performing a dozen or two insanities" (De Cervantes, 2013, p. 171). This time, the theatre of madness is brought under control by means of ritual staging testifying to the mastery Don Quixote has acquired in the course of his adventures. But the audience objects. Sancho is becoming fed up with the show, ceremonial or not. "I mean to go at once without seeing the fooleries your worship is going to do; I'll say I saw you do so many that [Dulcinea] will not want any more" (De Cervantes, 2013, p. 171). Don Quixote pleads with Sancho, asking him to see "a dozen or two of insanities", done "stripped to the skin", "in less than half an hour", since a ritual cannot be accomplished without a witness.

While Don Quixote is dedicating his efforts to helping Cardenio, Sancho has had enough of purification and does not care about the ceremonial man Don Quixote is preparing to become during their separation. "For the love of God, master mine, let me not see your worship stripped, for it will sorely grieve me, and I shall not be able to keep from tears [...]; but if it is your worship's pleasure that I should see some insanities, do them in your clothes, short ones" (De Cervantes, 2013, p. 171).

But Sancho cannot prevent a whiff of madness from taking hold of his master, facilitated by ritual regression and fasting. "I should not eat anything but the herbs and the fruits which this meadow and these trees may yield me."

"A tool rather than a fate", madness is no longer symptomatic—showing what cannot be said—but takes on a therapeutic role, in order to reconnect (*sumballein*, in Greek) that which perversion has torn asunder (*diaballein*). In the course of an analysis, this aspect is often blurred, since an analysis resembles a labyrinth more than a well-ordered structure. In the centre of the labyrinth, the Minotaur, who feeds on young people, is preparing to devour Cardenio. This is why Don Quixote supplies Sancho with an Ariadne's thread. "Observe the landmark well [...]; however not to miss me and lose thyself, the best plan will be to cut some branches of the broom that is so abundant about here, and as thou goest to lay them at intervals [...], after the fashion of the clue in the labyrinth of Theseus" (De Cervantes, 2013, p. 172).

But before heeding this advice regarding his return from the journey, Sancho's second thoughts just after taking leave prompt him to return in order to respect his oath. "He had not gone a hundred paces, however, when he returned and said: 'I must say, señor, your worship said quite right, that in order to be able to swear without a weight on my conscience that I had seen you do mad things, it would be well for me to see if it were only one; though in your worship's remaining here I have seen a very great one.'"

Clearly, in the time has come for the farcical transgression of the prohibition of pagan gestures by the Church, in an attempt to stem the excesses of pagan ceremonies. Don Quixote makes no fuss about mixing pagan and Christian metaphors: "Did I not tell thee so? Wait, Sancho, and I will do them in the saying of a credo" (De Cervantes, 2013, p. 172). In effect, the ritual is contained within a short paragraph. Quick as a wink, the knight proceeds to do just what the Church did not want to see. "[...] pulling off his breeches in all haste he stripped himself to his skin and his shirt, and then, without more ado, he cut a couple of *gambados* in the air, and a couple of somersaults, heels over head, making such a display [...]." We might note, in passing, the knight's agility, and remember the moments of the transference when the analyst finds himself heels over head, making such a display ... or worse! For this circus scene with its somersaults and back flips confirms, if it is not yet clear, that we have landed head first in full-fledged paganism.

The spell of the Sierra Morena

According to Wittgenstein, ceremonial man creates a theatrical space in order to fend off dangers threatening the social link. Retreating into the bowels of the mountain, and the calculated separation between madness and ritual regression, provide Don Quixote with the distance necessary to act ritually, naked, half-man, half-animal, making "such a display" shamelessly and altogether innocently of the *pudenda* Sancho was so unwilling to see "that [he] wheeled Rocinante around" and went on his way. The knight's modesty is safe, preserved from the fascination with the *fascinum*, the phallus displayed in mystery rites, to which Sancho only gives a sidelong glance, like the glance Perseus threw the Gorgon Medusa. Likewise, when the analyst claims the right to perform such stunts and acrobatics, the analysis may find its way out of the labyrinth. Thanks to the somersaults of its naked jester, the Sierra Morena will exert its true spell and accomplish miracles. "[…] and so we will leave [Sancho] to follow his road until his return, which was a quick one." The plural body separates, to be replaced by the theatre of fools whose tall tales will trip up the perverse mechanism, until it can do no more harm.

Now the plot follows the thread of the disguises which, starting with Don Quixote's strip-tease, go on to exchanges of clothing allowing each character to indulge his whims, and even change his gender. On the stage of the theatre of fools, the turnover of identities mimics traumatic depersonalisation, when one forgets one's own name and even one's gender. Like death in a macabre dance, madness leads the saraband, acting as a great equaliser. But before the music starts, the narrative slows down.

Don Quixote needs time to think: "[…] when he found himself alone, […] je climbed up to the top of a high rock, and there he set himself to consider" (De Cervantes, 2013, p. 173). The madness he decides to enact is that of Amadis, which as he foresaw, caused him to weep his fill "without losing his senses".

The advantage of Amadis' depression—in an era when drug molecules were not yet polluting rivers and the ground-water sheet—was that it was much less harmful to the planet than the disasters brought about by Roland the Furious. "[…] why should I now take the trouble to strip stark naked, or do mischief to these trees which have done me no harm, or why am I to disturb the clear waters of these brooks which will give me to drink whenever I have a mind?" (De Cervantes, 2013, p. 174). Thus, without doing nature much harm, Don Quixote is content to write on the sand, or carve on the bark of trees a multitude if rhyming verses, calling on "the fauns and satyrs of the woods and the nymphs of the streams [...]. And here it will be well to leave him, wrapped up in sighs and verses [...]" (De Cervantes, 2013, p. 175). The only drawback is that his vegetarian diet is so limited and unbalanced that he becomes unrecognisable. "[...] has [Sancho's return] been delayed three weeks, as it was three days, the Knight [...] would have worn such an altered countenance that the mother that bore him would not have known him" (De Cervantes, 2013, p. 175).

Mother folly at the inn

Fortunately, the squire's mission was cut short at the inn to which his craving for a hot meal had led him, where he encountered the barber and the curate, instead of Dulcinea. This meeting was to inspire Beaumarchais, Mozart and Musset. The two inquisitors wasted no time before questioning Sancho, who was "determined to keep secret the place and circumstances where and under which he had left his master" (De Cervantes, 2013, p. 176). But he quickly relented and told them everything, "offhand and without stopping", when faced with the barely disguised threat of being accused of a crime. "[...] if you don't tell us where he is [...], we will suspect as we suspect already, that you have murdered and robbed him, for here you are mounted on his horse." The need to produce proof of the lost letter provides an opportunity to introduce the spectacular gestural array of the art of mime at its finest. "[...] his face grew deadly pale, [...] he seized his beard with both hands and plucked away half of it, [...] and without stopping, gave himself half a dozen cuffs on the face and nose [...]. Sancho [...] stopped to scratch his head to bring back the letter to his memory, and balanced himself now on one foot, now the other, one moment staring at the ground, the next at the sky, and after having half gnawed off the end of a finger [...] he said, after a long pause, 'Exalted and scrubbing Lady [...], the wounded and wanting of sleep, and the pierced [...]'" (De Cervantes, 2013, pp. 176–177). To obtain this intelligence, Sancho is bribed by the two head-hunters with the prospect of becoming squire to an archbishop-errant, and he ponders on this new career, "wiping his nose from time to time" (De Cervantes, 2013, pp. 176–177).

The loss of the original text of the letter enables the passage from the primary process of traumatic revival to the secondary process of inscription, in which the founding agency of the Lady falls from her pedestal. Wearing a carnival disguise, she will lead us from jugglers to minstrels, and from farce to oratorios. "[…] the curate hit upon an idea very well adapted to humor Don Quixote […]; and this notion […] was that he himself should assume the disguise of a wandering damsel, while the [barber] should try as best he could to pass for a squire" (De Cervantes, 2013, p. 178).

The necessary garments were quickly found: a red petticoat with wide black bands, a quilted nightcap, a black taffeta mask, a broad-brimmed hat—these items constituted the curate's paraphernalia when he "seated himself woman-fashion on his mule" (De Cervantes, 2013, p. 180), while the barber mounted his with a long beard of mingled red and white. The official purpose of the mission was still to bring the hero back home, using the charm of the false damsel in distress. But this was without reckoning with the therapeutic play of masks, which ultimately will cause this trick to fail and perform their true symbolic and therapeutic function. The beard made of an ox tail attached to the chin, reproducing the ass-head figures seen in medieval sacred art, puts the reader in mind of Saturnalia or the Feast of the Ass. "Maritornes, who, sinner as she was, promised to pray a rosary of prayers that God might grant them success in such an arduous and Christian undertaking", may have prevailed on the curate's conscience. As he was leaving the inn, it struck him that he was doing wrong in indulging his desire for travesty, and he changed places with the barber, preferring to impersonate the squire. Madness is now more comical than ever. "Sancho […], on seeing the pair in such a costume was unable to restrain his laughter." He then proceeded to tell them about the existence of the other fool, Cardenio.

The next day "they reached the place where Sancho had laid the broom branches as markers", and he took the lead, according to their plan "to rescue his master from the pernicious life he had adopted [and bring] him back to a better mode of life", in their view (De Cervantes, 2013, p. 181). He leaves the two friends in the shade, in a glen "through which there flowed a little gentle rivulet". It is three in the afternoon on a beautiful August day. Suddenly, a voice rises in the afternoon heat, heard only by the masks.

Cardenio changes analysts

The voice sings that madness still holds sway on earth. "[...] it is but folly to seek a cure for melancholy: ask where it lies; the answer saith in Change, in Madness, in Death" (De Cervantes, 2013, p. 182). The sonnet which follows predicts the reign of hypocrisy and strife:

> This earth will be prey of strife once more,
> As when primeval discord held its reign.

Having set off in search of the bard announcing this apocalypse, the two masks come upon the madman described by Sancho, Cardenio, who "stood still with his head bent down upon his breast like one in deep thought" (De Cervantes, 2013, p. 183). He glanced at them sideways, judging these "false faces", as the Iroquois call their masks, to be crazy enough to guarantee them free passage. In fact, patients in the grip of madness are often more indulgent towards their analysts' eccentricities than conformists might imagine.

The curate, an expert spiritual advisor, with or without a cassock, feels compelled to preach and to try to obtain a confession. "The curate, [...] being a man of good address, [and] aware of his misfortune [...] urged him to quit a life of such misery, lest he should end it there [...]." Cardenio, who was usually suspicious, did not hesitate to answer. He was speaking to clowns, that is, to Heaven-sent beings. When fraud is in command, why not trust surreal encounters, including these false faces, as they indeed reveal themselves to be? Thanks to his first analysis with Don Quixote, Cardenio understands the benefits that can be gained from unexpected encounters. Thus, he continues the account of his loss of reason where he left off. But this time, he is the one who has a request. Speaking to them as anonymous witnesses, he entreats them "to hear the story of my countless misfortunes" (De Cervantes, 2013, p. 184). When an analysis is taken up again, we often have the impression of starting from the beginning, but in fact the possibility of narration has been strengthened in the first stage, although the analysis was abruptly ended—here, four chapters earlier.

Even though he has lost all hope, Cardenio knows that he needs his fiancée's guilt to avoid confronting "what I did not do [but] should have done". If Luscinda was as innocent as Queen Madasima, Cardenio would be forced to acknowledge that he did not come to her defence, as Don Quixote did. Thoughts of suicide emerge when a fit of madness subsides, bringing the awareness of having been "carried away" for some time. Cardenio knows this very well. The two accomplices have training in listening. Contrary to Don Quixote, they remain neutral and do not interrupt. Therefore, they offer the madman no chance to overcome his madness. Yet, Cardenio is not fooled by their humanitarian mission. Organised primarily to capture Don Quixote, this mission will pick up all the "crazies" along the way. Cardenio recognises, in the lofty words, the usual technique used in rescue missions: to "draw [him] away from this to some better retreat".

Cervantes makes it clear that the first part of his analysis with Don Quixote has already allowed him to speak. As a result, he can now tell his story without triggering the least traumatic revival: "[…] but now fortunately the mad fit kept off, allowed him to tell [his tale] to the end" (De Cervantes, 2013, p. 184). In a similar situation, Aby Warburg, while in the grip of madness, found someone to talk to as well: first Fritz Saxl, his disciple and faithful "Sancho", who never let him collapse under the weight of labels; and then the patients of Binswanger's clinic, to whom he presented his Lecture on Serpent Ritual. It was on this occasion that he used the phrase "*Symbol tut wohl*" [the symbol heals] (Binswanger & Warburg, 2007, p. 42).

Traditional analysis

Here, the aim of confession is to put an end to Cardenio's humiliation when he is thought to be stupid, "a week-minded man, or, what is worse, one devoid of reason" (De Cervantes, 2013, p. 184). In truth, most often a diagnosis of psychosis is equated with a defective brain. This is why Cardenio must save face by exposing the felony that pushed him over the edge. He might be irresponsible, but he is not guilty. "[…] all I can do is […] plead for my madness by telling how it was caused, to any that care to hear it; for no reasonable beings on learning the cause will wonder at the effects; and if they cannot help me at least they will not blame me, and the repugnance they feel at my wild ways will turn into pity for my woes" (De Cervantes, 2013, p. 184). Before meeting Don Quixote, Cardenio had not exposed the cause of his madness. But once this is done, causal reasoning becomes a stumbling block for healing. In any case, its cause is no mystery to him.

An important principle is stated here. Identifying the traumatic event is essential but not sufficient, as is insufficient the odd, perceptive, and likeable team which treats him. What is more, Cardenio does not want to be cured, because madness prevents him from "[falling] into another [evil] still greater, [...] to become at times like a stone, without feeling or consciousness". He hesitates to give up a state that protects him from catatonia and terror.His own case history, told to the barber and the curate, clearly proceeds from a traumatic memory. "Oh memory, mortal foe of my peace!" (De Cervantes, 2013, p. 189), which repeats the story ceaselessly "in nearly the same words and manner in which he had related it to Don Quixote". But this time, having finally found analysts who are willing to listen religiously, he can tell his story to the end. He takes up the thread of the story where it had been left off in Chapter XXIV (De Cervantes, 2013, p. 154), at the point where Don Fernando finds Luscinda's note in a volume of *Amadis of Gaul*, lent to Cardenio. In her note, Luscinda encourages Cardenio to ask he father for her hand in marriage. Instead, the rake is able to obtain this consent, because Luscinda's father is ready to sacrifice her to his ambition.

The difference between the letter Sancho has just lost and the letter Don Fernando stole on that occasion illustrates the distance between madness and perversion. The former does not aim at possession of the Lady, while the latter sets a predatory process in motion. "Traitor, cruel, vindictive and perfidious" (De Cervantes, 2013, p. 185), Don Fernando is only capable of mafia-style fraternising built on the ruins of the name of the father, trampling on three fathers at once: his own, who is unaware of his actions, Luscinda's father, from whom he buys the young girl, and Cardenio's father, who had entrusted his son to him. "Who could have thought that Don Fernando, [...] bound to me by gratitude for my services, one that could win the object of his love wherever he might set his affections, could have become so obdurate [...] as to rob me of my one ewe lamb that was not even yet in my possession?" Luscinda is fated to be thrown away as soon as she is conquered, just as Dorothea, the peasant girl, had been.

Clinical description of a perverted link

Cervantes enumerates the different elements of a perverse social link, which Hannah Arendt identified in a political context (Arendt, 1951).

Betrayal of the commanding body: "The promise Don Fernando gave you […], he has fulfilled much more to his own satisfaction than to our advantage." Powerless indignation, which excites the pervert: "O, treacherous […] Judas! What offense did I commit?" The unexpected swiftness of the attack: "Could I have anticipated this treachery? Could I by any chance have suspected it?" The victims' sense of foreboding: Luscinda's eyes filled with tears, and the lump in her throat; Cardenio's sadness and dejection, "[his] heart filled with fancies and suspicions, but not knowing well what it was [he] suspected or fancied" (De Cervantes, 2013, p. 186). The complicity of the family: five days later, Luscinda's marriage to "the treacherous Don Fernando" had been organised by her "covetous father". Finally, the distinction between the sacred and the profane is abolished: "[…] the bridegroom entered the hall in his usual dress, without ornament of any kind."

From political analysis, Cervantes goes on to the psycho traumatic analysis of an experience of terror. Cardenio keeps reliving "this memory of hell-fire like hell-fire of memory", as Claude Barrois (Barrois, 1993) puts it, because traumatic memory records every detail. "Be not weary sirs, of listening to these digressions; my sorrow is not one of those that can or should be told tersely or briefly, for to me each incident seems to call for many words." His two listeners assure him that all the details interest them greatly.

Cardenio has withdrawn from the subject who says "I should have done what I did not do" (De Cervantes, 2013, p. 189). All that is left in his place is a feeling of shame. "I stood stupefied, wholly abandoned, it seemed, by Heaven, declared the enemy of the earth that bore me, the air refusing me breath for my sighs, the water moisture for my tears; it was only the fire that gathered strength so that me whole frame glowed with rage and jealousy." The desire to kill is transformed into suicidal self-aggression. "[…] and so, without seeking to take vengeance on my greatest enemies (which might have been easily taken, as all thought of me was so far from their minds), I resolved to take it upon myself, and on myself to inflict the pain they deserved." Death has entered his being. "[…] sudden pain is soon over, but that which is protracted by tortures is ever slaying without ending life" (De Cervantes, 2013, p. 190). When his mule, the only companion he had left, dies, Cardenio goes berserk: his being disintegrates: this "undoing of character", as Jonathan Shay calls it, causes him to lose consciousness. "I lay stretched on the ground, how long I know not, after which I rose up free from hunger, [...] and [...] I had been uttering ravings that showed plainly I had lost my reason" (De Cervantes, 2013, p. 191).

Like Er, the traumatised Greek soldier in Plato's *Republic*, or like Orpheus, when Cardenio regains consciousness, he is a stranger to the human world. Monteverdi, Cervantes's contemporary (1567–1643), composed *The Legend of Orpheus* in Mantua at the same period, in 1607, the year when he lost his wife. *Orpheus* is also a myth which concerns traumatised soldiers returning from the hell of war, since Monteverdi had accompanied Duke de Gonzague, during the Ottoman-Hungarian Wars. Orpheus' music attracts wild animals, while Cardenio becomes one, taking refuge in the wilderness, snatching food from the goatherds and dwelling in the hollow of a cork tree, like a tree-man. Having regained his senses, Cardenio is no longer himself, but rather the incarnation of *Nemesis*, the goddess of revenge for the betrayal of trust.

Refusing therapy is logical, since traumatic memory cannot be erased. It is impossible to undo what was done. So Cardenio desires the impossible: either that "Heaven's will [...] order [his] memory no longer [to] recollect", or that Luscinda be his once again, though she is now married to Don Fernando. "[...] do not trouble yourselves with urging or pressing upon me what reason suggests as likely to serve for my relief, for it will avail me as much as the medicine prescribed by a wise physician avails the sick man who will not take it. I have no wish for health without Luscinda [...]; let it be mine to be a prey to misery [...]" (De Cervantes, 2013, p. 192).

Understandably, psychoanalysis is not likely to be useful in such cases. It is clear that this second analysis failed, despite the benevolent attitude of the masked listeners, which allowed Cardenio to finish his story. But both are disqualified by their patient, for they remain outside transference, strangers to any true proximity, to the *philia*, needed to challenge the Furies that haunt him, causing him "greater sorrows and sufferings, for [...] even in death there will not be an end to them".

The suspense is at its peak. There is no hint of what is written in the note discovered in Luscinda's bosom after she fainted. Fortunately, the shallow comforting words the curate proffers are brought to a close "by a voice that reached his ear, [speaking] in melancholy tones". A fourth voice is added to the polyphony, above Don Quixote's ground bass and the curate's hollow words, as a counterpoint to Cardenio's solo.

In the first Book of *The Aeneid* (Virgil, 1952), Virgil speaks of tears in the universe, *sunt lacrimae rerum*, and of "mortal things [which] touch the mind"—*et mentum mortalia tangunt*—the mind which is mortally devastated in equal measure, allowing the inscription of events otherwise left unrecorded. This is the end of the Third Part, stopped by a voice unaware of being a response to Cardenio's monologue.

CHAPTER EIGHT

Regenerating the social link

Hisayasu Nakagawa

In the fourth and final part of the novel, Don Quixote restores his ancestors' castle and, as his final feat, succeeds in saving the chivalry books. At the end of his treks through the Sierra Mountains, we can presume that he is a psychoanalyst, with all the transference required, including to his books. The therapeutic function of books is universal, so it is not surprising that I should find it in a book I just received from Japan. The story of this book, received "when I least expect it" and echoing what I was in the process of writing, deserves to be told.

In 1986, at the end of June, we met Professor Hisayasu Nakagawa and his wife Yoko. An expert on Diderot, Professor Nakagawa taught at the University of Kyoto. During dinner, I must have mentioned my recent hospitalisation for intestinal obstruction, one year after a previous surgical procedure.

The professor leapt to his feet and asked me to place myself next to him. He took off his trousers and, in his boxer shorts, firmly instructed me to join him in executing some yoga movements. Yoko joined us, laughing, putting me at ease with her indulgent attitude, so different from what I expected of Japanese tradition. So I executed as best I could the four postures her husband showed me, while throwing sidelong glances at her in the pancake pose. After this we all returned to the table to enjoy a dessert of melon with berries, which this unexpected event has rendered unforgettable for me.

As we were leaving, Mr. Nakagawa advised me to execute the four movements regularly, implying that this practice had saved his life. He did not explain further, but said I could call him during their month-long stay in Paris. Before they left, he sent me a book with photographs of yoga postures described in Japanese.

After summer vacation, one day I came home so exhausted from the psychiatric hospital—where I worked every Monday for thirty years—that I lay down on the floor to execute the four yoga movements, breathing deeply like Mr. Nakagawa had taught me. I got up so refreshed that I continued to use this method ever since, without looking for another teacher. A few years later, I even had occasion to help a woman I did not know by showing her these postures.

One evening, I was sitting in the waiting room of a group of doctors, waiting to see an ophtalmologist. At one point, a woman about my own age came in and sat down across from me. She looked as if she was in great pain. I asked her what the problem was. She said she sometimes had intense abdominal pain, and that she now suffered from an attack of this kind, while she was visiting her daughter in Paris. After a battery of tests, the doctor in her home town had told her there was nothing wrong. Remembering my own experience, I asked her whether she had had surgery recently. She said yes.

In a flash, I got up, lay on the floor, asked her to lie beside me and pull up her skirt, since both of us wore the narrow skirts fashionable in those years, over our tights. Then I showed her slowly how to make my four yoga movements, telling her to breathe deeply. Soon her pain subsided. I told her how I had learned the postures, and the story made her laugh out loud. I suggested she contact someone with more serious training than me, back in her home town. A few months later, at Christmas, I received a thank-you gift in the mail: a soft blue and white bathrobe made by her husband's firm. She had asked the doctor's secretary for my address. Later, I in turn thanked Mr. and Mrs. Nakagawa.

"Mémoires d'un 'moraliste passable'"

Professor Nakagawa sent me his latest book, "*Mémoires*", written in French, while I was writing my *Don Quixote*. In his Preface, Mr. Nakagawa explained that at the age of seventy he wished to bequeath the story of his life, which he entitled *Memoirs of an Acceptable Moralist*. On the cover, the reader sees two sculpted heads: one of the authors at twenty-five, the other a Noh theatre demon mask. With the same determination he showed when he taught me the four yoga movements, in the book he transmits all that is essential to him. First, his family history. (Nakagawa, 2007, p. 20). He is a forty-second generation descendant of Daimyos, who descend in a straight line from Emperor Seiwa-Genji (850–880) of the Minamoto clan. The clan's history was punctuated by two eras that brought reversals of fate.

The first was the modernisation of Meiji's imperial government, which destroyed the feudal system and restructured aristocracy in Japan based on the Western model. In 1871, fearing armed uprisings in the provinces, the Emperor ordered the demolition of the clan's Oka-jô castle, built at the top of a hill on Kjûshû Island, where his family had lived since 1594, about the time when Don Quixote came into being.

The second change occurred in 1946, when the New Constitution abolished the aristocratic regime. Now no longer part of the nobility, the members of his paternal lineage were already ruined. This, however did not prevent his father, a biologist, "from criticising the sly and hypocritical character of courtisans"—just as our knight did. The only vestige of the splendour of the past is a song, reproduced at the end of the book: "The moon over the castle in ruins". The music was composed in 1900 by a famous musician who had spent his childhood at the foot of the hill.

As for Hisayasu Nakagawa, as a child he coped with the overturning of all hierarchical systems by developing an all-consuming passion for books, "persisting throughout his school years in neglecting everything he learned in class, in order to live in the imaginary world of European writers and thinkers". The countless books he read day and night were as many stones that would one day allow him, he thought, to build "a castle he could call his own", that he would be able to contemplate in his old age (Nakagawa, 2007, p. 60).

This castle would be built on the international site of the "Republic of letters", but who can say in which era the foundations were laid? After having felt "naturally drawn by the Renaissance", he fell in love with the French eighteenth century and wove ceaselessly, *andante*, ties of cultural exchange, up to his recent encounter, literally staggering, with Japanese space research, careful not to exclude literature from its adventure.

But the Noh mask is there, on the cover, to serve as a reminder of the demons that assailed him after the war, when he was about twenty years old and felt "ill-adapted to society", and when these demons pushed him to desire death. He was placed in a psychiatric hospital, from which he escaped by climbing over a wall, only to pursue the same desire on another nearby hill.

The book provides a map of the hospital and of his escape route, which follows the buildings of the university where he would later teach. When he was hospitalised for the second time, a Cardiazol injection brought on such violent seizures that he understood that the doctor had "settled [his] score" (Nakagawa, 2007, pp. 64–65). No one asked him if, finding himself in an impasse, he had had to cross the bridge of Noh theatre to reach a beyond from which his ancestors could come back to help him built "the castle of [his] books".

This castle, standing now (on the uncertain ground) at the crossing of French and Japanese literature, was rebuilt from its ruins thanks to the encounter with his Lady, Yoko. In a cavalier fashion, as is his habit, let us suppose that Don Quixote enters this castle and hears, perhaps, the sound of the *biwa* accompanying songs of heroic deeds in the genre of thirteenth century narrative poetry or chivalry novels, like The Tale of Gengi (Shibiku, 1990), written around the year one thousand by a young woman, Lady Murasaki.

As we continue to read *Don Quixote*, the Fourth Part starts with a hymn addressed by Cide Hamete to the knight, aiming to revive joy in the hearts of suicidal youths. This is when a new, youthful voice is heard in the Sierra.

Amoebaen singing: trauma speaks to trauma

The mountain resonates with the sound of streams, leaves, birds, as well as the voices of voluntary exiles from the society of men. During his retreat in the Sierra, Don Quixote climbed to higher regions to reflect, and above all to do what Cardenio could no longer do: think about his lady love.

For the young man, the agency of the Lady has literally fallen in the dust, since at this point in his narrative Luscinda is lying on the floor, in a faint. As for him, because he ran off without attempting to lift her up, he does not know that the wedding ceremony was interrupted. Having removed himself from the scene, he has disappeared as a subject, and can no longer imagine anything or think ahead. Just as he is describing this defeat he cannot overcome, a new, unknown voice falls upon his ear.

The voice is not yet identified as an echo. Still, the two voices that are strangers to each other are already singing a duet from the reader's perspective, thanks to Don Quixote's presence in the background. In fact, all this while the knight has steadfastly composed for Dulcinea verses that act as charms, *carmina*, to force her to hold on. And she is in fact the one—through the lost letter addressed to her—who has entered the sphere of the mountain, in the guise of a curate and a barber dressed as a woman, to tie together these two voices which do not know each other, miraculously singing the same misfortune, the same tears, in the heat of a summer in an early year of the seventeenth century.

In the summer of 2005, viol player Jordi Savall recorded texts and songs from *Don Quixote*. In the Presentation of his book-recording *Don Quijote de la Mancha, Romances y Musicas* (Savall, 2005), he states that "music is always an essential element of the tales told by Cervantes, who was ill-treated and humiliated by his contemporaries"; this is particularly true of Carolingian and Arthurian epic songs which, thanks to the recent advent of the printing press, were distributed through the countryside on loose sheets that could be peddled.

Whistled, sang or danced, this music comes back over and over in the *intermes* which Cervantes brings to a close with songs he composes himself. They are present in all his plays, like the blues sang by the choir of Christian slaves in *The Bagnios of Algiers*, a play written immediately upon his return from captivity, and which "has this sad tone that accompanies our rejoicing".

This is why "the melodies which accompany us since childhood and throughout our lives", as Jordi Savall says, are vital for the voices which alternate in the Sierra Morena. Here, as a last hope, they call out to the forces of nature, from the loneliness which reduced them to silence, and they defy "with their sad tones" the banishment of speech, which a pervert holds in bondage.

Oratorio: Cardenio on the mend

In the Sierra, the odd little gathering which now included Cardenio, hearing a plaintive and melodious voice "got up to look for the speaker" (De Cervantes, 2013, p. 193). Stealthily, like Sioux Indians, they advanced towards the singer of the swan song looking for a "secret grave for the weary load of this body that I support so unwillingly" (De Cervantes, 2013, p. 193). This body was betrayed, the reader soon learns, and has given up hope of ever being heard, "for there is none on earth to look to for counsel in doubt, comfort in sorrow or relief in distress!"

The commando, lying in wait, wants nothing more than to take up this challenge. In fact, it soon comes upon a youth busy bathing his white feet, which look like "shining crystal". Concealed behind the curate, like special forces hidden in the mountains, "they approached so silently that he did not perceive them; [...] and so, finding they had not been noticed, the curate, who was in front, made a sign to the other two to conceal themselves behind some fragments of rock that lay there". From there, they could observe the object of their curiosity closely.

In a wink, the youth took off his montera, revealing a mass of flowing long hair. The creature before them was clearly a fairy, seated, naturally, at the edge of a fountain. Cardenio concluded: "As this is not Luscinda, it is no human creature but a divine being", eliciting instant tranference that intensified their desire to learn who she was, so that "they resolved to show themselves" (De Cervantes, 2013, p. 194). Unlike the three men who had approached her before, allegedly for her own good, none of these three seems intent on raping her. Strange, very strange, she thinks, alarmed, since the circumstances lend themselves to such a deed. The curate, used to offering comfort, tries to reassure her, taking her hand and enquiring about the "no trifling cause that has disguised your beauty in a garb so unworthy of it".

Stunned, she in turn stares at the strange group, "spellbound, looking at them without opening her lips or uttering a word" (De Cervantes, 2013, p. 195), and finally decides to give them an explanation, for the same reasons that Cardenio had. "[...] that my honor may not be left a matter of doubt in your minds, now that you have discovered me to be a woman, and see that I am young, alone, and in this dress, [...] I feel bound to tell what I would willingly keep secret if I could." With no illusions about a possible therapeutic effect of this confession, she checked her emotion and making "an effort to restrain some tears that came to her eyes, in a clear and steady voice began her story [...]".

Reference to Don Fernando

Her story first tells of a noble family in Andalusia, a family whose vassals include her own parents. They are peasants, "settled on their land", as my grandmother used to say, people "of means". She, being their only child, "was the mirror in which they beheld themselves"; she received instruction in the arts and trades, as well as music and literature. Mistress of their possessions, she managed the household, practiced embroidery and weaving, but also acted as an intendant, engaging and dismissing servants, keeping the accounts and returns of what was sown and reaped, and administering the oil mills, wine presses, flocks, herds and beehives. At seventeen, everything passed through her hands; she also found recreation in reading and played the harp, for "music soothes the troubled mind and relieves weariness of spirit". Thus, she lived in the seclusion of her parents' home and was veiled when she left it. But, as La Boétie says, the "means" of simple people awaken the greed of tyrants. "[…] the eyes of love, or idleness, more properly speaking, […] discovered me, with the help of the assiduity of Don Fernando."

Don Fernando's name triggers a neuro-vegetative reaction in Cardenio. Sweating and paleness are described clinically: he "changed colour and broke into a sweat, with such signs of emotion that the curate and the barber, who observed it, feared that one of the mad fits which they heard attacked him sometimes was coming upon him" (De Cervantes, 2013, p. 196). But contrary to all expectations, the attack of traumatic revival did not occur. "Cardenio showed no further agitation and remained quiet, regarding the peasant girl with fixed attention, for he began to suspect who she was." This is the first identification, the beginning of suspense.

Laub and Feldman call it "testimony" (Feldman and Laub, 1992, p. 75), an occurrence where a stranger testifies and describes an event you believe you alone witnessed. After this, everything changes. Shame at your own stupidity is now part of a more general story of power abuse, perpetrated over and over, freely, in secret in young girls' bedrooms, or even in the offices of despicable therapists, each girl believing herself to be the favourite. But naming the abuser annuls the confidentiality of perverse contracts.

Cardenio, who believed he was the only one who had been had, now knows better. The young girl who unwittingly opened his eyes continues her story. She blames idleness, which promotes corruption, spreading downward through the social strata. The *otium*, the idleness of Don Fernando, destroyed the *negotium*, the activity of the young girl who, once devoured, becomes disposable.

That is when Dorothea looks for refuge in the wilderness, where she attempts to be heard, despite her denials. Here, her words reach the ears of a half-crazed man who, unbeknowsnt to her, shares her shame—the *mancha* (stain)—of not having been able to resist the monster, and having succumbed to the same seduction. "[…] it gave me a certain sort of satisfaction to find myself so sought and prized by a gentleman of such distinction, and I was not displeased at seeing my praises in his letters (for however ugly we women may be, it seems to me it always pleases us to hear ourselves called beautiful)" (De Cervantes, 2013, p. 197). We hear echoes of Gretchen speaking in Goethe's *Faust*, or Margarita in Berlioz's *The Damnation of Faust*.

Voluntary servitude wins out, abolishing her reservations, despite her parents' (warning) mistrust. Considering "the disparity between [them]", they warn her—"little one, little one"—not to believe his words, which have "for their aim his own pleasure rather than [her] advantage". Less self-serving than Luscinda's father, they offer to marry her as quickly as possible to some neighbour of her choice. But too late!

The perverse mechanism is stimulated by the maiden's resistance, and feeds on scandal. Suddenly, the pace accelerates wildly. As victims everywhere attest, their perception of events is always delayed, since rape and soul murder are not only already plotted in secret, but carried out before one has time to imagine them. Don Fernando "learned that my parents were contemplating marriage for me in order to put an end to his hopes of obtaining possession of me, […] and this intelligence or suspicion made him act as you shall hear."

Chronicle of a rape foretold, complete with the element of surprise: "One night, as I was in my chamber with no other companion than a damsel who waited on me, with the doors carefully locked", this servant bribed by Don Fernando enabled him to suddenly appear in the space of purity, like a demon who can walk through walls. "I found him standing before me", causing terror and absolute astonishment that "deprived my tongue of speech. I had no power to utter a cry, nor did he give me time to utter one". Taking advantage of her shock, he took hold of her body "taking me in his arms" and mind "[making] such professions to me that I knew not how falsehood could have had the power of dressing them up to seem so like truth". Her protestations sealed her submission. The more she struggled, spoke, argued, the more tightly she was held in the net, to the point of classic identification with the aggressor: "I, a poor young creature alone, ill versed among my people in cases such as this, began, I know not how, to think all these lying protestations true […]." She is now "in the claws of a fierce lion" (De Cervantes, 2013, p. 198).

The declaration of her virtuous intentions is what excites him, with no need to wait for Sade's *Juliette*. "[…] if you hold my body clasped in your arms, I hold my soul secured by virtuous intentions. […] I am your vassal, but I am not your slave", and on and on. The innocence of the lamb only makes it more alluring. "[…] low-born peasant as I am, I have my self-respect as much as you, a lord and gentleman." As for him, the only thing he has is the desire to subdue her quickly, without wasting more time.

Her name is Dorothea

The narration is interrupted again when the young girl recounts a sham marriage—her own, saying: "the name of this unhappy being" (De Cervantes, 2013, p. 198) is Dorothea. Hearing this name, Cardenio "showed fresh agitation", but did bid her to continue her story. "[…] he was unwilling to interrupt the story, and wished to hear the end of what he already all but knew." In this simplistic and repetitive predatory process, the foreseeable outcome is the encounter with the next victim.

In his universe of travesty, Don Fernando marries left and right, whenever he chooses, on the fly, and then takes off. Using sacred images as bait, to his own ends, he "[took] an image that stood in the chamber [and] placed it as a witness of our betrothal". A similar scene would later be seen in Tirso de Molina's play *The Trickster of Seville* (*El Burlador de Sevilla*). At the time when Spain started to lose its predominant position among European nations, it also suffered the loss of its ethical values (De Molina, 1986). Don Fernando, like Don Juan, personifies the addictive desires of a society experiencing literal bankruptcy, since Spain suffered three bankruptcies during the Golden Age.

The prey has now been hooked. "[…] with the most binding words and extravagant oaths [he] gave me his promise to become my husband", his treacherous words accompanied by sighs and crocodile tears. "[He] shed more tears, redoubled his sighs and pressed me closer in his arms, from which he had never allowed me to escape; and so I was left by my maid, and ceased to be one, and he became a traitor and perjured man" (De Cervantes, 2013, p. 200).

An extremely expeditious way to recount a rape! Don Fernando gives the girl a gold ring, *post coitum*, "though not with as much earnestness and fervour as when he came", as if this trinket suffices to pay his debt. Then he disappears. "[…] when desire has attained its object, the greatest pleasure is to fly from the scene of pleasure." Now, she bores him. Without feeling, after performing his deed quickly, with brutal efficacy, he is out on "the street before daybreak", hiding his face behind his cape, like the "trickster" Tirso de Molina calls "a man without a name".

The depersonalisation afflicting Dorothea is of the same nature as Cardenio's condition. Her dreams destroyed, her fantasy life in pieces, she becomes unable to make the simplest distinctions: "I was left, I know not whether sorrowful or happy, […] agitated and troubled in mind and almost bewildered" (De Cervantes, 2013, p. 200). Waiting leaves her empty and deepens her melancholy. "[…] he came no more, nor […] could I catch a glimpse of him […] while I wearied myself with watching for one, although I knew he was in the town." She feels like enslaved, while he goes hunting: "[…] almost every day [he] went out hunting, a pastime he was very fond of, indifferent to her agony. She sinks into a slow death: 'How sad and dreary those days and hours were to me; I remember well how I began to doubt […], and even lose confidence in [his] faith […]; and I remember, too, how my maid heard those words [of] reproof […], and how I was forced to put a constraint on my […] countenance [for] my parents'", until the fatal blow of Don Fernando's marriage to Luscinda, which he had plotted to bring about practically at the same time.

Reference to Luscinda

The third name to be revealed is Luscinda, which wounds Cardenio again; he is affected to the core of his being: "[…] he only shrugged his shoulders, bit his lips, bent his brows, and before long two streams of tears escaped from his eyes" (De Cervantes, 2013, p. 200). But he continues to listen to Dorothea's story, until it intersects with his own.

Two letters left in suspense are finally going to intertwine, thanks to the young girl's account: the note taken from Luscinda's bosom, whose content was unknown to Cardenio, and the letter he wrote when he left the city in despair, in which he "[declared] the wrong Luscinda had done him". Dorothea and Cardenio compare their stories, and even intertwine them, to construct coherence and reason. This intertwining creates the *logos*, speech and reason—as Socrates says in the

Theatetus—and create a link between the three young people isolated by a perverse manoeuvre.

At this moment when the heart fails, Dorothea emerges as Cardenio's uncanny double, strangely familiar. Disguised as a shepherd, accompanied by a servant, she sets forth for the city where her enemy is said to be, and reaches it in two days. The mystery of the note found in Luscinda's bosom is quickly solved, since she has become "the talk of every knot of idlers in the street. [...] A paper in her own handwriting [...] said and declared that she could not be Don Fernando's bride, because she was already Cardenio's [...]" (De Cervantes, 2013, p. 201). A dagger found in her clothes confirmed her will "to kill herself on the completion of her betrothal", like Lucretia had done after being raped by Tarquinius.

Once unmasked, the narcissistic pervert often turns into a psychopath. "Don Fernando, persuaded that Luscinda had [...] trifled with him, assailed her before she had recovered from her swoon, and tried to stab her with the dagger". By trying to kill her in a swoon, as one would rape a corpse, Don Fernando shows how little distinction he makes between the animate and the inanimate.

The young girls have become public property; they are treated like whores and made the subject of gossip. They must flee: one to an unknown destination—which turns out to be a convent—the other into the mountain wilderness. In addition, a "Wanted" notice has been issued to find Dorothea, who is said to have run away from her father's house with a servant.

In fact, the latter proves to be another *burlador*. After having sworn to bear her company "as he said, to the end of the world", just two pages further he "sought to take advantage of the opportunity" of the solitude of their retreat. Cast out from society, his mistress is now ready for the brothel. But although she has lost her rank and good name, Dorothea disagrees. When he "began to use violence", she defended herself resolutely. "[...] with my slight strength and with little exertion I pushed him over a precipice, where I left him, whether dead or alive I know not" (De Cervantes, 2013, p. 202). Later, she would be unable to do the same thing to the third abuser, a herdsman who tried to rape her as well, after hiring her to take his herds to pasture. Pastoral romances have their limits, and "[having] no precipice or ravine at hand down which to fling [her] master", she goes off to hide in the mountains.

Dorothea ends her confession in total despair. "With these words she became silent, and the colour that overspread her face showed plainly the pain and shame she was suffering at heart." She feels shame at appearing before her parents, at having brought shame upon them, and at exposing them to the vicious talk of those who envy them. This feeling of shame, which cannot be appeased by any maternal comforting, will be alleviated when Cardenio pronounces the name of her father.

The space of wilderness

What Cardenio says is: "So then, señora, you are the fair Dorothea, the only daughter of the rich Clenardo?" (De Cervantes, 2013, p. 204). But the name of the father cannot be reinstated by just anyone. Thus, she replies in a flash: "And who may you be, brother, who seem to know my father's name so well?" Only one who bears the same stain she does, a man without rank, without clothing, without relations and even without reason can claim to recognise her.

He then consents to making himself known, and tells her his name is Cardenio. Dorothea's account bears witness to his own story, which has almost disappeared into insignificance. "I am the unfortunate Cardenio […], who had not courage enough to see how her fainting fit ended, or what came of the paper that was found in her bosom." Their fortuitous meeting and the confession of their errors finally lead to a glimpse of hope. "But fate [contented] itself with robbing me of my reason, perhaps to preserve me for the good fortune I have had in meeting you" (De Cervantes, 2013, p. 205). The future opens, there is expectancy. "[…] it may be that Heaven has yet in store for both of us a happier termination […] than we look for [and] will restore to us what is ours."

Like the young warriors of the Crazy Dog Society, who confess to each other the motives of their shame before going on the warpath, the two of them can now go back into combat. The prized possession they must recover urgently is the integrity of the given word (Sullivan, 1974, p. 248). "I swear to you by the faith of a gentleman and a Christian not to desert you until I see you in possession of Don Fernando." Invested with Quixotic determination, Cardenio now takes on the only mission that can re-establish the priority of the pledge. In case Don Fernando does not keep his word, he promises "to avail myself of the right which my rank as a gentleman gives me, and with just cause challenge him on account of the injury he has done you, not regarding my own wrongs […]".

Cardenio is no longer alone. His case is no longer that of a deranged mind, but rather that of a shared injury perpetrated by a tyrant. Now that masks are thrown off, the barber and the curate also reveal their true identity. Speaking in kindly tones, they offer the two outcasts shelter in their community, with the ulterior motive of getting Don Quixote away from there "in spite of himself". But the two young people have no need for reintegration; what they need, when they leave the mountain, is recourse to a much greater power, in order to regenerate the broken social link. In fact, this demonic force manifests itself with a great hue and cry: "At this moment they heard a shout" (De Cervantes, 2013, p. 205) and recognised Sancho Panza's voice.

The Sierra Morena has played the role of a space of wilderness, "the bush" into which young Athapaskans of the Canadian Northwest Territories make ritual forays in search of spirits. When they return, they are welcomed into the dream of an elder, who can articulate their secret visions. Throughout life, secrets become known to a widening circle of people. This process produces myths, which serve to heal torments, along a "trail of telling secrets" (Ridington, 1982, pp. 213–219).

Dorothea was able to share her secret with the wild man who gave her back her name, as she gave him back his. Both of them prepare to confront danger, linking their fate to Don Quixote's visions, in the ceremonial space of the theatre of fools.

The cry of mother Folly's consort

Sancho has found his master, more ghostly than ever, "stripped to his shirt, lank, yellow, half dead with hunger, and sighing for his lady Dulcinea". He is still obsessed with worthy deeds, and is determined to heal Cardenio. In truth, his objective is about to be achieved, although the patient has no inkling of this intention. When the barber speaks of "the strange nature of Don Quixote's madness", and of his burning desire to find Cardenio, the latter is astounded. He had no idea that his analyst was so concerned about him. "Like the recollection of a dream, the quarrel he had with Don Quixote came back to Cardenio's memory, and he described it to the others; but he was unable to say what the dispute was about."

This scene is an excellent description of the analyst's disarray when, after having fretted and worried about a patient who stopped coming to his sessions, the latter makes another appointment and shows up as if nothing happened, explaining that, thanks to a certain hormone, diet, fitness programme, jogging or other technique, his whole life has changed. Still, the analyst tells himself, if he came back despite all these postmodern miracles, it means that the work is not finished after all. We can't stop halfway. So the work resumes. Here, the second part of the encounter teaches us how to resist scoundrels without being crushed.

The stage is set now for the theatre of Fools, a political theatre showing the abuses of power. The plot will unfold in mythical style, in the ancient tradition of Greek tragedies, to prevent traumatic revivals triggered by the current situation. In a flash, the famous scenario of the damsel in distress is acted out by Fool number five, in this case Dorothea, who dons her own feminine attire once again. The curate directing the play decides that the role suits her perfectly. "[…] she could play the distressed damsel better than the barber; especially as she had there the dress in which to do it to the life." Moreover, she knew her lines well, "for she had read a great many books of chivalry, and knew exactly the style in which afflicted damsels begged boons of knights-errant".

The actor's paradox

But the Carolingian and Arthurian epics, of which Don Quixote makes indiscriminate use, take hold of her and transform the masquerade meant to fool the knight into catharsis for Dorothea herself. In a dramatic turn of events, the young actress playing the lead in the collective psychotherapy, is caught in the intrigue of the sottie and thwarts the intentions of the barber and the curate. Despite the agreed upon plan, the story takes control and manipulates those who intended to manipulate it.

As soon as Dorothea puts on her beautiful dress—which she took with her when she left disguised as a shepherd—the young girl, still distressed, finds herself affected by the relevance of the scenario she has agreed to act out. Seeing her, Sancho is awestruck, for "in all the days of his life he had never seen such a lovely creature" (De Cervantes, 2013, p. 206). He conceives the idea that in order to obtain the position of governor quickly, his master should marry this flesh-and-blood Dulcinea.

The condescending curate is amazed at seeing "what a hold the absurdities of his master had taken on his fancy". But he would be better advised to admire Don Quixote's therapeutic prowess. Without elaborating a plan of any kind, the knight succeeds in creating a space of safety in this remote place, allowing each person to play his role.

The synopsis provided by the curate bears a close resemblance to Dorothea's own story. She plays a princess from Guinea, Micomicona, who has come to beg Don Quixote to redress a wrong done her by a wicked giant, a barely disguised Don Fernando. The princess makes a solemn entrance on her mule, followed by the barber with the oxtail beard fixed to his face, while Cardenio and the curate remain at a distance, behind some bushes. Dorothea, sure of herself, told them that "they might make their minds easy, as everything would be done exactly as the books of chivalry required and described" (De Cervantes, 2013, p. 207). After that, the stage is set for improvisation.

Commedia dell'arte

The prelude to the damsel's request proceeds rather cheerfully. Dorothea, feeling more like herself again, "whipped her palfrey, [...] dismounting with great ease of manner advanced to kneel before the feet of Don Quixote", to request the might of his strong arm. She then declaimed a series of superlatives to describe herself—"the most disconsolate and afflicted damsel the sun has seen" (De Cervantes, 2013, p. 208)—and Don Quixote agrees, in the ritually appropriate terms, to avenge her betrayal by a traitor. For she has indeed been betrayed.

Right away, Don Quixote understands that he is being solicited to carry out therapeutic work. "[...] and so, lady, you may from this day forth lay aside the melancholy that distresses you, and let your failing hopes gather new life and strength" (De Cervantes, 2013, p. 208). Later, Dorothea would confess that she had read so many books of chivalry because she too suffers from insomnia. "[...] my spirits are not yet tranquil enough to let me sleep when it would be seasonable."

Don Quixote needs to know no more to turn instantly to the Salmon principles. *Immediacy*: "'[...] and now hands to the work, for in delay there is apt to be danger.' [He] made her rise and embraced her with great courtesy and politeness." The knight is versed in prompt decision making, since he alone can right the ravages wrought by the lightning raids of felonious giants. Without delay, he ordered Sancho to arm him, and to check Rocinante's saddle girths. Cervantes—a former slave—has not chosen Guinea at random. Here, he takes the opportunity of expressing his opinion on the slave trade and racism.

In Algiers, Tunis, Alexandria, and Tripoli, ransomed slaves like Cervantes fetched a high price, while common slaves, as well as women and children, disappeared without a trace. Taken altogether, their numbers were higher than those of the African Slave Trade (Davis, 2004). It is in this context that Sancho reflects on colour while he speculates about his future once Don Quixote becomes king of Micomicon. "Not unless you go to sleep and haven't the wit or skill to turn things to account and sell three, six or ten thousand vassals while you would be talking about it! By God I will stir them up, big and little, or as best I can, and let them be ever so black, I'll turn them into white or yellow"—that is, into shining coins (De Cervantes, 2013, p. 209). Cardenio, like Dorothea, was treated like a thing. To signify his return to civility, the curate cut Cardenio's beard and lent him his own coat. The two of them are now ready to step on stage for the second act.

The decor has changed. The scene takes place on the plain, at the foot of the mountain. Once he crosses the threshold between wilderness and civilisation, the curate reveals his true identity once again. Reality reasserts itself, introducing mayhem reminiscent of a Marx Brothers movie, triggered by the curate's mule, "as it happened a hired one, which is the same thing as saying ill-conditioned" (De Cervantes, 2013, p. 210). What follows are kicks and tumbles, as well as the ungluing and regluing of the barber's beard, reawakening Don Quixote's obsession with learning new remedies, this one consisting of "a certain special charm for sticking on beards", a remedy of which Cervantes' father, the barber-surgeon, might have dreamed.

In the midst of all this havoc, subliminal messages are picked up by Don Quixote's seismometer which registers, unbeknownst to him, the farce in which he is supposed to play the fall guy. His unwavering selflessness deflates the hyperbolic style Dorothea uses to please him. "Enough; no more praise, for I hate all flattery [...] I will only say, señora, that whether it has might or not, that which it may or may not have shall be devoted to your service even to death" (De Cervantes, 2013, p. 211). The knight is impervious to seduction.

Politically correct interlude

Having abandoned his burlesque disguise, the curate becomes a professional inquisitor again, specialising in creating guilt. A scaled-down version of Torquemada, he takes advantage of the knight's madness to torment him. The indictment takes the form of an anonymous accusation, rather vague, made at the scene of the crime, at the outlet of the mountain where the right to asylum is suspended. Immunity is lifted. As if catching Don Quixote red-handed at the moment when he comes out of hiding, the curate accuses him in veiled terms of freeing the galley slaves: "[...] he must have been out of his senses, or he must be as great a scoundrel as they, or some man without heart or conscience to let the wolf loose among the sheep, the fox among the hens, the fly among the honey." Don Quixote is being tortured by an expert, who delights in his torment. "The curate [...] made the most of it to see what would be said or done by Don Quixote; who changed color at every word, not daring to say that it was he who had been the liberator of those worthy people."

At the outlet of the Sierra, Don Quixote struggles once again with the question of the duty to intervene. But Sancho comes to the aid of his master, who refuses to speak, and takes the bait: "In faith, then, señor licentiate, he who did that deed was my master; and it was not for want of my [...] warning him to mind what he was about" (De Cervantes, 2013, p. 213).

Unequivocal, Don Quixote's answer invokes the sacred right to refuse to torture "any persons [...], without regard to their rascalities". His concern is not with meeting out justice based on the letter of the law, but rather with acting according to unwritten laws which forbid cruelty, especially when this cruelty is robed in the garb of legal authority. Cervantes knows what he is talking about, from personal experience. "[...] it is no business or concern of knights-errant to inquire whether any persons in affliction, in chains, or oppressed that they may meet on the high roads go that way and suffer as they do because of their faults or because of their misfortunes."

"I encountered a chaplet or string of miserable and unfortunate people, and did for them what my sense of duty demands of me, and as for the rest be that as it may." As Don Quixote said this, his anger reached such a peak that he was ready to knock out the curate.

"Poetry as performance" (Nagy, 1996)

Dorothea was tempted to join those who were mocking Don Quixote. "Dorothea, who was shrewd and sprightly, [...] understood [...] that all except Sancho Panza were making game of him" (De Cervantes,

2013, p. 213). But contrary to the cynical duchess in Part II—a forerunner of the Marquise de Merteuil, (the main character in Choderlos de Laclos' Dangerous Liaisons)—Dorothea engages her own fate in the tales she makes up. The suspense is growing. Everyone was "eager to hear what sort of story the quick-witted Dorothea would invent for herself" (De Cervantes, 2013, p. 214). Finally, she refuses to take part in the collective mockery, and invents a story, like the games and drawings of children who show the analyst what they cannot say, by playacting what happened to them.

She starts by putting an end to the curate's sarcastic comments, asking him to "[bite] his tongue three times", and demanding silence in ritual fashion. Then she begins her story in an apparently Freudian manner, with the unconscious forgetting of her assumed name. Still, Don Quixote realises that the young woman is not an ordinary hysteric, but a political refugee. Therefore, he does not take this forgetting for a sign of repression, but rather for traumatic amnesia, since "such afflictions often have the effect of depriving the sufferers of memory, so that they do not even remember their own names".

Dorothea's tale confirms this. Not only has her father's name been dishonoured, but she herself has been banished, is an orphan and has fallen prey to a perverse giant hungry for conquest, Pandafilando of the Scowl, whose name signifies that he loves one and all. He never looks straight at anyone, but "always looks askew as if he squinted, and this he does out of malignity, to strike fear and terror into those he looks at". Lustful and violent, he overruns territories and borders, and has invaded the maiden's kingdom, "not leaving [her] even a small village".

However, the princess is not without resources, since she received instruction from her father, Tinacrio the Sapient. In fact, her strategy resembles that proposed by la Boétie. Never argue with a pervert, do not express indignation, simply get away. "I am not asking you to oppose him, but simply to refuse consent" (De La Boétie, 2012). Rather than die for ideas that kill people and are used by ideologues in their speeches, her father advises her that after his death, when "I saw Pandafilando about to invade my kingdom, I was not to wait and attempt to defend myself [...], but that I should leave the kingdom entirely open to him if I wished to avoid the death and total destruction of my good and loyal vassals, for there would be no possibility of defending myself against the giant's devilish power" (De Cervantes, 2013, p. 215). Dorothea too has followed this advice, joining a Maquis network headed by Don Quixote, whom she is to recognise by "a grey mole".

At this point, a second mistake reveals Dorothea's poor knowledge of geography; Don Quixote questions her immediately: "But how did you land at Osuna, señora, when it is not a seaport?" (De Cervantes, 2013, p. 215). Dorothea manages to correct her *faux pas* and avoids any other geopolitical considerations by getting straight to the happy ending, where she marries Don Quixote and makes his squire a nobleman. Wild with joy, Sancho "cut a couple of capers in the air with every sign of extreme satisfaction".

After inventing a Spanish Resistance, Dorothea distributes in advance titles and honours to her fellow (Resistance) fighters. Simply by narrating her story, she has succeeded in unifying their plural body. The foursome is now composed of Sancho, his master, herself, and Cardenio. Anxious to fight with them against giants who repudiate past promises, Don Quixote categorically refuses the hand of the fair Dorothea, whom Sancho urges him to marry. "In the devil's name, marry, marry, and take this kingdom that comes to hand without any trouble, and when you are king make me a marquis or governor of a province, and for the rest let the devil take it all" (De Cervantes, 2013, p. 217).

Knights-errant do not ask for compensation for the services they render, once they are solicited. They do not abuse transference, and do not ask young girls in need for payment in kind: "[…] when your fierce [enemy's] head has been cut off and you have been put in peaceful possession of your realm it shall be left to your own decision to dispose of your person as may be most pleasing to you." What matters to Don Quixote is to restore the damsel's freedom, not to take advantage of her. A servant of love, he has no interest in subjugating a bevy of enamoured maidens. "[…] for so long as my memory is occupied, my will enslaved, and my understanding enthralled by her—I say no more […]."

This ethical stance does not suit Sancho, for such selflessness deprives him, in effect, of bettering his status. It is as if Don Quixote, by refusing to marry Dorothea, is robbing him of his spoils. That is when he goes berserk, like Achilles from whom Agamemnon stole Briseis. Now, the squire goes so far as to commit a crime of lese-Dulcinea.

The Lady ever and again

When he compares Dulcinea to Dorothea, "and I will even go so far as to say she does not come up to the shoe of this one here", Sancho attacks the sacred foundation of valour. Don Quixote is outraged by this blasphemy: "[He] could not endure it, and lifting his pike, without saying anything to Sancho or uttering a word, he gave him two such thwacks that he brought him to the ground; and had it not been that Dorothea cried out to him to spare him he would have no doubt taken his life on the spot" (De Cervantes, 2013, p. 217).

These actions are no longer rooted in traumatic revival. They are intended to destroy assertions which misrepresent the art of chivalry by describing it in trivialising language. Interestingly, at the very moment when Spain is unable to enter the financial world of bankers in Bruges, Genoa, Augsburg, and England, Sancho takes it into his head to become a broker, negotiating the market value of Dulcinea. But Sancho's master is far from being a cool-headed investor. "[…] were it not for the might that she infuses into my arm I should not have strength enough to kill a flea. […] She fights in me and conquers in me, and I live and breathe in her, and owe my life and being to her" (De Cervantes, 2013, p. 217).

Nothing is held back in this personal quarrel acted out in public. Don Quixote roars: "Do you think, you vicious clown, that you are to be always interfering with me, and that you are to be always offending and I always pardoning?" Then he goes on to proffer insults, that Molière was to take up later: "[…] lout, vagabond, beggar, scoffer with a viper's tongue […], whoreson scoundrel […]." This argument renders the agency of the Lady more complex. Whereas previously she was an abstract notion, the designated site of inscription, now she represents the stakes in a joust carried out in public.

Who, then, is this agency that uses Don Quixote like an instrument within a plural body? Dulcinea is so minimally embodied that it is hard to see her as an object of worship, a passionate militant or a show-business idol.

She is the foundation of valour, but has no intrinsic value and has no interest in claiming any. She continues to exist solely as the foundation of a value system, a standard against which everything can be measured. Beautiful or ugly, brilliant or dumb, feminist or old-fashioned, she is the Mother Folly Sancho will describe, presenting a maternal function devoid of mothering qualities, the best and the worst, but one you call your own. Thus, the remote Lady, never seen, the foundation of the plural body, is only revealed through an unconscious slip.

Mad philosophy

In a burst of sincerity, Sancho lets slip: "I have never seen the Lady Dulcinea" (De Cervantes, 2013, p. 218). Don Quixote is enraged: "How!

Never seen her, blasphemous traitor!" Sancho tries to backtrack, claiming that he did not have the "leisure [to] take particular notice of her beauty". This rapid exchange makes it clear that the Lady, far from taking advantage of the situation, not only does not give a hoot, but is not even aware of her role. Dulcinea is faceless, and has only the indulgent smile of the "merry lady" who bolsters Don Quixote and lends him the perspective needed to analyse the unconscious: "[…] forgive me the injury I have done thee: for our first impulses are not in our control." To this, Sancho replies in frankly Freudian manner, that he is not always master of his tongue either. "[…] with me the wish to speak is always the first impulse, and I cannot help saying, once at any rate, what I have on the tip of my tongue". The reconciliation scene is now played out in formal ritual gestures: "Sancho advanced hanging his head and begged his master's hand, which Don Quixote with dignity presented to him, giving him his blessing as soon as he had kissed it." Each man has preserved what is essential to him: one his Lady, the other his donkey, which this ritual has elevated to the status of Apuleius' Golden Ass (Apuleius, 1999), the incarnation of a jolly discipline called "gay science" by troubadours.

Sancho's ass had disappeared when they entered the Sierra. But the animal's brilliant instinct drove the thief to an encounter with his legitimate owner. Sancho, "whose eyes and heart were there wherever he saw assess" (De Cervantes, 2013, p. 219), recognised Dapple, began to shout and chased away the thief, Ginés de Pasamonte, who made off speedily. The squire gave vent to his joy in the tenderest fashion: "How hast thou fared, my blessing, Dapple of my eyes, my comrade?—all the while kissing him and caressing him as if he were a human being. The ass held his peace, and let himself be kissed and caressed by Sancho without answering a single word" (De Cervantes, 2013, p. 219).

Don Quixote approves the reunion by keeping his word. He does "not cancel the order for the three ass colts" and shows himself to all those present to be "perfectly rational, [with a] mind quite clear and composed".

Delivery of the truth

Promises are kept and the hour of truth has arrived. "Señor", replied Sancho, "if the truth be told, nobody copied out the letter for me, for I carried no letter at all" (De Cervantes, 2013, p. 220). In any case, the letter lost by Sancho could not have reached its destination since

Don Quixote admits that he did not give it to his squire. He "found it in [his] own possession two days after" Sancho's departure. From then on, Sancho lets his imagination run wild, inventing the never encountered Dulcinea and the letter she never read, and painting an unflattering portrait of the Lady, so as to preserve his hope of a marriage between his master and Dorothea.

He describes Dulcinea as a tall, gangly girl, rough, mannish, and loud, whom Don Quixote strives to transform into a flower of rhetoric, as he did with Maritornes. Wheat becomes pearls: "Then depend upon it, the grains of that wheat were pearls [...]" (De Cervantes, 2013, p. 221). The damsel's indifference is transformed into discretion: "Lay the letter, friend, on the top of that sack"—"Discreet lady!" As for her lofty soul, she is as lofty as a giant: "And so lofty she is", said Sancho, "that she overtops me by more than a hand's breadth"; but for the knight, her "little odour, something mannish" smells like Arabian perfumes. Still, there is no denying that she is illiterate, since "she did not read [the letter], for she said she could neither read nor write" (De Cervantes, 2013, p. 222). As for the gift due, according to the rules of courtly love, to the messenger bearing news of a knight or a lady, it consisted of nothing more than bread and cheese, "and more by token it was sheep's milk cheese". It's safe to say that it was manchego, and the emblem of the madman, the wild man of the Middle Ages, whose brain ferments like cheese. "I told her how your worship was left doing penance [...] in among these mountains like a savage."

Once the sublimation process has been completed, Don Quixote must explain Sancho's quick return. His desire for loftiness leads him to envision aviation: "I find no difficulty in believing that you mayest have gone from this place to El Toboso and returned in such a short time, since, as I have said, some friendly sage must have carried thee through the air without thee perceiving it" (De Cervantes, 2013, p. 223). Here, the sage takes on the role of a "trickster", benevolent and nasty by turns. But never mind! The only thing that matters is to keep one's promise to an improbable Dulcinea, expecting nothing in return, and not knowing whether one is loved by her or not. Contrary to drugs that promise happiness, this antidepressant does not rely on the pleasure principle. "[...] the law of chivalry compels me to have regard for my word in preference to my inclination."

At the conclusion of this spiritual exercise, Sancho has an experience of enlightenment—*satori*, as it is called in Zen: the love of the Lady is mystical. "It is with that kind of love [...] we ought to love our Lord, for himself alone, without being moved by the hope of glory or the fear of punishment". (De Cervantes, 2013, p. 225) Don Quixote salutes this discovery of "pure love", *fin amor* in Occitan. "The devil take thee for a clown! and what shrewd things thou sayest at times! One would think thou hadst studied." "In faith, then, I cannot even read", answers Sancho. But the idealised image is quickly dispelled.

In this continuous reconquest of speech, the oral tradition regains its rightful place. Dulcinea is "the duchess in clogs", Anne of Brittany, who eventually became queen, transposed to El Toboso. When the three captains of the popular song Anne inspired, call her ugly, Dulcinea can reply as Anne did: "I am not so ugly, since (the king) Don Quixote loves me". But the knight, unlike Anne's king, is not so well-off. What is more, he will soon be scolded by Andrés, the young shepherd he saved at the beginning of his adventures, and who should presumably have established his reputation as a liberator of hostages.

In fact, his departure from the mountain is accompanied by the reproaches of Andrés, unwisely released in Chapter IV, who now makes an unexpected appearance: "On [your worship] and all the knights-errant that have ever been born God send his curse", because after Don Quixote's departure, his master beat him almost to death. Forced to give up his image as a saviour, Don Quixote is disconcerted by the youth's accusations. As a result, the next knightly deed, aimed at forcing Don Fernando to keep his word to Dorothea—duchess in clogs—shall be carried out *manu militari*. This deed will take place at the inn, during the next stage of the adventure, after the reinstatement of the word in the Sierras.

Don Quixote's patrol returns to the inn

The patrol which returns to the inn has increased in size. It includes Don Quixote, Sancho, Cardenio, and Dorothea, followed by representatives of medicine and the clergy in the persons of the barber and the curate "mounted on their powerful mules", as well as Rocinante and the donkey. And what awaits them at the inn? Books! The element so savagely cut out of the device of transference is found there, at last, forgotten by some traveller, so that Cardenio and Dorothea discover, in print, a sinister tale very similar to their own.

Thus, the books reappear at the crossroads of worlds not intended to meet, except in Don Quixote's dreams. This "crossroads of dreams"—characteristic of Nô theatre as well—provides a junction between the storms of History—wars against the Turks, slavery in Algiers—and the cruel story of three other young people on their way to destruction.

Once again, the inn, will allow our heroes to escape from the trap in which they were caught, and set out in search of the truth. This transformation underlines Don Quixote's authority, without which none of this would be possible. Like a true PI (Principal Investigator in scientific research), he brings together a number of researchers. Soon, his laboratory houses fifteen, twenty, and then even more people, as if the depressive deflation of voluntary servitude fills out again, the expansion passing from one person to the next in as little time as it took for the collapse to come about.

As soon as they arrive at the inn, the tone is set. Contrary to the atmosphere of "fear and dread" Sancho anticipated because of the blanketing he had suffered in this very place fifteen chapters earlier, the hospitable foursome composed of the landlady, the landlord, their daughter, and Maritornes gives them a warm welcome. In addition to shelter and nourishment, the inn provides a safe space in which, four chapters later, it will be possible to confront a third group of strangers, threatening, silent, and masked.

But for now, the inn offers asylum and refuge to victims of abuse, be it political or domestic, suffering the same loss of freedom. By contrast, through the story that will be read there, Cervantes takes his time to analyse the mechanism allowing three promising young people to be gradually driven out of their minds. Using the device of a book found at the inn, he develops his own theory of the "origins of totalitarianism", long before Hannah Arendt.

Don Quixote knows all this by heart, so the reading can take place while he sleeps. "[…] they thought it best not to waken him, as sleeping would now do him more good than eating" (De Cervantes, 2013, p. 228). From that point on, Cervantes has two superposed stages at his disposal—like in a *"corral"*—a two-tiered Spanish theatre of that period, which can still be seen today in the town of Almagro, in La Mancha.

On the upper tier, Don Quixote is sleeping, exhausted, and dreams while gathering strength for the task that awaits him, that of finally inscribing his father's wars. On the ground floor an anti-chivalry story is being read, whose plot destroys dreams.

Books of chivalry rediscovered

But the immediate result of the hero's slumber is to revive his precious allies, believed to have been turned to ashes. Don Quixote, Freud's favorite hero, embodies the question formulated in *Moses and Monotheism*, after the burning of his own books by the Nazis in Berlin: how can his work survive the forces of destruction? (Freud, S., 1955 [1939a]). Cervantes' answer to his future disciple is that writings can always be resuscitated thanks to those who are mad about reading, be they illiterate or not. "[...] writings", the landlord said, "are the very life, not only of myself but of plenty more" (De Cervantes, 2013, p. 229).

To keep him company, let us quote Hannah Arendt again, in Volume Two of *The Origins of Totalitarianism*: "Legends have always played a powerful role in the making of history. They offer a truth beyond realities, a remembrance beyond memories. [...] Only in the frankly invented tale about events did man consent to assume his responsibility for them, and to consider past events his past. [...] Legends, however, are not ideologies; they do not aim at universal explanation but are always concerned with concrete facts. [...] For legends attract the very best in our times, just as ideologies attract the average, and whispered tales of gruesome secret powers behind the scenes attract the very worst" (Arendt, 1951, pp. 207–209).

There is no better way to describe the role of the legend of Don Quixote, and the use which Don Quixote makes of legend. He assumes responsibility for the historical events in Cervantes' life, and establishes "a truth beyond realities, a remembrance beyond [traumatic] memories". For Don Quixote, legends are the space which can contain the same abominable monsters that in our own time propel the same vulnerable youth into suicide and self-destruction.

For stories take different shapes. Arendt distinguishes between legends and ideologies. To make this difference very clear, Cervantes invents the short story of "the ill-advised curiosity" (*la novela del Curioso impertinente*), which is inserted here as if to exorcise the "worst", thanks to the innkeeper's passion for reading.

The Quixoticised innkeeper

Dorothea has noted the innkeeper's enthusiasm, and whispers to Cardenio: "Our landlord is almost fit to play a second part to Don Quixote" (De Cervantes, 2013, p. 231). People can surprise us, and the innkeeper reveals certain qualities no one would have expected. He invites each person present to analyse his transference relating to the actions described in medieval chronicles in verse.

Books of chivalry are his hobby as well. They allow him to sublimate an explosive character through "furious and terrible blows". This is particularly true at harvest time, when thirty or more reapers gather around the one who can read, "and stay listening to him with a delight that makes our grey hairs grow young again". The harvest season, when the work is done with a flail or a thresher, fills the house with whiffs of hay, dust and memories.

"Are you reading again?" my grandmother would exclaim, sensing the threat of a rustic version of Madame Bovary taking possession of her granddaughter, who was hiding in a corner with a book. No doubt about it, the girl was going to become a sloppy housekeeper! When I shall meet her in the beyond where she told me she was going to be reunited with her ancestors, I will slip my *Don Quixote* under her nose, open at Chapter XXXII, where the landlady—who prides herself on being constantly busy with housework—sings the praises of reading. She would willingly see her husband listening to stories "night and day", she says, "because I never have a quiet moment in my house except when you are listening to someone reading; for then you are so taken up that for the time being you forget to scold".

For Maritornes and the innkeeper's daughter, the transference involves unconscious sexual desires. They are barely repressed in the case of the servant—who clearly relishes these stories which are "as good as honey", for she feels the duena's excitement while she keeps watch when a lady is in the arms of her knight. The maiden's desires are more discreet. But the curate uses his professional skills and soon has her confessing. "'And you, what do you think, young lady?' said the curate turning to the landlord's daughter." To which the ingenue replies cautiously: "I don't know indeed, señor […] and to tell the truth, though I do not understand it, I like hearing it."

Not as dim-witted as she seems, she understands the games of the ladies who show "such prudery" (De Cervantes, 2013, p. 229), to the point of driving their knights mad: "If it is for honour's sake, why not marry them? That's all they want." Dorothea presses her to reveal her own desire: "Then you would console them if it was for you they wept, young lady?" But the girl's mother is keeping an eye on her, and pulls down the shades of repression again. "Hush, child, it seems to me thou knowest a great deal about these things, and it is not fit for girls to know or talk so much." There would be a lot of work to do, for hysterics and psychoanalysts, later, when this emerging social class was going to be gentrified.

Ah the joys of murder! Things are going so well, so why stop now? The priest finally has the innkeeper open a valise full of books, forgotten by a traveller at the inn. Driven anew by an obscure desire to burn them, he lets the barber know it in veiled terms: "We want my friend's housekeeper and niece here now [...]—Nay, said the barber, there is a very good fire in the hearth."

Yet, the circumstances lend themselves to a new cultural revolution flare-up, since Don Quixote is sleeping, as exhausted as upon returning from his first sally, in which another innkeeper had dubbed him a knight. The two licentiates have not lost the desire to re-educate the working class, infected with the outdated influence of books of chivalry. But Don Quixote has done good work since the first sally, and he no longer has to face them alone.

While he is sleeping soundly, the innkeeper sees the threat emanating from these learned minds. Without shilly-shallying, he takes the offensive: "Are my books, then, heretics or phlegmatics that you want to burn them?—Schismatics, you mean, friend, said the barber.—That's it, said the landlord, [...] for I would rather have a child of mine burned [...]."

Like Hannah Arendt, he appoints himself spokesman of the truth found in legends. "It is a good joke for your worship to try and persuade me that everything these books say is nonsense and lies." The landlord defends the poetic "foolishness" dear to Descartes in his dreams, and to Socrates in *Phaedrus*, which "take away [his] senses" (De Cervantes, 2013, p. 231). Here, Cervantes presents an indictment against fanatics who condemn "the opium of the people" by issuing fatwas and blacklists. "I have told you, friend, that this is done to divert our idle thoughts", states the curate, who sets himself the task of reforming people's imagination. "[...] if it were permitted to me now, and the present company desired it, I could say something about the qualities books of chivalry should possess to be good ones" (De Cervantes, 2013, p. 231).

Don Quixote's madness also serves to fight against those who want to force people to be "right-minded", like the curate. The "sombre tale" that is about to be read at the inn is clear proof of this.

CHAPTER NINE

A sombre affair

The novel of "The Ill-Advised Curiosity" (La novela del Curioso impertinente)

Critics were to disapprove of the "exemplary novel" Cervantes inserts here, saying that it is extrapolated and external to his text. The story's disastrous ending, so different from the tone of the narrative, whose pace it interrupts, leaves the reader perplexed. Cervantes himself agrees with his critics, at the start of the Second Part, when the bachelor Sansón Carrasco recounts the reception given to the first adventures of the two heroes: "One of the faults they find with this history", said the bachelor, "is that its author inserted in it a novel called 'The Ill-Advised Curiosity'; not that it is bad or ill-told, but that it is out of place and has nothing to do with the history of his worship Señor Don Quixote" (De Cervantes, 2013, p. 417).

This defect in structure is attributed at once to the Moorish author, Cide Hamete Berengena, whose name Sancho mispronounces, while making him the scapegoat for all the imperfections of the novel. Does this mean that the story in question could only have been conceived there, in the hell of captivity? Did Cervantes learn from experience that friendship founded on the Lady's treason can only lead to ruin and death?

For this is the lesson to be learned from this strange tale. In the sixteenth century, "impertinent" meant "out of place" and "absurd". This adjective, associated with madness at that period, became less harsh over time until, in the classical era, it came to signify "impropriety", and today refers to no more than brash behaviour. But the ill-advised impertinence recounted in the story is not harmless, as it surfaces over and over in an unchanging, wearisome scenario. Here is the summary:

> In order to test the virtue of his wife Camilla, Anselmo asks his best friend, Lothario, to seduce her, without revealing her husband's secret plan. At first, Lothario objects, but is finally persuaded to indulge his friend. He courts Camilla with more and more genuine ardour. She resists, then softens and finally yields to Lothario, under her husband's nose. In the end, she leaves her home, not to start a new life with her lover—other days, other ways—but to shut herself away in a convent. Despite Lothario's virtuous protestations against his friend's ill-advised scheme, the plot bears a closer resemblance to Sade's *The Misfortunes of Virtue* (De Sade, 2013) than to the farce of the deceived, beaten and content husband.

But the initial enigma remains. What caused Anselmo to relinquish his hold on reality and become obsessed with testing his wife's virtue? In truth, his plan is elaborated like a laboratory experiment in psychology, observed through a one-way mirror. The story ends with the death of Anselmo's wife, and that of his friend, who were both used as guinea pigs; but the scheming husband is killed as well, falling victim to his own experiment.

We may ask whether there may not be some connection between this social experiment and the utopian fantasies of the knight, who also sacrifices his few possessions and his health.

What does the impossible demanded by Anselmo have in common with the impossible standard Don Quixote sets for himself?

At this point in the novel, the only difference lies in the enlivening energy of the knight, in stark contrast with the depressing, postmodern tone of the inserted tale. What, then, makes the impertinence in the novel pertinent at this stage? In effect, it serves to open a space for suspense, just when Dorothea and Cardenio are making strides, *andante*, towards recovering their honour. Here, Cervantes seems to be saying: when you undertake impossible missions, be careful to distinguish between pertinent and impertinent investigations!

The sacrifice of the Lady

We are seemingly invited to witness a rigorous theoretical demonstration. But does this story mean anything today, when the protagonists would simply have consulted a therapist and remarried, instead of entering a convent or precipitating a disaster? A century ago, this story could have been the theme of a bedroom farce in which an imbecile persists in offering his wife to his friend, while forbidding him to touch her. It could also have served as a pretext to discuss common psychoanalytic clichés like repressed homosexuality, the hysterical desire to have an unsatisfied desire, or trivial trafficking in living currency, on the Klossowskian (Klossowski, 2015) model. Unfortunately, not having access to this modern enlightenment, when his wife left him, Anselmo did not consider for a moment letting a new woman console him for his loss. How the devil did he come to find himself in such dire straits? Let us look at the end of the story, where we may find the key to our enigma.

Before taking his last breath, Anselmo wrote: "A foolish and ill-advised desire has robbed me of life. If the news of my death should reach the ears of Camilla, let her know that I forgive her, for she was not bound to perform miracles, nor ought I to have required her to perform them" (De Cervantes, 2013, p. 269). After making this written declaration of his strange passion, which caused the death of three young people—himself among them—victims "of a thoughtless beginning", Anselmo takes his last breath. At the same time, by rehabilitating his Lady, he seems to regain, *in extremis*, his status as a subject: "[…] she was not bound to perform miracles."

The miracle brought about by this story is directly related to the point at which it is inserted in Cervantes' novel. When the story is brought out of its valise, like a jack-in-the-box, Cardenio and Dorothea had been just about to suffer the same misfortune as the three young people in the story. Camilla, sacrificed to her husband's obsessive idea, reveals the disastrous fate that would have been theirs when they were subjected to Don Fernando's "foolish and ill-advised desire", had not someone like Don Quixote intervened.

Here, Camilla's sacrifice acquires a placating function identified by Anne Dufourmantelle in *La Femme et le Sacrifice* (Women and Sacrifice), which deals with "bringing a cancelled trauma onto the collective stage" (Dufourmantelle, 2007). Preceding the narration of Cervantes' traumas, soon to be brought into public view by the captive who would join them at the inn, this story holds a strategic position. A music lover, Cervantes introduces the sound of a funeral dirge just before the arrival of a masked party whose plans would be foiled. And the novel of the ill-advised curiosity plays the role of a sacrificial process, so that Joven, young love, can triumph.

Once this is achieved, Don Quixote can legitimately claim that the inn is a castle where beautiful damsels saved from rape and murder can count on being defended, a castle over which he "offered to mount guard" (De Cervantes, 2013, p. 323). This heraldic figure, serving as the protector of the agency of the Lady, is precisely what Camilla lacked.

A policy of love

Here, Cervantes forces us to hear a story that contradicts his novel, a story whose plot is mounted against Camilla, as a trick, to make a fool of her.

At the start of the story, everything is going wonderfully well for Lothario and Anselmo, who get along so well that they are called, in fact, "the two friends" (De Cervantes, 2013, p. 233). Both "gentlemen of wealth and quality", they spend their time pursuing pleasure. One enjoys the pleasure of the chase, while the other is more inclined to seek pleasure in love. In Quixotic terms, they can be classified in the general category encompassing all knights, although they are not "true knights-errant". This "second kind" of knight, though educated and cultured, is not "gold, [but] pinchbeck, and [although] all look like gentlemen, not all can stand the touchstone of truth" (De Cervantes, 2013, p. 431). In fact, the artifice of appearances exerts its power over these pinchbeck gentlemen and ultimately destroys them.

Contrary to the ill-matched duo constituted by the Knight of the Rueful Countenance and his uncouth squire, who are constantly arguing, the two friends are compared to a well-oiled mechanism, since "their inclinations kept pace one with the other with a concord so perfect that the best regulated clock could not surpass it". They keep their relationship free of dissonance and are skilled at maintaining harmony at any price. Down with discord! Everything always goes smoothly for these fortunate gentlemen whose lives unfold in the ease of a social relation allowing satisfied egos to be each-other's reflection and to combine their talents into a narcissistic masterpiece, so as to succeed at everything, gain admiration and, above all, impress the crowd.

It is in this context that Cervantes insists on showing that the only obstacle to this ideal social link is the agency of the Lady. She is the one who brings about the downfall of this kind of friendship by creating a gap so unforeseen that the attempt to close it by shutting her away in a convent is of no avail. The grain of sand in the cogwheels of the machine is the heterogeneity of the Lady. Whether she likes it or not, like the shepherdess Marcela, something in her nature undermines this power game.

As for Lothario, he is doubtless well-intentioned, but not blameless. Once Anselmo's marriage disrupts their previous complicity, he interferes, taking it upon himself to protect the serenity of the household and his married friend's honour, "a thing of such delicacy", by "[leaving] off going to the house of Anselmo" (De Cervantes, 2013, p. 233). His absence only serves to make him more present, and enables him to control the reputation of the young couple. In fact, the couple's friend introduces suspicion by invoking the precautionary principle. "He said, and justly, that a married man upon whom heaven had bestowed a beautiful wife should consider as carefully what friends he brought to his house as what female friends his wife associated with."

As an uninvited matchmaker, not unlike Celestina (De Rojas, 2009) some of whose traits Cervantes clearly borrows, Lothario controls his friend's private life on the pretext of protecting him from gossip. The plot could just as easily have been comical. Like Harlequin, Lothario is a randy devil, but instead of being flogged, he inserts himself between the newlyweds. His calculated absence drives Anselmo into elaborating a convoluted plan to draw him back into his home. Neither friend informs Camilla of the trap being prepared for her, since she has become the prey in their friendship.

The damage is done; Lothario, contrary to Don Quixote, who is always ready for combat, adopts the motto: "If you want war, speak only of peace"; he takes control by delivering lectures about abstract principles. Anselmo protests "that, if by the thorough harmony that subsisted between them [...] they had earned such a sweet name as that of 'The Two Friends', he should not allow a title so rare and delightful to be lost [...]; and so he entreated him, if such a phrase was allowable between them, to be once more master of his house [...], assuring him that his wife Camilla had no other desire or inclination than that which he would wish her to have". Cervantes indicates from the outset that she is not entitled to an opinion.

Elevated to the status of master of the household, Lothario is officially given the role he played in any case. He nourishes the doubt and suspicion that are the key elements of his occupation as image counsellor. "Lothario said, too, that every married man should have some friend who would point out to him any negligence he might be guilty of in his conduct [...]. But where is such a friend to be found as Lothario would have, so judicious, so loyal, and so true? Of a truth I know not. Lothario alone was such a one" (De Cervantes, 2013, p. 234). Entangled in this marriage that he undermines using a barrage of negative messages, his discourse is so massively constructed of altruistic formulas that any skepticism would be seen as the product of a twisted mind.

Anselmo's rhetoric is in complete contrast to Don Quixote's delusion. While Don Quixote fights for the honour of the Lady, Anselmo obliges her to fight in his place, supposedly for his honour, and without her knowledge. One defends the given word, the other destroys its foundation. In effect, the story exposes, in three chapters, the paradigm of an attack upon the link, and serves as a contrast to the process of recreation of the link, which will take place at the inn in the ensuing chapters. How have young people full of life been transformed into agents of death and destruction? Hannah Arendt is careful to point out that when considering such questions it is essential not to mix the social with the political.

From depression to the cult

After analysing PTSD, Cervantes undertakes to examine the other affliction of the twenty-first century. Presenting the semiologic characteristics displayed by Anselmo, depression emerges in fact as a political tool enabling the insidious introduction of a reign of terror.

Besieged, Anselmo is overwhelmed by the friendly intruder who takes up his time and insinuates the idea of possible adultery. "[...] so that a great portion of the day was taken up with complaints on one side and excuses on the other." Feeling guilty, Anselmo admits that he is fortunate, being "the son of such parents as mine were [...] and [having] thee for a friend and Camilla for a wife". His submission is inextricably tied to the unpayable debt made clear to him by the envious champion of his cause. Indeed, Anselmo complains of feeling oppressed and distressed. "And yet, with all these good things [...] I am the most discontented and dissatisfied man in the whole world" (De Cervantes, 2013, p. 235).

His anxiety takes the form of a "strange obsession". Entrapped in the scheme elaborated by his friend, he intends to put himself in his hands. "[...] by thy readiness as a true friend to afford me relief, I shall soon find myself freed from the distress it causes me." But this relief soon turns into addiction.

Once the symbolic bond of trust between husband and wife is abolished, since Camilla is excluded, reliability is tested in the imaginary realm, by endless demands of garantees and quantitative checks, always insufficient. "[...] the desire which harasses me is that of knowing whether my Camilla is as good and as perfect as I think her to be; and I cannot satisfy myself of the truth of this point except by testing her in such a way that the trial may prove the purity of her virtue as the fire proves that of gold." But purification carried out without the subject's knowledge is more like purging, a travesty of courtly love, where the Lady is subjected to experimental procedures and to espionage techniques.

Instituting terror is the main item on the agenda. Anselmo does not become aware of this until it is too late. Not only is he no longer master in his own house, but he is overwhelmed with fear as he disintegrates bit by bit under the influence of the smooth projections put forward by Lothario. When he lets him take over, Anselmo becomes entrapped in a totalitarian system applying to his domestic domain.

A logic of submission has been introduced by the insidious collapse of his own agency. At the same time, Lothario is frightened by the change in their characters, as if he was seeing the effects of brainwashing. "I verily suspect that either thou dost not know me, or I do not know thee; but no, I know well thou art Anselmo, and thou knowest that I am Lothario; the misfortune is, it seems to me, that thou art not the Anselmo thou wert, and must have thought that I am not the Lothario I should be" (De Cervantes, 2013, p. 236). Anselmo's reason is destroyed, like that of the fanatics "who can never be brought to see the error of their creed [...] by reasons which depend upon the examination of the understanding" (De Cervantes, 2013, p. 237). Yet this perverse process is the very one introduced and reinforced by Lothario.

Melusine

Now, "a secret society in plain sight", as Hannah Arendt calls it, is established, in which his friend advises Anselmo "not to communicate his purpose to any other". At this point, Lothario could have avoided disaster by telling Camilla the truth. But this possibility never occurs to him, since he is so busy manipulating the cues governing discourse. Cervantes portrays him as the "false friend" (De Cervantes, 2013, p. 249) he always was, "availing himself of the device the devil has recourse to when he would deceive one who is on the watch; for he being the angel of darkness transforms himself into an angel of light" (De Cervantes, 2013, p. 244).

The Mephistophelian mechanism of seduction is intertwined with the warrior metaphor—observation, eloquent silence, flattered vanity: "[…] for there is nothing that more quickly reduces and levels the castle towers of fair women's vanity than vanity itself upon the tongue of flattery" (De Cervantes, 2013, p. 249). We have come to the final assault, to gain the spoils. "Camilla yielded, Camilia fell […]; and thus each step that Camilla descended toward the depths of her abasement, she mounted, in [her husband's] opinion, toward the summit of virtue and fair fame" (De Cervantes, 2013, p. 252).

In a dramatic turn, no sooner has Camilla given free rein to her desire to free herself from patriarchal rule, than she falls under the domination of her servant and confidante: "[…] ladies' imprudences make servants shameless […]; they make themselves the slaves of their own servants, and are obliged to hide their laxities and depravities" (De Cervantes, 2013, p. 253). Then Camilla takes action, turning suddenly from "weak woman" to "violent desperado" (De Cervantes, 2013, p. 258).

Different times, once again? According to Cervantes, who is as old-fashioned as Don Quixote, Camilla has been had by Lothario: "I fear that he will think ill of my pliancy or lightness, not considering the irresistible influence he brought to bear upon me." Cuckolded, Anselmo has become "the most charmingly hoodwinked man there could be in the world. He himself, persuaded he was conducting the instrument of his glory, led home by the hand him who had been the utter destruction of his good name" (De Cervantes, 2013, p. 261). If we transpose the story in a political context, from a social context focusing on the evolution of mores, this observation can be applied to entire populations which in our times are masterfully led astray, to the point of genocide, by seductive rhetoric courting humanity.

Politically speaking, Camilla is not Melusine (D'Arras, 1980). The story of this wyvern, half woman, half fairy, written by Jean d'Arras in the fifteenth century, tells the same tale of impertinent curiosity insidiously introduced by a friend of Melusine's husband, Raymondin. The fairy has consented to marry a mortal man and transmit to their offspring her powers as a pioneer and builder on condition that he does not see her or enquire after her on Saturdays. In fact, on that day, in her bath she happily becomes a serpent fairy again.

All goes well until the husband, whose jealousy has been aroused by an envious friend, looks through the keyhole on two occasions on Saturday and is horror stricken by what he sees. But here the outcome is very different than it was for Camilla. Melusine does not forfeit her authority. Taking back her powers as a serpent fairy, she soars up, like a dragon, into the air, from where she watches over her children, instead of hiding away in a convent, where Camilla "shortly afterward died, worn out by grief and melancholy" (De Cervantes, 2013, p. 269).

This comparison brings us back to the agency of the Lady, so dear to Cervantes. Like the fairy, she has a certain monstrous quality which triggers fury when she is betrayed. In fact, contrary to the Virgin Mary who never threw a fit, and even to Eve, the mother of humanity, whose "impertinent curiosity" drove the human race out of the Garden of Eden, she "seems […] to savour somewhat of heathenism", as the rascal Vivaldo puts it.

Melusine has more in common with the shepherdess Marcela. She has remained an untamed creature, and woe to anyone who attempts to manipulate her. Camilla lacked the ability to trigger this rage against the violation of the agency of the Lady. As for the rest, whether she took a lover or not, as Sancho says, "if [she] did, what is that to me? […] who can put gates on the open plain?"

But it is precisely this unbearable demonic force that makes Don Quixote lose his reason as the reading of the story is about to end, and he is suddenly heard shouting at a ferocious giant. The all-purpose giant can personify the ogre who destroyed Anselmo's household, or Pandafilando who threatened Dorothea, or Don Fernando, who was about to make an entrance. What is gigantic is the impertinence which presumes that omnipotence will triumph over the most fragile social element: the alliance.

From Anselmo's madness to Don Quixote's madness

Don Quixote's screams pull the listeners out of the lethargy induced by the story. Once again, his extraordinary energy lifts them out of the demoralising influence of the tale. The curate recovers his equanimity by adopting an aesthetic perspective. "I like this novel, but I cannot persuade myself of its truth [...]. As to the way in which the story is told, however, I have no fault to find" (De Cervantes, 2013, p. 269). These two attitudes, one shouting blame, the other choosing to be conciliatory, reflect two reactions to the same situation. Don Quixote's madness is used by Cervantes more than ever as a stylus to draw the distinctions without which, as Artaud said in 1938, "our societies commit suicide without noticing it" (Artaud, 2009).

For instance, is there a good and a bad madness? Are there good madmen, *locos lindos*, as the Argentinian analyst Pichon-Rivière calls them, bad madmen, *locas de mierda*, and even killers, recognisable or not? To this question, Cervantes answers "yes". Once again, his assessment is political. He enacts it by making the knight rise with a start from his bed and carry out an imaginary attack in his sleep, when "there remained but little more of the novel to be read" (De Cervantes, 2013, p. 263). This is the famous episode of the battle against the skins of red wine, reminiscent of the wine-skin escapade in Apuleius' *Metamorphoses* (Apuleius, 1999). Sancho asserts that the knight has indeed given "the giant, the enemy of my lady the Princess Micomicona, such a slash that he has sliced his head clean off as if it were a turnip". From that point on, a casuistic discussion ensued on the different ways of making heads roll. The curate asks himself if Sancho and his master are as crazy as Anselmo in the story.

But, just at the moment when the listeners, fascinated by this sombre tale, could easily react with a resigned "that's life", the Quixotic insults addressed to all swindlers awaken the audience. "Here they heard a loud noise in the chamber, and Don Quixote shouting out, 'Stand, thief, brigand, villain; now I have got thee, and thy scimitar shall not avail thee!'". While the plot of the story unfolds surreptitiously, the knight bursts into the room with great fanfare, leading an attack stemming from unconscious foreclosure, or what we call the cut out unconscious.

Moved by the same impulse which had propelled him, in this very place, to defend Maritornes, he now slays the monsters who threaten not only Camilla, whose downfall filtered into his awareness while he slept, but also Luscinda, whom Cardenio talked of, and above all Dorothea, who steps back at the strange sight of her hero, bare-bottomed, "in his shirt, which was not long enough in front to cover his thighs completely and was six fingers shorter behind".

A veritable *daimon*, "his legs were very long and lean, covered with hair, and anything but clean; on his head he had a little greasy red cap that belonged to his host, round his left arm he had rolled the blanket of the bed, to which Sancho, for reasons best known to himself, owed a grudge" (De Cervantes, 2013, p. 263). The sleepwalking trance is described with clinical precision. "[…] his eyes were not open, for he was fast asleep, and dreaming that he was doing battle with the giant. For his imagination was so wrought upon the adventure he was going to accomplish." As for Sancho, he confirms it all, diving in head first.

Before the pitiful end of the story inserted in the novel, Cervantes has recourse to the relentless logic of the theatre of fools. Don Quixote pays tribute to Mother Folly by kneeling before the curate, say-ing: "Exalted and beauteous lady, your highness may live from this day forth fearless of any harm this base being could do you" (De Cervantes, 2013, p. 264). His mission accomplished, the knight fell asleep again, to return, like after a trance, to his own self after the turbulent intrusion of the god. "[…] the barber, Cardenio, and the curate contrived with no small trouble to get Don Quixote on the bed, and he fell asleep with every appearance of excessive weariness."

The episode ends with the curses of the innkeeper's wife, furious about the spilling of the wine, with the curate's promises to make good all the losses, with Dorothea's comforting of Sancho and, above all, with the close-up of the adolescent face of the innkeeper's daughter, who "held her peace and smiled from time to time" (De Cervantes, 2013, p. 265). A reflection of Don Quixote's child-like soul, she was smiling at a youthful soul like her own, in the midst of the upheaval, proof that joy triumphs over the deathly sadness of the novel of the "ill-advised curiosity".

Still, can we agree with the curate, who considers, when he finishes reading, that "the author's invention is faulty, for it is impossible to imagine any husband so foolish as to try such a costly experiment" (De Cervantes, 2013, p. 269). We know that at the same period there were men of the cloth foolish enough not only to deny that Amerindians have a soul, a subject debated in the 1550 Valladolid Controversy, but also to oblige them to repudiate their goddesses. A Peruvian analyst, Maria Celina O'Campo, told me that the *susto*, a term used in Latin America for melancholia of the heart, which the Quechuas call *mancharisca*, refers back to the deadly fear of the Indian populations when the Spanish demanded that they abandon Pachamama, the goddess of the Sierra.

Don Quixote came to be read as far away as New Spain, where Cervantes would have liked to emigrate, and where the second part of one of his plays, *El Rufian Dichoso* (The Fortunate Ruffian), (De Cervantes, 2000) takes place. The play tells the story of the conversion of a delinquent youth from Seville—who died in Mexico in Cervantes' lifetime—into Friar Cristobal de la Cruz. In the play, Cristobal takes upon himself all the sins of a deathly ill woman, becoming a leper to save her soul. It is safe to say that his infallible remedy for the pain of life, the restitution of the agency of the Lady, is about to take place at the inn. Indeed, a masked party has just arrived, bringing with them a lady who seems about to faint.

Don Quixote's well-advised curiosity

Everyone falls silent upon seeing the third black-veiled party arrive at the inn. Dorothea covers her face and Cardenio retreats into Don Quixote's room. The man leading the party is no other than Don Fernando, who places a lady dressed in white in a chair. Cardenio recognises Luscinda when he hears her voice through the door. Cervantes directs a choreographed scene of recognition, amazement, attraction, and confrontation between the characters, resembling a warrior dance called *kata* in Japanese martial arts, in which attacks coming from all sides have to be pushed back.

When the masks fell, all movement ceased. Dorothea fainted, and the curate revived her with cold water. They all became linked in a mutual stare and "stood in silent amazement scarcely knowing what had happened to them. They gazed at one another without speaking, Dorothea at Don Fernando, Don Fernando at Cardenio, Cardenio at Luscinda, and Luscinda at Cardenio" (De Cervantes, 2013, p. 272). The improbable meeting reveals Luscinda's secret abduction.

A young woman has indeed been kidnapped. In the deadly showdown that follows, anything might happen between three or four armed men on one side, and Cardenio, Sancho, the barber, and the curate—all unarmed—on the other. The tension mounts to a fever pitch, and then gives way to speech used by the women to keep the weapons at bay.

Dorothea and Luscinda, once they recover, remind Don Fernando of his Quixotic duty to his own name: "The first to break the silence was Luscinda, who addressed Don Fernando: 'Leave me, Señor Don Fernando, for the sake of what you owe to yourself; [...] leave me to cling to the wall of which I am the ivy [...]'". Once Dorothea comes to herself, she finds the strength to remind him of the promise he has made to her, concluding: "[...] these are my last words to thee: whether thou wilt, or wilt not, I am thy wife; witness thy words, which must not and ought not to be false" (De Cervantes, 2013, p. 273).

Floods of tears bespeak the softening of all hearts. His secret scheming exposed for all to see, Don Fernando relents, saying: "Thou has conquered, fair Dorothea, thou hast conquered, for it is impossible to have the heart to deny the united force of so many truths" (De Cervantes, 2013, p. 274). Opening his arms, he releases Luscinda who, on the point of falling to the ground in a swoon, is caught instead in Cardenio's arms.

The confrontation is brought to an end by an exchange of "dance" partners, like in the quadrille—perhaps the Lancers Quadrille my great-grandmother was so fond of. But another crisis interrupts the dance, marking a second peak of tension. René Thom illustrates this tempo in his catastrophe theory by referring to the critical moment when the prey enters the field of a predator, propelling the latter into action (De Cervantes, 2013, p. 274). Recourse to weapons seems imminent again when, despite his veneer of civility, Don Fernando reacts to seeing his prey get away. "Dorothea fancied that Don Fernando changed colour and looked as though he meant to take vengeance on Cardenio, for she observed him put his hand to his sword."

This impulse to take murderous action strongly resembles the start of Don Quixote's sallies, when he is ready to charge with couched lance, with his legs straight in the stirrups. And yet there is a difference. But it will not be until later, in the speech "on arms and letters", that the text will establish the distinction between the two parallel fields, that of trauma and that of perversion.

In the meantime, Cervantes leaves it to Dorothea to create, again and again, the field of speech, this time in the classical posture of supplication, as "she clasped the knees" of the armed man, "kissing them and holding him so as to prevent his moving" (De Cervantes, 2013, p. 275). Her second tirade focuses on presumptuousness. At the crucial moment, when danger is greatest, she displays an insight she acquired at great cost, and which allows her to foresee the murderous reaction of a pervert caught in the act. "I implore thee, let not this open manifestation rouse thy anger; but rather [...] calm it [...] and the world shall see that with thee reason has more influence than passion."

Reason: the word has been spoken. For Don Quixote, reason is the culmination of a long search, in the quasi mathematical sense of the "reason" of a harmonic relation achieved by defeating unreason. For Don Fernando, reason is that which opposes the passion that devours people at a rate directly proportional to the magnitude of their appetites. Cardenio, like Dorothea, knows that a sudden attack is still possible. "Cardenio, though he held Luscinda in his arms, never took his eyes off Don Fernando, determined, if he saw him make any hostile movement, to try to defend himself and resist as best he could all who might assail him, though it should cost him his life."

At the height of danger, we hear the voices of the spectators' choir—Sancho, the barber, the curate, and the three riders who arrived with the party—joined by Dorothea now ready to fight, for she has nothing to lose. They surround the dangerous character and transform their chance encounter into a divine sign the Ancient Greeks called *kledon* and the Christians call providence. "[...] they firmly believed [...] that it was not, as it might seem, by accident, but by a special disposition of providence that they had all met in a place where no one could have expected a meeting."

What the curate has to say is inspired less by the Council of Trent than by the story of Tristan and Isolde. He reminds Don Fernando "that only death could part Luscinda and Cardenio; that even if some sword were to separate them they would think their death most happy". And he goes on to admonish him "that if he prided himself on being a gentleman and a Christian, he could not do otherwise than keep his plighted word" (De Cervantes, 2013, p. 275). This sentence is truly the leitmotif of the whole novel.

But Luscinda and Cardenio have already taken up the sword, so to speak, by forcing the schemer to rise to the obligations of his rank.

"[...] Cardenio and Luscinda went and fell on their knees before Don Fernando, returning him thanks for the favour he had rendered them in language so grateful that he knew not how to answer them" (De Cervantes, 2013, p. 276). In truth, he is the one who must obey the rule of the given word. Courtesy is reinstated. The brutal lover confesses his aggression and admits to breaking into the convent with his accomplices to kidnap Luscinda, who had taken refuge there. Only Sancho is left stranded "with no little sorrow at heart to see how his hopes of dignity were fading away and vanishing in smoke, and how the fair princess Micomicona had turned into Dorothea, and the giant into Don Fernando" (De Cervantes, 2013, p. 277).

The collapse of the perverse windbag goes hand in hand with disillusionment. But does this radical change in his discourse lead to the bitter-sweet resignation that accompanies the return to reality?

Cervantes is determined to prevent this. He endeavours to show us that the warrior's art is the only thing than can oppose hostage-taking. Of course, Don Fernando would not have backed off without Dorothea's determination, but without Don Quixote's obstinate readiness for battle, none of these things could have taken place.

In summary, without the well-advised resolve of the knight to speak to a madman deemed to be hopeless, the inn could not have become the place where agreements considered impossible were concluded. The major themes of Quixotic delusion—wrongs to be righted, damsels to rescue and perverts to slay—not only can be carried out in reality, but best of all, remain feasible even while the knight is fast asleep. Clearly, his objective is not to gain some advantage from a well-planned, spectacular liberation. The knight has a score to settle with the inconsequence of despicable stratagems, and he has only just begun.

CHAPTER TEN

History makes its entrance

"The hard reality of fiction" (Devos, 1989)

The couples are reunited and their happiness is complete. "Dorothea was unable to persuade herself that her present happiness was not all a dream" (De Cervantes, 2013, p. 277). The same is true of Cardenio, Luscinda, and even Don Fernando, who realises that he has barely escaped the fate of a criminal. Don Quixote, on the other hand, has to stop dreaming. The medico-social scheme concocted by the barber and the curate is still in effect: their plan to lock up the knight so that the others can live real lives, lives which, in their opinion, can do without madness and its visions.

As a result, Sancho, like a child who has just discovered that there is no Santa Claus, wants to warn his master of the disaster. "Sancho [...] was the only one who was distressed, unhappy, and dejected; and so with a long face he went in to his master, who had just awoke [...]" (De Cervantes, 2013, p. 277) to inform him that their dreams had no chance of coming true.

The situation is critical. Don Quixote's efforts are now dismissed by the entire company, which maintains its diagnosis, a diagnosis supported, first of all, by those who like a good laugh. "[...] the curate gave [all those] present an account of Don Quixote's madness and of the stratagem they had made use of to withdraw him from the Pena Pobre (Poor Rock) where he fancied himself stationed [...] they marveled and laughted not a little, thinking it, as all did, the strangest form of madness a crazy intellect could be capable of."

No one seems to understand what they all owe to this crazy intellect, which had proven to be the only power capable of reuniting them all and extricating them from the traps in which they were stuck. Now, they all seem to want to participate in the "stratagem" aiming at "getting him home". Ousted from the realm of those who are normal, after having been exploited, the only thing left for Don Quixote is to be confined to his home, receiving no recognition for his efforts on their behalf. So it goes, as is bluntly pointed out by Jean Cassou in *La Mémoire courte*, and by Kurt Vonnegut in *Slaughterhouse-Five*.

Don Quixote to the rescue

But Don Quixote is now ready to face all threats to the integrity of his intelligence, disguised as care offered for his own good. His psychic survival is at stake. Once again, he chooses direct confrontation and orders Sancho: "[...] hand me my clothes and let me go out, for I want to see these transformations and things thou speakest of" (De Cervantes, 2013, p. 278). At that point, he seems to have come back from the beyond, a character from Nô theatre, masked and wearing clothes of another era, to dance at the betrayal of his memory. "At this moment Don Quixote came out in full panoply, with Mambrino's helmet, all dented as it was, on his head, his buckler on his arm, and leaning on his staff or pike."

A figure from another time, from a realm beyond conformity, he fills the entire company with amazement. "The strange figure he presented [...], his lean yellow face half a league long, his armor of all sorts, and the solemnity of his deportment" all contribute to make him a phantom of the betrayed word, ready to fight against absurd reductionist interpretations. Like his demeanour, the moment is solemn. "They stood silent waiting to see what he would say."

What the knight has to say is addressed first to Dorothea. He reminds her of the transference which came to her rescue: "I am informed, fair lady, by my squire here that your greatness has been annihilated and your being abolished, since, from a queen and lady of high degree as you used to be, you have been turned into a private maiden" (De Cervantes,

2013, p. 279). He constrains her to respect the status of disinherited queen, which was hers in the language play they enacted together, and he sets her a challenge. Will she disavow their work and adopt the common opinion that all this is nothing but fiction, empty words, ridiculous nonsense?

Far from giving in to the slayers of analytic discourse, Don Quixote persists in defending the value of his books as therapeutic tools. Thanks to these "annals of chivalry [...] read and gone through [...] attentively and deliberately [...], there is no peril on earth through which [his] sword will not force a way", for indeed: "It is no great matter to kill a whelp of a giant, however arrogant he may be." How can she deny this and participate in the ambient scientism? He challenges her to recognise what he has done for her, saying that otherwise "[he] will not speak of it, that they may not say [he is] lying". Not wanting anything to disrupt the collective entertainment, Don Fernando tells the landlord to keep quiet, when the latter brings up the reality of the wasted wineskins.

But Dorothea knows where her allegiances lie. Taking advantage of the opportunity Don Quixote offers her, she assures him that she has not forgotten what she owes him. Using the words of their shared language, she admits that he saved her, and tells him that she has not changed. "Whoever told you [...] that I had undergone any change or transformation did not tell you the truth, for I am the same as I was yesterday. [...] I have not [...] ceased to be what I was before". Her acknowledgement reinstates the value of their common search publicly. "I believe, señor, that had it not been for you I should never have lit upon the good fortune I now possess" (De Cervantes, 2013, p. 279). This is how the order of analytic discourse is validated in the transitional space of theatrical play, which made the deed possible "and in this I am saying what is perfectly true; as most of these gentlemen who are present can fully testify".

Don Quixote admits that he had a scare. Without this testimony, he would have been precipitated into "the greatest perplexity I have ever been in all my life, I vow". His efforts were about to be disqualified, with the complicity of all those present. On a small scale, a totalitarian system was in the process of denying the obvious, destroying the evidence, falsifying the story and, above all, abolishing outright the initial event, that of the transferential encounter with the madman of the Sierra Morena.

Dorothea, being more intelligent than Camilla, has decided not to echo her husband's simplistic arguments. She acknowledges the "invincible arm" of the man who saved her life and her sanity.

Greatly relieved, the knight discharges his tension on his squire: "I declare now, little Sancho, thou art the greatest little villain in Spain", letting his anger mount until he is ready to knock him out on the spot for misleading his master, and to "play the mischief with thee, in a way that will teach sense for the future to all lying squires of knights-errant in the world". Let future analysts be warned! Then tempers cool and the mood becomes forgiving. "[…] forgive me, and that will do." Don Fernando agrees, putting an end to the incident: "That will do, […] let us say no more about it […] because it is too late" (De Cervantes, 2013, p. 280). It is best to forget all these silly affairs in which he came off as the villain.

But we soon have to reckon with the trick Cervantes was to play on him, and on readers too prompt to stop speaking, once peace returns, of the follies carried out to bring about freedom.

"We call out Christmas till 'tis here" (Villon, 1906, pp. 15–17)

Now, Cervantes sends off his hero—confirmed in his function as ferryman negotiating the passage between worlds—to bring back the protracted memories of old wars and of the bagnios in Algiers. In fact, is it not Cervantes himself who appears, disguised as the traveller on the threshold of the inn, "who seemed from his attire to be a Christian lately come from the country of the Moors, [and whose] appearance was such that if he had been well dressed he would have been taken for a person of quality and good birth"? Here, Cervantes describes the scene of his own return, in a decor reminiscent of a Christmas eve: "Behind him, mounted upon an ass, there came a woman dressed in Moorish fashion, with her face veiled […]." He speaks to her in Arabic; her name is both Zoraida and Maria, and like in the Bible, there is no room for them at the inn.

The veiled woman's silence (Garcés, 2002, pp. 202–211) creates a transition from Don Quixote's battles to the real universe of the wars fought by the soldier Cervantes once was. From one war to the other, in the course of the "long week-end" measured out by Bion, victory changes to defeat and the battle of Lepanto is followed, seventeen years later, by the disaster of the Invincible Armada. We have only to remember the "roaring twenties" and post-war periods with their boisterous night life and youth eager to put the dark years behind them. But their rejoicing cannot prevent the surreptitious return of a spectral survivor of the slave camps.

The history of the bagnios, veritable gulags in Algiers and on Ottoman shores around the Mediterranean, was most often denied outright. Still, it is precisely this story of slavery, long shrouded in silence, that slips into the novel wordlessly and in veiled fashion. The captive returning from the hell of the bagnio and from his exile from language is accompanied by a veiled Dulcinea. Luscinda and Dorothea offer her the hospitality one is "bound to show all strangers that stand in need of it, especially if it be a woman to whom the service is rendered" (De Cervantes, 2013, p. 281). Having been ostracised themselves, they are not about to intrude in the life of a refugee just to satisfy their curiosity. The debriefing can wait until those who seek asylum have been provided with nourishment and rest. Despite their desire "to know who the Moorish lady and the captive were, [...] no one liked to ask just then, seeing that it was a fitter moment for helping them to rest themselves than for questioning them about their lives" (De Cervantes, 2013, p. 282). When Zoraida would finally remove her veil, she was going to be revealed as the one to whom the captive owes his freedom.

For the same reason, it is best not to be in a hurry to lift the poetic veil of delusion which creates a means of speaking with the unspeakable. But Don Quixote has just been poetically acknowledged by Dorothea. Therefore, he no longer needs delusions to bear testimony as the son of a traumatised soldier. The discourse he is about to deliver, as well as the captive's narrative which follows, have real documentary value for historians.

The discourse on Arms and Letters

Now, the setting resembles a banquet, a symposium on war trauma. Supper is served. Despite his reserve, Don Quixote is asked to take "the seat of honor at the head of a long table like a refectory one". He presides over the gathering. Suddenly, he leaves off eating, for this position of authority inspires him to address those present.

Let us summarise. Thirty-seven chapters were needed before Don Quixote succeeded in bringing together, at the inn, "gentlemen, to whom arms are an appurtenance by birth, [who] listened to him with great pleasure" (De Cervantes, 2013, p. 284). Only then, in this setting of *philia* linking those who know what he is talking about, can he share the knowledge he acquired in the hell of war. "Don Quixote delivered his discourse in such a manner and in such correct language, that [...] he made it impossible for any of his hearers to consider him a madman."

His role is to prepare the audience to hear the tale of the wars fought by Cervantes, and of his captivity in Algiers, by ushering in the epic tale—*epos* means speech in ancient Greek—in solemn fashion, through an introductory discourse on Arms and Letters. First, he discourses on the topic "life is a dream", which was to be taken up a few years later by Calderón de la Barca (De la Barca, 2012). "Say, what being is there in this world, who entering the gate of this castle at this moment, and seeing us as we are here, would suppose or imagine us to be what we are?" (De Cervantes, 2013, p. 282).

The gathering at the inn of all these people destined, in all likelihood, never to meet again, has an uncanny quality very like the strangeness which propels Don Quixote into each episode of traumatic revival. Thus, he begins by invoking the theme of the surreal: "Verily, gentlemen, if we reflect upon it, great and marvelous are the things they see, who make profession of the order of knight-errantry."

This introduction establishes the theoretical framework of what he calls knight-errantry, a concept on which it is time to shed some light. It encompasses visions of "great and marvelous things" in which we glimpse surviving forms emerging at the edge of the unspeakable. Knight-errantry is a profession, an art, a calling requiring true discipline; ordinary mortals have little understanding of it. "[...] there can be no doubt that this art and calling surpasses all those that mankind has invented, and is the more deserving of being held in honor in proportion as it is the most exposed to peril." Because this profession is always intimately linked with danger, it can claim a status of extraterrestriality, which authorises the question: "What being in this world would suppose us to be what we are?"

Here, the being who enters through the door of the book first is the reader, who now understands how Dorothea can be Don Fernando's wife and, at the same time, a princess in her kingdom, reclaimed by the extravagant knight Don Quixote, the only one who can restore the rights of exiled subjects.

This reader is startled by Don Quixote's conjuratory words when he says: "Away with those who assert that letters have the pre-eminence over arms; I will tell them, whosoever they may be, that they know not what they say." Should the learned take this personally? Who would dare to argue nowadays that the art of Arms is nobler than that of Letters and even that of Sciences? Upon reading his first words, would we not agree that Don Quixote's discourse is extremely outdated?

Cervantes chooses to produce this effect, making no concessions to snobbism. Indeed, the injunction "away with those" acts as a magnet, attracting a multitude of readers who perhaps bear the scars of wars in their family line, or who are waging battles against shady giants, big or small.

Now, Don Quixote goes on to describe, in three segments, life aboard a galley in Lepanto when it encounters an enemy galley in the open sea, comparing this with the hardships of student life. It may be that Cervantes is reflecting on the great difference between the university life he left at the age of twenty-two, in 1569, and his experiences as a soldier in the ten years that followed.

When he returned to Spain in 1580, at the age of thirty-three, as destitute as the captive entering the inn, he may not yet have been aware of the contempt in which veterans are held, owing to the stain—*mancha*—of spilled blood. This is why now Don Quixote describes the intelligence required by the warrior, the objectives of war and the labour of the soldier as compared to that of the student.

In defence of the mind

First, Cervantes entrusts his son with speaking on behalf of the soldier's intelligence. Presented as a singular attribute of those who face death, it demolishes the conventional opposition between brain and brawn. Don Quixote's argument seeks to destroy the preconception—still persistent today—which holds that "the labors of the mind are greater than those of the body, and that arms give employment to the body alone; as if the calling were a porter's trade, for which nothing more is required than sturdy strength" (De Cervantes, 2013, p. 283). Here, Cervantes is delivering a veritable treatise on martial arts.

He refers first to the engineers of artillery and architects of fortifications—much admired later by Tristram Shandy's Uncle Toby (Sterne, 1999)—for their contributions to research in physics and mathematics. Then he goes on to praise the intelligence required in battle, to outwit the enemy, analyse one's impressions, be able to anticipate, and save one's life. "[...] see whether by bodily strength it be possible to learn or divine the intentions of the enemy, his plans, stratagems, or obstacles, or to ward off impending mischief; for all these are the work of the mind, and in them the body has no share whatever." The profession of arms requires the body to be the seat of mental processes relying on somatic markers—as neurologist Antonio Damasio (Damasio, 2005) calls them—able to inform the mind with the speed of lightning.

Indeed, these same abilities are often found among the offspring of former soldiers, in the form of symptoms reproducing hypertrophied capacities directly inherited from their fathers. Don Quixote's discourse is itself an illustration of this form of intelligence which, despite scorn and ridicule, allows thinking to triumph over peril. Once this is established, the knight goes on to the next point of comparison: "Since, therefore, arms have need of the mind, as much as letters, let us see now which of the two minds, that of the man of letters or that of the warrior, has most to do" (De Cervantes, 2013, p. 283).

The soldier and the student

The comparison between the man of letters and the warrior is extended to eliminate the dichotomy between the presumed creativity of the former and the destructiveness of the latter. From the start, Don Quixote condemns the pseudo-pacifist rhetoric advocating collaboration: "[...] the end of [letters] is to establish distributive justice, give to every man that which is his, and see and take care that good laws are observed [...], [while] arms have for their end and object peace, the greatest boon that men can desire in this life." This reflection on the object of the use of force refers not only to Cervantes' wars, but also to the battles of his son. "This, then, being admitted, that the end of war is peace [...], let us turn to the bodily labors of the man of letters, and those of him who follows the profession of arms, and see which are the greater."

Now, Don Quixote evaluates the tasks of the student and those of the young soldier. The Quixotic demonstration would impress any PhD defence committee. The comparative study focuses on each one's professional future, quality of life and wages. Despite their poverty, the most destitute students are eventually rewarded by having the possibility to "reach the rank they desire, and [...] we have seen them, I say, ruling and governing the world from a chair" (De Cervantes, 2013, p. 284). This is rarely the fate of veterans with PTDS, about whom Don

Quixote says that "in poverty itself there is no one poorer", and that their hardships can in no way be compared to those of the student.

Don Quixote describes in minute detail the privations endured by the soldier, who "is dependent [...] on what he can plunder", has to defend himself against the cold and "the inclemency of the weather in the open field with nothing better than the breath of his mouth, which I need not say, coming from an empty place, must come out cold, contrary to the laws of nature". Always hungry, he sleeps under the stars on the ground, a bed "[...] which never sins by being over narrow". And then there are the wounds—like those received by Cervantes: "[...] suppose the day of the battle to have arrived, when they invest him with the doctor's cap made of lint, to mend some bullet hole, perhaps that has gone through his temples, or left him with a crippled arm or leg" (De Cervantes, 2013, p. 285).

The lack of any compensation or recognition echoes a trauma Cervantes suffered thirty years earlier, upon his return from war. "For tell me, [...] by how much do those who have gained by war fall short of the number of those who have perished in it?"

The physical pain is equalled only by the moral torment produced by the ever-present fear of the soldier "who finds himself beleaguered in some stronghold mounting guard in some ravelin [...]" (De Cervantes, 2013, p. 286). It was, in fact, in just such a ravelin in Namur, that captain Toby Shandy "had the honour" of receiving his wound in the groin, which would heal eventually thanks to his talking cure with his own Sancho Panza, Corporal Trim.

In his *Notebooks* (Wittgenstein, 1979b), written on the front lines, Wittgenstein describes the conditions of which Don Quixote speaks, when he had to "stand his ground in fear and expectation of the moment when he will fly up to the clouds without wings and descend into the deep against his will". Decorated for having defended heroically an observation post in a dangerous mission for which he volunteered and during which he was constantly the target of enemy fire, Wittgenstein remembers that he "was praying to God for the courage to look death in the eye without fear".

Cervantes can never forget the day of the naval battle of Lepanto, in which, thirty-five years earlier, he was gravely wounded in an inferno of artillery fire. The invention of new weapons has repeatedly made people believe that the end of the world is near. "Happy the blest ages that knew not the dread fury of those devilish engines of artillery, whose inventor I am persuaded is in hell receiving the reward of his diabolical invention" (De Cervantes, 2013, p. 286). An anonymous death, or death by friendly fire, which "cuts off the life of one who deserved to live for ages to come".

The battle of Lepanto

Only a son driven mad by his father's traumas can be trusted to make real and depict vividly the naval battle involving "the encounter of two galleys stem to stem, in the midst of the open sea, locked and entangled one with the other". His father's galley was called *La Marquesa*, and we know that he was in the bow. "And what is still more marvelous, no sooner has one gone down into the depths he will never rise from till the end of the world, than another takes his place; and if he too falls into the sea that waits for him like an enemy, another and another will succeed him without a moment's pause between their deaths" (De Cervantes, 2013, p. 286).

The battle recounted by Don Quixote in a single breath, on behalf of his father, literally as he speaks, in a fusion of identity characteristic of the epic tale, is carried off in two twenty-line episodes he separates only to catch his breath. These lines intone the moment when Cervantes faced his own death, and paint an epic portrait of the moments when his comrades drew their last breath. Paradoxically, the rhythm could also be that of a lullaby, like *Ruht Wohl* repeated endlessly at the end of the *St. John Passion*.

The previous three hundred and fifty pages constitute the time the son needed to experience as many traumatic revivals as there were surviving images to reanimate his father's wars, followed each time by real debriefing sessions with Sancho. It is also the time Cervantes needed to "digest death" and weave a shroud of words for those who were given no graves, his fellow soldiers for whom he feels deep love.

This recollection carries no incitement to war. Cervantes knows, like all those who have experienced it, that there is nothing worse than this pit of hell, constantly dug by the increasingly more terrifying advancements in weaponry. The stories all resemble each other: a comrade's death that haunts you, whose life and thoughts were cut short when he was barely twenty, the total dependence on stupid decisions made behind the lines, physical and moral mutilation, hunger, thirst, stench, filth, insomnia, terror, backup that does not arrive and, above all, the complete loss of your bearings, which turns everything into a mirage in the midst of chaos and deafening noise.

There is no doubt that the novel was written to attest to the madness inherent in survival. Don Quixote's fits are what Cathy Caruth (Caruth, 1996) calls "crises of life". They enact the critical threshold between intense awareness of mortal danger and an acute faculty to imagine and anticipate danger. This is why veterans are quite capable of punching anyone who tells them they are fantasising or having hallucinations; in fact, they are righting the wrongs that keep coming back in their nightmares.

Belleface and Roc Noir

The March 31st, 1945 attack on Roc Noir at an altitude of 2,342 metres, and the attack on Belleface at 2,800 metres—just above my birthplace— by the Alpine Hunters of the Paganon battalion (Bogonet, 2005)— grouping together at the Little St. Bernard Pass various factions of the Resistance into the First Regular Alpine Battalion—are an exact illustration of Cervantes' words. As is always the case, this battle was considered perfectly useless by some, and decisive by others. While the major offensives of the war targeting Berlin were being carried out in Italy and Alsace, the role of the Alpine Hunters was to stop the advance of the SS battalions in the Afrika Korps and the Austrian Gebirgjäger, to assist the Allies on the other side of the Alps. But events do not follow established stratagies.

At Roc Noir (Gaide, 1996), they crossed over a narrow, frozen mountain ridge, and stood on a narrow ledge no wider than two feet, facing German mortar shelling. They climbed the mountain, were shot down, and fell: "[...] no sooner has one gone down [...], than another takes his place; and if he too falls into the [abyss] that waits for him like an enemy, another and another will succeed him", says Cervantes, "without a moment's pause between their deaths". Forty men died one after the other at Belleface, climbing the precipice in minus twenty degrees Celsius.

While experts argue over the importance of these battles, trying to decide whether they are insignificant events or time bombs, I can say that I know what it means to be an offspring haunted by dead companions, whether I knew them or not. Each year, I must walk along the slopes surrounding *Lac Sans Fond* (Bottomless Lake) at the foot of

Roc Noir and Belleface, in a seemingly innocent decor, and wander around the Roman road that goes up the pass and comes down on the other side, crossing the pre-Celtic circle of stones bearing witness to a much earlier route. *Andante*!

The epic tale of the captive

After Don Quixote's discourse, it is the captive's turn to relate his odyssey. He is prompted to speak and encouraged by Don Quixote's affirmation of the priority of arms over the peaceful professions chosen by his two younger brothers, as will be revealed by his story. Both brothers became successful, one as a tradesman and the other as a lawyer. The choice of the eldest, the profession of arms, which can bring no such success, receives unexpected approval from the knight, restores his identity ravaged during his captivity, and reconnects him with his family line. Now he can be questioned about the missions in which he was engaged. His account unfolds, crescendo, throughout the three chapters that follow, rising against the oblivion into which the bagnios almost buried them.

He belongs to a linage of warriors, *bellantes*, in the Indo-European triad also comprising *orantes* and *laborantes*, characterised by the voluntary sacrifice of one's life. Thus, worth is not associated with accumulation, but with loss and the reputation gained by it. In fact, Cervantes' description of the captive's father remains true today. "This tendency of his to be liberal and profuse he had acquired from having been a soldier in his youth, for the soldier's life is a school in which the niggard becomes free-handed and the free-handed prodigal; and if any soldiers are to be found who are misers, they are monsters of rare occurrence." No doubt, Cervantes is also speaking for himself and for others, perhaps his own father, the barber-surgeon who had served in war. "My father went beyond liberality and bordered on prodigality, a disposition by no means advantageous to a married man who has children to succeed to his name and position" (De Cervantes, 2013, p. 288).

Unable to control his spending, he wants to assure his sons that he loves them "like a father", and will not ruin them "like a stepfather". Therefore, he divides his property between them, giving up his immediate pleasures, on condition that his sons do not spend their inheritance at once, but invest it in one of three professions, according to the proverb "The church, or the sea, or the king's house" (De Cervantes, 2013, p. 288).

One of his sons chose the clergy and became a student at the Law School of Salamanca, another chose international trade and became wealthy in Peru, while the eldest chose the profession of arms, in which the only thing one can gain is honour. They wasted no time putting their plan into action. "As soon as we had come to an understanding, and made choice of our professions, my father embraced us all, and in the short time he mentioned carried into effect all he had promised." Each of the younger sons gave back a third of his share to their father; the future captive gave him two thirds of his. Then they separated to find their own way in the world, and had no news of each other for twenty years.

Twenty-two years passed between 1575, when Cervantes was captured by Barbary Coast pirates, and 1597, when in the prison of Seville Cervantes was visited by a surviving form from his military past, a figure with ghostly weapons, from another era—betrayed like Hamlet's phantom—whose story would also become a best seller.

The captive is also a phantom, returning without a maravedi. All he has is the young, beautiful Moorish lady, the agent of his escape and witness to events which could have caused him to disappear without a trace in Constantinople, where Cervantes was about to be sent away for good the day before his ransom was paid at last.

Called to order by Don Quixote, History returns on the double. The captive recounts his military exploits at a hasty pace, in two pages that take the reader to Genoa, Milan, Piedmont, and finally Flanders, where he enrolls in the troops of the Duke of Alba, grimly remembered in connection with the battle against the Sea Beggars, which made Till Eulenspiegel (De Coster, 2010) famous. After witnessing the execution of the Count of Egmont and the Count of Horne—condemned to death as supporters of Dutch independence, the captive served as an ensign in a regiment led by Diego de Urbina, who had been Cervantes' captain as well. In Italy, the captive joined the league under the command of John of Austria, to fight the Turks, who had just invaded Cyprus. Finally, he took part in the battle of Lepanto, in which "all the nations of the earth were disabused of the error under which they lay in imagining the Turks to be invincible on sea" De Cervantes, 2013, p. 290).

It was there that the captive was captured, when he leaped alone on board the enemy galley of El Uchali, which sailed off towards

Constantinople before his men could follow him. The Grand Turk, Selim II, son of Suleiman the Magnificent, made El Uchali general of the Turkish fleet. "[…] on the night that followed that famous day I found myself with fetters on my feet and manacles on my hands."

History seen from the Turkish perspective

The opposite historical perspective provided by a galley slave introduces the Turkish exploits needed to complete the plot. The reader learns that Navarino failed to be captured by the Spanish fleet thanks to El Uchali's cunning, and that the badly treated slaves of the son of the famous corsair Barbarossa, who had brought wealth to Algiers, tore their master to pieces, "passing him on from bench to bench, from the poop to the prow, [and] so bit him that before he had got much past the mast his soul had already got to hell". We learn about the capture of Tunis from the Turks by Don John of Austria in 1573, and about the defeat of the Spanish troops at The Goletta—battles in which Cervantes participated—the following year.

The story of the fall of The Goletta, a fort reckoned impregnable until 1574, presents recurring themes of veterans' narratives. That is, the precise number of men involved: 7,000 soldiers in the fort (more likely 9,000, specifies a note in the French translation) (De Cervantes, 2001, p. 1574), against 75,000 Turks in pay and 400,000 Moors and Arabs from all parts of Africa; the criticism of comments made by those who were not there: "It was a common opinion that our men should not have shut themselves up in The Goletta, but should have waited in the open at the landing place; but those who say so talk at random and with little knowledge of such matters"; the strategic analysis that considers it a useless distant outpost, very costly for Spain, a "hiding place for mischief, […] devourer, sponge, and moth of countless money [having] no other purpose save preserving the memory of its capture by the invincible Charles V; as if to make that eternal, […], these stones were needed to support it" (De Cervantes, 2001, p. 1574).

In one sentence, Cervantes states what is needed to make a lasting inscription: not enormous sums of money invested in the upkeep of a useless fort, but epitaphs for those who died there. Each of the fallen cited—who all have historical existence, says the same note—is immortalised by an attribute. Thus, the text specifies that Pagan Doria was killed by a traitor, executed in turn by the admiral of the Turkish fleet, proving the truth of the proverb: "Though the treason may please, the traitor is hated."

Enumerating the names produces the effect of a resurrection. "The instant the captive mentioned the name of Don Pedro de Aguilar, Don Fernando looked at his companions and they all three smiled" (De Cervantes, 2013, p. 293). One of them recognised his brother in this galley slave, "who had in particular a special gift for what they call poetry". The captive learns that this man was able to escape, and offers to recite two sonnets composed by this soldier poet, dedicated to the men fallen at The Goletta, saying: "I have them by heart."

One of the sonnets, built around an oxymoron, turns absurd death into victory through the grace of Cervantian poetry, which does away with victimisation:

> It was the ebbing life blood first that failed
> The weary arms; the stout hearts never quailed. (De Cervantes, 2013, p. 294)

The captive, a symbolic figure of naval warfare and slave trade, in which so many disappeared without a trace, insists on affirming that the soil where the dead are resting is sacred.

> Up from this wasted soil, this shattered shell,
> Whose walls and towers here in ruin lie,
> Three thousand soldier souls took wing on high,
> In the bright mansions of the blest to dwell.

Cervantes wished to inscribe the actual place and date of the event by demarcating the perimeter of this poetic tomb made of verses and rhythms, to provide a shelter for the fallen who have no burial monuments.

Anthropology of life in the bagnios

The story of El Uchali (Bennassar, 2001, p. 370) continues with a tribute rendered to the former slave. A Calabrian renegade, for fourteen years he was a galley slave under the Grand Signor, until he renounced his faith at the age of thirty-four, finally becoming "general-on-the-sea" in the Ottoman Fleet. "[…] worthy man morally, […] he treated his slaves with great humanity. He had three thousand of them [...]" (De Cervantes, 2013, p. 295). The opposite was true of Hasan Pacha, "one of his most favored youths", whom he designated as his successor and who proved to be "the most cruel renegade I ever saw" (De Cervantes, 2013, p. 295), as the captive testifies. We have already described the sadism of the terrible Bey of Algiers, both towards the slaves held for ransom, forerunners of today's hostages, and towards the slaves who were "public property", forgotten by all, for "there is no one with whom to treat for their ransom, even though they may have the means".

Cervantes inserts his signature in the text when the captive mentions a Spanish soldier named Saavedra. He only allots himself nine lines, like the Renaissance painters who would include a tiny portrait of themselves in a corner of their paintings. Nine little lines telling a story left in suspense by the captive. "[...] and only that time does not allow, I could tell you now something of what that soldier did, that would interest and astonish you much more than the narration of my own tale" (De Cervantes, 2013, p. 296). The surname Saavedra, referring to a warrior's feats, was adopted by Cervantes after his captivity to name the other, a stranger to himself, that he had become. (Garcés, 2002, p. 195 & 198) As a subject embodying History, Saavedra holds but a very precarious role ; historical events had no need of him to unfold, but without him no one would know they took place.

The captive's escape introduces a major theme of both parts of Cervantes' *Don Quixote*, but particularly of Part Two, written as an "Art of the Fugue" from mental torture at the ducal castle.

A true anthropology of life in the bagnios, the episode begins in a courtyard where the slaves are confined, and where a reed is glimpsed through the lattice-covered window of the wealthy moor Hadji Morato's house—a man reputed to have been very powerful in Algiers at that period. The reed is used by someone in the house to pass gold coins to captives seeking to gain freedom; the coins are accompanied by a letter containing a proposal to escape with the daughter of the household. She wishes to become a Christian, at the risk of being "[flung] down a well and [covered] with stones" (De Cervantes, 2013, p. 299) if her father finds out. The intermediary assisting in the mission is a renegade wishing to acquire certificates of worthiness in case he should find himself before the Inquisition once he returns to Spain— documents which would become invaluable sources of information for future historians.

The captive's traumatic memory constitutes another document which recounts in detail and with great precision the adventure of the escape, "for nothing of importance that took place in this affair has escaped my memory, or ever will while life lasts" (De Cervantes, 2013, p. 300), to put it in his own words. This exceptional recollection can be cut out entirely, only to resurface unexpectedly "when you least expect it", even one or several generations later. Don Quixote demonstrates this, since this type of memory, with no oblivion, is what constitutes the thread of his successive adventures.

Cervantes presents a clinical analysis of suppression, which is different from repression. Captives who are able to escape do not remember the promises made to their fellow captives to come back and free them. The renegade advises them to escape all together, without dividing their plural body, a veritable organism of survival. Indeed, as soon as their survival is no longer at stake, "experience had taught him how ill those who have been set free keep promises which they made in captivity, [to] return for the others who had ransomed [them]" (De Cervantes, 2013, p. 301). The reason for this forgetting is primarily fear. "[…] recovered liberty and the dread of losing it again efface from the memory all obligations in the world" (De Cervantes, 2013, pp. 301–302). Dread is still lurking.

Zoraida, the daughter of Hadji Morato, pays the ransom of the captive and his comrades with her father's money, "for [he] had so much he would not miss it" (De Cervantes, 2013, p. 302), and asks them to meet her in the garden. The reader now learns that "Moorish women do not allow themselves to be seen by any Moor or Turk, unless their husband or father bid them; with Christian captives they permit freedom of intercourse and communication, even more than might be considered proper" (De Cervantes, 2013, p. 304).

The scene is infused with terror when four Turks leap over the fence of the garden. "The old man was alarmed and Zoraida too, for the Moors commonly, and, so to speak, instinctively have a dread of the Turks, but particularly of the soldiers, who are so insolent and dominieering to the Moors who are under their power that they treat them worse than if they were their slaves" (De Cervantes, 2013, p. 307).

Cervantes' account of daily life in Algiers confirms that of his contemporary, Dr. de Sosa, in *Topography of Algiers*, and those of other slaves like Emmanuel d'Aranda (D'Aranda, 1997) and Joã Mascarenhas (Mascarenhas, 1993) a century later. Still, he does not reveal the secret of his survival, given that he attempted to escape four times, making one attempt each year, and that this would have surely exposed him to great risk of torture and death.

As a result, the reader is tempted to try to solve the mystery by imagining a romance between the one-armed slave and the woman presented as Zoraida (Garcés, 2002, p. 207). Her real name was Zahara and she was the daughter of Hadji Murad, a renegade Slavonic slave, governor of a fort near Oran and entrusted with carrying out many more or less secret alliances with the other side of the Mediterranean (De Cervantes, 2001, p. 1575). She was the granddaughter of a Christian slave from the Baleares, on her mother's side. Quite young, she became the widow of the Sultan of Morocco and married Hasan Pasha, the Bey of Algiers.

We might imagine that she could have fallen in love with a slave as alluring as Cervantes, could have permitted "freedom of [...] communication, even more than might be considered proper", and could have been able to persuade her ferocious husband, on several occasions, to spare his life. Be that as it may, Cervantes was determined to make her known, since he refers to her several times under her real name in *The Bagnios of Algiers*, one of the plays in the volume of plays published in 1619.

Escape

The escape episode is narrated from the tragic standpoint of a father betrayed by his only daughter, whom he "had loved so dearly". Seized, tied up, gagged and "not knowing how willingly she had placed herself in our hands (De Cervantes, 2013, p. 310), he only begins to understand in the ship that carries them away. Now the reader perceives the extent of Zoraida's violent desire to convert, a renegade to her religion, affirming her free will: "Allah knows that I could not do otherwise than I have done [...] so eagerly did my soul urge me on to the accomplishment of this purpose, which I feel to be as righteous as to thee, dear father, it seems wicked" (De Cervantes, 2013, p. 313).

A conversion on this side of the Mediterranean, but a disavowal beyond it: her father can only curse her decision. Once again, Cervantes presents opposing perspectives: "[...] it is only because she knows that immodesty is more freely practiced in your country than in ours [...]", cries her father. "Infamous girl, misguided maiden, whither in thy blindness and madness art thou going in the hands of these dogs, our natural enemies? Cursed be the hour when I begot thee! Cursed the luxury and indulgence in which I reared thee!" When he realises that she has truly crossed over to the side of the enemy, he jumps overboard. After being saved from drowning, as he is about to be set on the shore of a cape aptly called "*Cava rumia*", meaning "the wicked Christian woman" (De Cervantes, 2013, p. 312)—the one who betrayed Spain—he shouts maledictions followed by words of forgiveness. Again, Cervantes highlights the viewpoint of the adversary, avoiding any simplistic comparisons.

Since foes other than Turks and pirates from Algiers can be encountered at sea, the fugitives escape one danger only to run into another. Their vessel is attacked by French corsairs from La Rochelle, whose desires, fortunately, "do not go beyond money, but of that their covetousness is insatiable" (De Cervantes, 2013, p. 314). The trunk containing Zoraida's wealth is dropped into the sea before the pirates can discover it, for the future delight of marine archaeologists. After having taken from them "everything [they] had, as if they had been our bitterest enemies", the captain gave them a skiff in which to make the short voyage to the coast of Spain, near Malaga. Now, sudden oblivion sets in. "[...] on coming in sight of the Spanish coast [...], all our suffering and miseries were as completely forgotten as if they had never been endured by us, such is the delight of recovering lost liberty."

Seeing them appear suddenly, in Moorish dress, a shepherd cries out the warning which, almost unchanged, was still used not so long ago to frighten children on Greek and Italian shores: "The Moors—the Moors have landed! To arms, to arms!" (De Cervantes, 2013, p. 316). This cry warned of raids by pirates who, for three more centuries, continued to take shiploads of slaves on the shores of the Mediterranean.

But the cavalry, as Western films teach us, always comes to the rescue. One of the captives, taken from this coast, recognises his uncle on horseback, and learns that his family believes him dead. Happy endings where people are reunited, which abound in literature, are not always *deus ex machina* events, as we were taught in school. The return of the captive also signals the resurgence of the social link interrupted by slavery and hostage-taking, phenomena we would like to believe are in the past.

The inn, once a brothel, has become a place of refuge and alliance for refugees from political and domestic abuse, often considered commonplace. Abusive practices, which are in fact frequent, perpetrated by the Don Fernandos of the world, are likened here with human trafficking and hostage taking. Still, unexpectedly, the return of those we would rather forget in order to live undisturbed lives suddenly opens a space in which young, vibrant voices resonate with unheard-of tones which call forth unexpected harmonies.

Music!

A third group now arrives at the inn, composed of a judge of appeal, his daughter Clara and their servants. But the inn is full, despite its "discomfort and want of luxuries, for it is the way of roadside inns to be without them" (De Cervantes, 2013, p. 281). Indeed, the conditions of travel of that age forced the most refined ladies to content themselves with garrets no modern travel guide would dare recommend, even for the sake of local colour. Moreover, these scanty accommodations would soon have to hold another four servants, entrusted with finding the sixteen-year-old youth who has run away, disguised as a muleteer, to be with his beloved Clara.

When the "voice [...] musical and sweet" of this youth rose in the night singing "Love's mariner am I" (De Cervantes, 2013, p. 325), the young girl confessed to Dorothea her own love for the boy: "I have never spoken a word to him in my life; and for all that I love him so that I could not live without him."

This adolescent love song is the note on which was brought to an end the Quixotic enterprise of resuscitating "Joven" "in so detestable an age as we live in now". This song emerges as praise of Don Quixote's madness, which succeeded, with ingenuity and genius—words sharing a common Latin root—in bringing together over thirty people who had lost all hope of finding each other.

When he sees the judge, the captive's heart leaps in his chest, "telling him somehow that this was his brother" (De Cervantes, 2013, p. 320). He does not dare to approach him, fearing that "his brother, seeing him so poor, would be ashamed of him".

Don Quixote's knight-errantry is, in fact, the central element and hub of all these encounters. A source of stories to be told, it has gradually loosened tongues that had fallen silent, and has revived social links in danger of disappearing. The results are undeniable for once, since they can actually be counted.

Let us do the sums, starting with the initial foursome composed of Don Quixote, Sancho, Rocinante, and the ass, with Dulcinea, more present in thought than any other lady of one's thoughts could be; this procession followed by their ambulatory care assistants, the barber and the curate, to be relieved at home by the niece and the housekeeper. Then come Don Quixote's two patients, Cardenio and Dorothea, who are met at the inn by the enemy foursome composed of Don Fernando and his three accomplices, escorting the swooning Luscinda. Once they all reconcile, they can greet the captive and Zoraida, and their incredible story, followed by the judge holding his daughter Clara by the hand, with their attendants on horseback, and their servants, among whom is the young boy Don Luis, who ran away disguised as a muleteer, and who has four of his father's servants hard on his heels; and we must not forget the innkeeper, his wife, their daughter, Maritornes and, last but not least, the second despoiled barber who soon arrives and claims his barber's basin and his pack-saddle, to say nothing of the holy brotherhood and the whole crew launched in search of the scoundrel who freed the prisoners, together with the Devil and his clan.

A careful count shows at least thirty people gradually crowded into the inn, which comes to resemble the ship's cabin in the Marx Brother's movie *A Night at the Opera* (Wood, 1935), a space even smaller than the inn, into which an equivalent number of passengers is packed.

A remarkable achievement of knight-errantry, whose first sally was made in utter solitude! The reunion of the two brothers evokes the intensity of feeling Cervantes must have experienced when he was reunited with his brother Rodrigo, ransomed two years before Miguel. Perhaps his younger brother did not recognise him after five years of captivity, just as my father did not recognise his brother Emile at the Hotel Lutetia, when the latter returned from a concentration camp he refused to name.

The reunion of brothers separated for twenty-five years is artfully prepared, by means of a story which serves to avoid abruptness and protects the returning captive from shame, and from the fear that his successful brother may look down on him. The curate, never out of ideas, invents another scheme to test the feelings of the judge for his lost brother. He pretends to have been the captive's comrade in Constantinople. As he tells his story, the captive watches from a distance, to see the reaction of the brother who had not recognised him. Very soon, joy replaces apprehension. "The words the brothers exchanged, the emotion they showed can scarcely be imagined, I fancy, much less put down in writing" (De Cervantes, 2013, p. 323). "You would have had to live through it to understand it" is a phrase I heard a million times.

CHAPTER ELEVEN

Farewell to arms

"How to get rid of [him]?" (Ionesco, 1965)

Cervantes has one problem left to solve: how to end his book and get rid of its overly cumbersome hero who brought about all these miracles. Just as the curate discards the scenario he invented to bring the two brothers together, the author attempts to let go of the character he created. But Don Quixote has no intention to comply, and despite the fact that his father has reached a venerable age, being well over sixty, he will compel him to produce another five hundred pages, published ten years later, in 1615.

For the moment, the one who is the true author of all the events seen at the inn is content to stay in the background; as modest as his father, he claims no credit for any of them. "And there was Don Quixote observing all these strange proceedings attentively without uttering a word, and attributing the whole to chimeras of knight-errantry" (De Cervantes, 2013, p. 323). He does not take credit for the results of his work, any more than an analyst takes credit for the success of an analysis. In that case, what can be done with this "estrangement" in which he finds himself? Cervantes' answer is to send him back to madness, whence he came. Indeed, this appears to be a logical choice when we remember that the theatre of fools of that era was the precursor of analytic discourse.

As if sensing that he would be betrayed by his own friends, Don Quixote offers to stand guard outside the castle-inn, to protect them all from danger while they sleep. Very soon, all their "sufferings and miseries were as completely forgotten as if they had never been endured". Their joy is so great that they mock the one who freed them from their suffering, and who, in any case, has no desire for formal acknowledgement.

"[...] they gave the judge an account of his extraordinary humor, with which he was not a little amused." Still, we must admit that this amusement provided by madness in those times is preferable to the sinister reactions it automatically evokes in modern times. Today, the judge would no doubt have pulled a tranquiliser out of his pocket, or offered Don Quixote the name of a specialist to help him get rid of this "humor" which, let us not forget, brought him back his brother.

However, when Cervantes decides to do away with his hero, the options available are much more brutal, after all, than those of our pill-oriented world. Various strategies will be carried out mercilessly in order to discourage his main character from staying in the novel.

The strappado

The first attempt consists of transforming him, by means of a trick Maritornes and the innkeeper's daughter play on him, into one of those figures from Sicilian puppet theatre based on poems of chivalry. Hanging by a rope deviously tied around his wrist while he stands on Rocinante's back to try to hear the whispers of the two nit witted girls, he is suddenly transformed into a lovelorn puppet. Hanging in the air, "bellowing like a bull" (De Cervantes, 2013, p. 331), he was still tied up at dawn, when his horse moved, to smell another horse which had entered the courtyard of the inn with a group of servants sent in search of Don Luis. He was now suspended by the arm and his "agony [was such] that he believed either his wrist would be cut through or his arm torn off; [...] just like those undergoing the torture of the *strappado*, when they are fixed at 'touch and go'. [...] So loud [...] were the shouts of Don Quixote [that] Maritornes untied the halter by which [he] was suspended" (De Cervantes, 2013, pp. 332–333).

Knight-errantry, like psychoanalysis, can be rather torturing work—*tripalium*—for it sometimes falls into the trap of struggling hopelessly, when the interlocutor has slipped away. For the first time, Don Quixote is in the grip of despair. He proclaims in vain, as is his custom: "Whoever shall say that I have been enchanted with just cause, [...] I challenge him and defy him to single combat." No one takes up the challenge.

Once again he finds himself alone in the midst of all these people. There is no use protesting against the trick that turned him into a puppet; since the puppet is no longer amusing, no one pays it any heed. "The newly arrived travelers were amazed at [these] words; but the landlord removed their surprise by telling them who he was, and not to mind him as he was out of his senses". Even Sancho has abandoned him. "[...] buried in sleep and stretched upon the pack-saddle of his ass, [he] was oblivious, at that moment, of the mother that bore him."

Don Quixote's isolation, this time, is not comparable to that of Amadis doing penance on Poor Rock; the knight can more easily be compared to a furious Achilles fuming under his tent, "[seeing] that not one of the four travelers took any notice of him or replied to his challenge" (De Cervantes, 2013, p. 334). Not so naive after all, Don Quixote lets thieves leave the inn without paying, and even lets them beat the innkeeper, invoking a chivalric pretext formulated in these terms: "[...] it is not lawful for me to draw sword against persons of squirely condition" (De Cervantes, 2013, pp. 336–337). In truth, he is expressing his exasperation with stupidity.

For once, Don Quixote and Cervantes agree, considering that there is no use casting pearls before swine. "But let us leave him there; for he will surely find someone to help him, and if not, let him suffer and hold his tongue who attempts more than his strength allows him to do; and let us go back fifty paces [...]." The tracking shot moves backward.

The sottie

Without knowing it, Cervantes is already foreseeing his second novel, which was going to place emphasis on a variety of theatrical forms, like Master Peter's puppet show (De Cervantes, 2013, p. 542). Thus, Cervantes' second strategy to get rid of his hero is to place him on stage, to face judgement in a morality play. In a mock trial, we encounter the fools named Barber number one and Barber number two, and await the decision that officially recognises the second barber's basin—stolen in Chapter XXI—as Membrin's helmet.

After this, objects run the show and wreak havoc in the world. The trial degenerates into a full-fledged brawl, masterfully directed by the author, who takes great pleasure in perturbing the symmetry of the amorous coupling and in breaking off the lachrymose cooing which fills the inn.

When Barber number two arrives at the inn, he immediately confronts those who stole from him, demanding that they return his basin and packsaddle. Barber number one, followed by his accomplice, the curate, decides "to back up [Don Quixote's] delusion and carry on the joke for the general amusement" (De Cervantes, 2013, p. 340). Therefore, they initiate a naming procedure, to rename the packsaddle and the basin, and call them caparison and helmet.

In France, a century earlier, this theatre of fools brought fame to Villon, Marot, Pierre Gringoire, and André de la Vigne, (Zumthor, 1978) and produced marvellous physical and linguistic juggling or mock trials called sotties, in which, through a veritable rapture of polyphonic virtuosity, Mother Folly and her henchmen would judge abusive people and get even.

From the start, Barber number one, the curate's acolyte, produces his credentials in the barber's art: he has had a license to practice for over twenty years, and is proficient with barber's implements, having probably been an army surgeon. "I was likewise a soldier for some time in the days of my youth, and I know also what a helmet is, and a morion". After that, he starts to quibble, saying that "this piece we have now before us, [...] not only is no barber's basin, but is as far from being one as white is from black, and truth from falsehood; I say, moreover, that this, although it is a helmet, is not a complete helmet." It is one of the functions of the sottie to restore the word, by mocking the way the "establishment" can twist it out of shape.

Although the lesson is farcical, it retains its linguistic value. Thus, Barber number one demonstrates that signifiers acquire conventional uses disconnected from the objects they signify. As for us, we are free to call analytic discourse in a context of trauma and madness "Quixotic", as long as this becomes the agreed-upon usage among our peers. How do we bring this about? Let us begin.

Validation by the scientific community is crucial. Why should physicists be free to give their particles preposterous names, while the same right is refused to analysts, and even to Don Quixote, who invented new paradigms that disturb the space-time conception of normalcy in order to let other dimensions emerge?

In the matter of the renaming of the objects discussed, Don Fernando strives to obtain the collective agreement of those present in the inn. To do this, he carries out, in secret, an electoral campaign, admittedly somewhat corrupt. Nobody is perfect, as Marilyn Monroe declares at the end of *Some Like it Hot* (Wilder, 1959)—and things are about to get hot. To put an end to this lesson in the trappings of knight-errantry, Barber number 1 gave his colleague Barber number 2 "eight *reales* for the basin, and the barber executed a full receipt of engagement to make no further demand then or thenceforth for evermore, amen" (De Cervantes, 2013, p. 346).

No doubt, such a renaming process requires colossal energy. It is not easy to reintroduce into the symbolic exchange that which cruelty or scorn has taken away. In fact, Don Quixote is ready to knight Sancho for the gallantry with which he defended the noble signifier "harness", instead of the specific designation "packsaddle", associated with an ass, which Barber number two would rather have chosen. "[…] highly pleased to see his squire's stoutness, both offensive and defensive, and from that time forth he reckoned him a man of mettle, and in his heart resolved to dub him a knight on the first opportunity that presented itself" (De Cervantes, 2013, p. 338).

Let us place this naming process in context. In fact, it corresponds to the vital need, for Don Quixote, to recover the name of the father, together with the barber's basin used as an emblem. "As regards the assertion that this is a basin and not a helmet I have already given an answer; but as to the question whether this is a packsaddle or a caparison I will not venture to give a positive opinion, but will leave it to your worships' better judgement" (De Cervantes, 2013, p. 341). Far from acting like a fanatic, he concedes that with the exception of the signifiers which matter to him, everyone is free to call things by whatever name he wishes. "Perhaps as you are not dubbed knights like myself, the enchantments of this place have nothing to do with you, and your faculties are unfettered, and you can see things in this castle as they really and truly are, and not as they appear to me".

Hellzapoppin! (Potter, 1941)

Now, everything could have gone smoothly had it not been for the law enforcement officers of the Santa Hermandad, who arrived at the inn and created even greater havoc than they had on a previous occasion. An archer of the Brotherhood, of whom it is said that "he was not a quick reader", felt compelled to contribute his two cents to this highly intellectual discussion. He threw oil on the fire by affirming: "It is a packsaddle as sure as my father is my father, and whoever has said or will say anything else must be drunk" (De Cervantes, 2013, p. 342).

This is all it took to start a general brawl, after Don Quixote almost stretched the archer flat on the ground with his pike, so that soon "the whole inn was nothing but cries, shouts, shrieks, confusion, terror, dismay, mishaps, sword cuts, fisticuffs, cudgelings, kicks, and bloodshed" (De Cervantes, 2013, p. 343). Young Don Luis takes advantage of the confusion to escape from the servants sent by his father to bring him back.

Once more, Cervantes comes close to inventing filmmaking. His third attempt at getting rid of his character, by knocking him out, turns to the hero's advantage again. Not only does he find renewed energy, but he discovers the supreme role of his chivalric calling. The ultimate referee in this muddled entanglement, "Don Quixote took it into his head that he had been plunged into the thick of the discord of Argramante's camp". The first stage of the peace process: "[...] at length the uproar was stilled for the present; the packsaddle remained a caparison till the day of judgement, and the basin a helmet and the inn a castle in Don Quixote's imagination. [...] Thus by the authority of Agramante and the wisdom of King Sobrino all this complication of disputes was arranged" (De Cervantes, 2013, pp. 343–344). Agramante and King Sobrino, in Ariosto's epic poem Raging Roland, were worthy Saracen leaders who succeeded in appeasing a discord sent into their camp by the archangel Michael, while they were besieging Charlemagne in Paris.

But, of course, this kind of respite is usually short-lived, for the Devil never sleeps. "[...] but the enemy of concord and hater of peace, feeling himself slighted and made a fool of [...], resolved to try his hand once more by stirring up fresh quarrels and disturbances." One of the officers of the Brotherhood has turned out to be a policeman carrying a description of Don Quixote, who is to be arrested as a delinquent.

But the hero, rendered invulnerable by the magical helmet made of the same symbolic metal as the fool's cap, now wears on his head the heraldic figure of a name of the father. For this reason, any attack on his honour makes him go berzerk. "[…] worked up to the highest pitch of wrath, and all his joints cracking with rage, with both hands [he] seized the officer by the throat with all his might", indignant and showering insults on the agents of law and public order. "Come now, base, ill-born brood; call ye it highway robbery to give freedom to those in bondage […]? Infamous beings!"

Here, Don Quixote, like Anigone, is engaged in the uncompromising battle to defend unwritten laws. For the sake of avoiding even greater disaster, the peace process brings about a remarkable resolution. "The curate settled all amicably, and Don Fernando paid", the least he could do to show his contrition, after all, and "it was universal opinion that their thanks were due to the great zeal and eloquence of the curate, and to the unexampled generosity of Don Fernando". Not a peep about Don Quixote; he has disappeared from the scene.

Entrapment

The preceding episode is a perfect illustration of what it means to save a situation. The consensus, as usual, supports political appropriation by the former tyrant of the hero's efforts. As for the hero, he doesn't care.

Thus, Cervantes has attempted for the second time to get rid of his character by recourse to the manipulation of public opinion. But Don Quixote refuses to yield and he exhausts his author with his constant desire to rekindle the spark of adventures for which there is no longer any need. He urges Dorothea to accompany him "in quest of fair fortune" (De Cervantes, 2013, p. 347), declaring that "in delay there is danger", when in fact there is no more danger anywhere. Therefore, his calls to action remain unheeded. "[…] and as neither heaven has created nor hell seen any that can daunt or intimidate me, saddle Rocinante, Sancho, […] and let us take leave […] this very instant" (De Cervantes, 2013, p. 348). What can persuade him to lay down arms?

This time, it is clear that Cervantes counts on Sancho's collaboration in dispelling his master's illusions, by revealing that the lady Micomicona is not a queen, "no more so than my mother" (De Cervantes, 2013, p. 348), for he has seen her billing and cooing in dark corners with Don Fernando. But his arguments are in vain. They are brushed aside, as are all assaults on the agency of the Lady, which meet with an onslaught of insults too lengthy to reproduce here.

Instead of making a discreet exit, Don Quixote turns into a demon: "he knitted his brows, puffed out his cheeks, gazed around him, and stamped on the ground violently with his right foot, showing [...] the rage that was pent up in his heart" (De Cervantes, 2013, p. 349). Feeling hopeless this time, Dorothea does not try to deny the facts. She just convinces Don Quixote to forgive Sancho, without taking "the trouble of going back with [them] to [their] village" (De Cervantes, 2013, p. 350).

Still, the problem remains: how to get rid of the damned knight? If he will not leave willingly, like it or not, he must be made to leave by force. The plan elaborated by the curate to trap him took two days to be carried out, the time needed "[to arrange] with the owner of an oxcart who happened to be passing that way to [construct] a kind of cage with wooden bars, large enough to hold Don Quixote comfortably".

Thus, Cervantes has decided that the best way to eliminate such a tenacious survivor is to reduce him to the condition of a savage man or a wild beast, on the pretext of a medical condition. The declared objective is to "take his madness in hand at home".

The forceful internment is carried out by masked men. "[...] by the directions and advice of the curate, [they] covered their faces and disguised themselves [...]. This done, in profound silence they entered the room where he was sleeping tranquilly." Covered faces to induce terror is a strategy still in vogue today, as we all know: "[...] they seized him firmly and bound him fast and and foot [... and] bringing in the cage, they shut him up in it and nailed the bars so firmly that they could not be easily burst open."

The classic brainwashing techniques follow: sensory and cognitive dissonances which torture the mind: "They then took him on their shoulders, and as they passed out of the room an awful voice—as much so as the barber [...] was able to make it—was heard" (De Cervantes, 2013, p. 351).

Waking with a start, Don Quixote "was unable to move, and could only marvel and wonder at the strange figures [...] which his crazed fancy conjured up before him". Of course, the craziest fancies are not those self-important people believe. Their perverse plan did not allow for the slightest improvisation. Everything unfolded "precisely [as] the curate, the concocter of the scheme, expected would happen". Indeed, the supremely stupid scheme against one of the most brilliant minds of

La Mancha was very carefully devised. Then "the apparitions lifted the cage upon their shoulders and fixed it upon the oxcart" (De Cervantes, 2013, p. 352).

But this time, contrary to the book burning episode, the capture is not unwitnessed: Sancho, who is no fool, decodes the trickery by trusting his senses which do "not fail to perceive who all these disguised figures [are]". Instinctively going underground, "he did not dare to open his lips until he saw what came of this assault and capture of his master". He looks at all these apparitions with suspicion, for they do not even smell of brimstone, as they would if they were devils. On the contrary, "one smells of amber half a league off"—as is befitting to a Spanish grandee. The squire recognises Don Fernando, "who, like a gentleman of his rank, was very likely perfumed as Sancho said".

In this mortal extremity, in the cart of infamy reminiscent of the Knight of the Cart (De Troyes, 1997), Don Quixote holds on to the only solid value left, that of the given word, and concentrates on his promise of paying Sancho's wages, a sum established "not by his many faithful services, but by the means at my disposal". In any case, his will is already made, and in return he relies "upon [Sancho's] goodness and rectitude", trusting that the squire will not abandon him in good or evil fortune, as indeed he has not done so far.

The immediate mobilisation of the plural body prevents Don Quixote from becoming dejected. Very resistant to brainwashing, he starts to dream of another, more rapid and more elegant way of being carried off than in an oxcart, at the pace of such slow animals. For the second time, he invents aviation. "[…] never yet have I read, seen, or heard of their carrying off enchanted knights-errant in this fashion, or at the slow pace that these lazy, sluggish animals promise; for they always take them away through the air with marvelous swiftness, enveloped in a dark thick cloud" (De Cervantes, 2013, p. 353). In technical language, this is called flying blind. "[…] or on a chariot of fire, or it may be on some hippogriff or other beast of the kind." While he is at it, he also invents fighter planes, the exterior of their cabins decorated with fantastic beasts like tigers, dolphins, chimeras or other hippogriffs.

But Sancho, firmly rooted in his century, is convinced the enchantment is humbug. He does his best to make Don Quixote perceive his actual sensations, despite the deliberate obfuscation. As rigorously arranged as a march to the scaffold, the procession is set in motion in this order: first the cart, on which "Don Quixote was seated in the cage, with his hands tied and his feet stretched out, leaning against the bars as silent and as patient as if he were a stone statue and not a man of flesh", at each side the officers of the Brotherhood, then Sancho on his ass following behind, leading Rocinante by the bridle, and at the end of the procession "came the curate and the barber on their mighty mules, with faces covered, and a grave and serious air" (De Cervantes, 2013, p. 355).

Books of chivalry are dead, long live books of chivalry!

Of course, the marvellous adventure has to end sooner or later.

The transferential apparatus is worn and exhausted, but still alive. Looking jaundiced and emaciated in his madman's cage, the hero has not given up. The undestructible Dulcinea remains, in and of herself, the destination of his thoughts, always vitally present in his worn-out body. Sancho, riding close to Don Quixote on his ass, is more faithful than ever to his master. Soon, he would fight to defend him tooth and nail, and later, before his wife who is not one to mince words, he would defend errant psychoanalysis using statistical arguments. "[…] there is nothing in the world more delightful than to be a person of considera-tion, squire to a knight-errant, and a seeker of adventures. To be sure […], out of a hundred, ninety-nine will turn out cross and contrary. Still, for all that […]" (De Cervantes, 2013, p. 387).

But for all that, the transference apparatus—not at all eradicated—has preserved a crucial element. The ghosts of the burnt bodies of books of chivalry have not given up either. For the grand finale, on the arid soil of La Mancha, they are reborn like another Phoenix—nickname of the great poet Lope de Vega—"when you least expect it". Wandering souls of warriors-errant, the books continue to show their therapeutic efficiency until the end of the novel, even and especially when they are cursed.

Don Quixote never lets this point be disputed. To provide a gran-diose ending to "the book of books"—as Laurence Sterne calls his *Tristram*, a hero in the line of the knight—Cervantes stages a situation of enslavement he has experienced many times in Algiers. Tied up, una-ble to move, he preserved his spirit by conversing with fellow captives who, like himself, had a passion for reading. Doctor de Sosa , author of "A Topography of Algiers", was one of them (Garcés, 2002, p. 98).

This time, his interlocutor is a canon of Toledo, whom Cervantes brings onto the scene just in time, as he is about to overtake the slow procession. Witnessing the extent of the mistreatment inflicted on the hero, he reacts as Don Quixote did when he saw young Andrés mistreated by his master; he expresses surprise at seeing a man carried like "some desperate highwayman" (De Cervantes, 2013, p. 355).

The contest begins with Don Quixote's traditional challenge, this time on expertise pertaining to books of chivalry: "Haply, gentlemen, you are versed and learned in matters of errant chivalry? Because if you are I will tell you my misfortunes; if not, there is no good in my giving myself the trouble of relating them." He has learned from experience that it's no use talking to people who don't understand anything. Given the state in which he finds himself, in order to survive he must save his energy for more essential things.

To his surprise, the canon takes up the challenge: "In truth, brother, I know more about books of chivalry than I do about Villalpando's elements of logic." Villalpando taught theology at the University of Alcala de Henares, near Madrid, where today Cervantes' house can be seen by visitors. Now we witness the presentation of a dissertation in due form: thesis, antithesis, synthesis, which would do justice to any student of this university defending a PhD thesis on books of chivalry. It is a serious matter, since the entire content of the novel is at stake. As a concession to the solemnity of the occasion, Cervantes reduces the harshness of his son's treatment, since defending literature and the spirit of chivalry is their shared priority. Therefore, it is important for Don Quixote to be able to stand up and recover all his intellectual and sensory faculties, free of the torture inflicted on him.

Physical and emotional liberation

Sancho liberates his master's reasoning faculties, starting with the ones rooted in the body. He begins by unmasking the barber and the curate. "Ah, señor curate, señor curate! Do you think I don't guess and see the drift of these new enchantments? Well, then, I can tell you I know you, for all your face is covered, and I can tell you I am up to you, however you may hide your tricks" (De Cervantes, 2013, p. 357). Unmasked, the barber threatens to place Sancho in the cage as well, telling him: "[…] you are of the same fraternity as your master". But Sancho is not intimidated: "I am [not] a man to let myself be got with child, if it was by the King himself. Though I am poor I am an old Christian, and I owe nothing to nobody."

In surprisingly prophetic fashion, he reminds the barber-surgeon that medicine should not treat patients like things. "Mind how you talk, master barber, for shaving is not everything, and there is some difference between Peter and Peter." Thus, he makes the travelling canon and his servants witnesses to the situation. "I have said all this […] only to urge [you] to lay to your conscience [the] ill-treatment of my master" (De Cervantes, 2013, p. 357).

But to no avail. There is no reasoning with narrow-minded people, even if they are educated and respectable. Seeing this clearly, Sancho also perceives the real reason for the sadism deployed against his master's madness: stupid and bitter enviousness aroused by his freedom of thought. "After all, where envy reigns virtue cannot live", says Sancho, echoing his master's opinion that "such things never happen to knights of little renown and fame, because nobody in the world thinks about them; to valiant knights they do, for these are envied for their virtue and valor by many princes and other knights who compass the destruction of the worthy by base means" (De Cervantes, 2013, p. 354). This interpretation seems delusional, unless its basis in reality can be proven.

Sancho takes it upon himself to provide proof in a final venture which reveals not only the key to the mystery of the enchantments, but also the cognitive distortions created to make Don Quixote lose his wits. Starting with the book burning episode, Don Quixote has used the term "enchanters" to designate a "secret society in broad daylight" (Arendt, 1951, p. 414) which is attempting to control him. The squire informs his master of the subterfuge. "Señor, […] these two here, with their faces covered, are the curate of our village and the barber; and I suspect they have hit upon this plan of carrying you off in this fashion, out of pure envy […]; and if this be the truth it follows that you are not enchanted, but hoodwinked and made a fool of" (De Cervantes, 2013, p. 365).

Once proclaimed, this truth, not so easy to accept, is supported by a quasi-Socratic dialogue: "And to prove this I want to ask you one thing; and if you answer me as I believe you will answer, you will be able to lay your finger on the trick, and you will see that you are not enchanted but gone wrong in your wits." It took Sancho some time to ask the question, for it relates to body image and to sensations that the masked schemers have deliberately perturbed, anesthetising hunger, pain, and even the need to relieve oneself.

You nasty thing! Pooh pooh!

In an analysis, becoming aware of having been had by villains, as is often the case, is always a rude awakening. Often the delusions take stronger hold, as the confrontation with Cardenio has shown. So in this instance Don Quixote maintains his version at all costs, be it complete denial of reality, rather than be seen as hoodwinked and a fool. "[...] it is very possible that they may seem to be those same persons; but that they are so in reality and in fact, believe it not on my account; what thou art to believe and think is that, if they look like them, as thou sayest, it must be that those who have enchanted me have taken this shape and likeness" (De Cervantes, 2013, p. 365).

The same is true of fraudulent beliefs fostered by totalitarianism regimes, when the most enlightened minds accept outrageous lies despite evidence to the contrary. Anything is better than admitting that one has been had. Sancho's work consists of replacing falsehoods with the concrete reality of a sensation so basic and undeniable that even babies experience it.

He describes the reigning ideology as a cardboard fabrication, having more to do with "malice [...] than enchantment". Proof of this will be based on a return to the bodily certainties. Sancho forces Don Quixote to acknowledge, when the latter is running at full speed "in his head"—as one does when one has lost touch with one's body and tries to make sense of fallacious nonsense. Appealing to his master's "goodness and truth", he asks "speaking with all reverence, whether since your worship has been shut up and, as you think, enchanted in this cage, you have felt any desire or inclination to go anywhere, as the saying is?" (De Cervantes, 2013, p. 366).

But one does not discard devitalising absurdities so readily in order to recover sensations, as Don Quixote innocently admits: "I do not understand 'going anywhere', explain thyself more clearly, Sancho, [...]."

Sancho repeats his question patiently, placing the discussion at the level of nursery school: "Why, the schoolboys know that from the time they were babes. Well then, you must know I mean have you had any desire to do what cannot be avoided?" It is only then, after the aptly-named Panza (equivalent of "belly") has brought him back to his own body, that the knight understands, coming out of his artificially induced haze and acknowledging his sensations. "Ah! Now I understand thee, Sancho. Yes, often and even this minute; get me out of this strait, or all will not go right." Quite a lesson for anyone who must escape from deadly ideologies which rely on sensory manipulation!

Escape, then, is the second step. Sancho has broken through the identification with the aggressor which had paralysed his master: "Aha, I have caught you. This is what in my heart and soul I was longing to know." Don Quixote resists, once again in classical fashion, since abandoning his theory would force him to admit that he was infantilised. "I know and feel that I am enchanted, and that is enough to ease my conscience." But Sancho insists, remaining firm—as is sometimes necessary at a certain point in an analysis, when the unknown is frightening and it seems best to stay in a drug-induced torpour—for there is no time to lose: "[...] it would be well if your worship were to try to get out of this prison, and I promise to do all in my power to help, and even to take you out of it". He exhorts the knight to mount again his "good Rocinante, who seems to be enchanted too, he is so melancholy and dejected" (De Cervantes, 2013, p. 367). His proposition includes even the vector of transference.

In effect, it is urgent to reactivate the psychodynamic apparatus neutralised by perverts. Don Quixote finally realises that he and his buddy must stick together, and decides to trust Sancho, who has taken the lead. "I am content to do as thou sayest, brother Sancho, and when thou seest an opportunity for effecting my release I will obey thee absolutely." Negotiations with the hostage-takers are based on the argument that "the prison might not be as clean as propriety [...] requires". Sancho offers to guarantee the knight's return, and promises the curate to answer for his not running away. The curate relents, encouraged by the canon, who is delighted to converse with Don Quixote, particularly if he gives his word as a knight not to leave without consent. "I give it", answers Don Quixote, who had listened to all this.

The canon then proceeds, solemnly, to free the captive; he "took his hand, tied together as they both were", a gesture still charged with emotion for Cervantes. Don Quixote "rejoiced beyond measure" and went to his steed. He passes his exaltation on to Rocinante, "giving him a couple of slaps on the haunches [and saying] 'I still trust [...], O flower and mirror of steeds, that we shall see ourselves, both of us, as we wish to be'". This desire for freedom, that no secret plot can suppress, is what leads Don Quixote to defend Cervantes' true theory on books of chivalry, no matter what anybody says.

Cervantes' theory on books of chivalry

The theory uses the three elements of rhetoric in a scene involving four characters: the canon of Toledo, the curate, Sancho, and Don Quixote. Before the knight was freed, he had a brief exchange with the canon, who, upon his arrival, presented himself as a knowledgeable lover of books of chivalry. Both of them agreed that the renown of these books equals that of "all the magicians of Persia, or Brahmans that India, or Gymnosophists that Ethiopia ever produced". Such was their erudition.

Their dialogue has reached a spiritual level soon to be interrupted by the curate, anxious to gain the canon to his cause. That is when Sancho intervened to reveal the scheming and trickery. "Well, sirs, [...] the fact of the matter is, my master, Don Quixote, is just as much enchanted as my mother. He is in his full senses, he eats and he drinks, and he has his calls like other men" (De Cervantes, 2013, p. 356). The truth uttered by the *gracioso* was quickly denied by the barber, who did not want to answer Sancho "lest by his plain speaking he should disclose what the curate and he himself were trying so hard to conceal". Forced to give the canon an explanation, the curate led him away from the others "so that he might tell him the mystery of this man in the cage, and other things that would amuse him" (De Cervantes, 2013, p. 357). Shared amusement creates greater complicity.

Now, two paradigms confront each other: on one side the transferential apparatus of fools, and on the other the medicine of the clergy, which the canon might be expected to represent. He is given a very succinct description of Don Quixote's case. "The canon [...] listened with attention to the account of the character, life, madness, and ways of Don Quixote." The semiology and "moral treatment" of the case are presented in academic fashion: "[...] the beginning and origin of his craze [...], together with the plan they had of taking him home to try if by any means they could discover a cure for his madness."

Again, for the umpteenth time, we hear the same refrain. The cause of Don Quixote's madness is to be found in books of chivalry, whose medieval obscurantism causes softening of the brain. At first, the canon agrees with this opinion; being a defender of reason, he considers "what they call books of chivalry to be mischevious to the State. But he confesses having given in to "idle and false taste", and having "read the beginnings of almost all that have been printed", without managing "to read any one of them from beginning to end". Finally, he comes to the same conclusion as the curate, saying that these books should be condemned in the name of what seventeenth century French theatre has begun to call the rules of verisimilitude and propriety.

Outright assassination of medieval literature follows.These novels "are harsh in their style, incredible in their achievements, licentious in their amours, uncouth in their courtly speeches, prolix in their battles, silly in their arguments, absurd in their travels". Not much is needed, after this, to declare that "they deserve to be banished from the Christian commonwealth as a worthless breed" (De Cervantes, 2013, p. 359). This small, but devilishly Platonic, step is promptly taken by the two learned characters.

The curate welcomes the canon's assessment, seeing him now as an ally. Certain that they are "on the same side", he impetuously confesses his iconoclastic deeds. "[…] so he told him that, being of the same opinion himself, and bearing a grudge to books of chivalry, he had burned all Don Quixote's, which were many."

Here, the Castilian proverb applies once again: "Though the treason may please, the traitor is hated." The canon "was amused", but did not fail to notice the curate's stupidity.

Antithesis

"[…] the canon [added] that though he had said so much in condemnation of these books, still he found one good thing in them". The good thing, which is useful on the spot, is that they provide an escape from the curate's inanity. The canon now praises the freedom of writing and "the opportunity [these books] afforded to a gifted intellect for displaying itself; for they presented a wise and spacious field over which the pen might range freely". We recognise again the vital desire to open the field—wide, spacious, airy—of the sea, the mountain, offering physical, emotional, heuristic, and creative adventures.

Aware of the difference between himself and his colleague, the canon admits that he is not speaking solely as a reader, but also as a writer.

"I myself was once tempted to write a book of chivalry [...]; and if I must own the truth I have more than a hundred pages written." But he did not pursue this good start, finding it inconsistent with his profession, but above all because he had no desire "to submit [...] to the stupid judgement of the silly public". But let us be wary: the silly public is right there, embodied by the two imbeciles in front of him.

He has no doubt tried his hand at depicting nautical adventures like *The Trials of Persiles and Sigismunda* (De Cervantes, 2009), Cervantes' posthumous work, which slips into the novel through an allusion. The canon explains that authors are free to "[describe] shipwrecks, tempests, combats, battles, portraying a valiant captain", and the inevitable beauteous lady, the muse who inspires all styles of literature. The unrestricted scope of writing "enables the author to show his powers, epic, lyric, tragic, or comic [...]; for the epic may be written in prose just as well as in verse" (De Cervantes, 2013, pp. 359–360).

Indifferent to epic poetry, the curate understands not a word of this laudatory discourse. "It is as you say, señor canon", said the curate, "and for that reason those who have hitherto written books of the sort deserve all the more censure". Throughout Chapter XLVIII, the discussion focuses on playwriting which had initially brought Cervantes success some twenty years earlier, when *La Galatea* was published, but later led to disappointment. Overshadowed by Lope de Vega's nova comedia, the plays written after *Don Quixote* were never performed. Jean Canavaggio's hypothesis (Canavaggio, 1977) is that Cervantes' theatre was ahead of its time.

Prevented from being staged by the cultural policies of his era, Cervantes' theatrical ingenuity will triumph in The Second Part of *Don Quixote*, where Don Quixote uses different genres such as an *auto sacramental*, puppet theatre, short *entremes*, plays involving machines, musical comedies, farces, morality plays, and even the dreary theatre of political trials.

Nevertheless, for the moment, the situation is critical; the book is coming to an end and Don Quixote is more determined than ever to go on. In this desperate situation, an unthinkable scheme starts to take shape in Cervantes' mind (this, at least, is what I think): why not make his character disappear behind the screen of a seminar, which he compels him to give, to defend his thesis against stupidity for centuries to come?

Don Quixote's seminar on books of chivalry

The topic of the seminar is obvious. Are books of chivalry, or are they not, the cause of the knight's madness? In other words, should Don Quixote be kept away from poetry and fancy? After a debate between the canon, a sharp-witted critic, and the curate, a dim-witted dunce, Don Quixote tends first to the matter of expelling waste. "[…] he withdrew to a retired spot, from which he came back much relieved and more eager than ever to put his squire's scheme into execution" (De Cervantes, 2013, p. 368). Then he appointed Sancho moderator, and even speaker in the intellectual joust that was about to take place.

Both physically and emotionally relieved, Don Quixote conversed with the canon brilliantly, drawing admiration from all those who listened. "The canon gazed at him, wondering at the extraordinary nature of his madness, and that in all remarks and replies he should show such excellent sense, and only lose his stirrups, as has been already said, when the subject of chivalry was broached." An improvised symposium is about to take place. The canon invites the entire party to stop at a pleasant green spot to listen to their discussion. "And so, moved by compassion, he said to him, as they all sat on the green grass awaiting the arrival of provisions: […]" (De Cervantes, 2013, p. 368).

Ouch! The speaker is off to a bad start. The organisers of the symposium should have included in their preliminary address the warning that madness in general and Don Quixote in particular are not likely to respond well to a pitying or compassionate tone. And for good reason. The condescending sympathy shown to psychic suffering is a poor cover-up for the rejection of madness with its combative intelligence. In short, the "all is well, we don't want any trouble" attitude is the one shown by the canon, who adopts a pacific approach intended to promote neutrality and objectivity.

Like a good positivist, but in contrast with Auguste Comte—who was Quixotic enough to claim that his philosophy had its roots in the attack of madness he experienced in his youth, and which made him run away from Dr Esquirol's clinic (Gouhier, 1997, pp. 142–159) against medical advice—the canon develops a scientific argument for the search for historical truth. "Is it possible, gentle sir, that the nauseous and idle reading of books of chivalry can have had such an effect on your worship as to upset your reason so that you fancy yourself enchanted, and the like, all as far from the truth as falsehood itself is?"

The goal of the symposium is very ambitious. It intends to establish the status of myth and epic writing in regard to the truth. To illustrate his position, the canon chooses Amadis—a fortunate choice!

In prophetic anticipation of modern school programs, the cleric goes so far as to imagine stripping the classrooms and the cabinets which contain these books. "I fling the very best of them at the wall, and would fling it into the fire if there were one at hand, as richly deserving such punishment as cheats and impostors." He is clearly no advocate of the opium of the people. These books, he says, are "teachers that lead the ignorant public to believe and accept as truth all the folly they contain".

Then, treating Don Quixote like a doctoral student, he quickly draws up a list of serious and accurate history books, as a suitable bibliography: the book of Judges about the wars of Israel at the time of early settlements in Palestine in the twelfth and eleventh centuries BC, Julius Caesar's War of the Gauls, the exploits of Valencia's El Cid Campeador, Rodrigo Diaz de Bivar; those of Garcilaso de la Vega, the ancestor of the writer, and so on. Don Quixote listened with the greatest attention to the canon's words, and when he found he had finished, after regarding him for some time, he replied to him. This focused reflection traditionally precedes combat.

As usual, the knight does not beat around the bush by using scholastic arguments, and gets straight to the point. In summary, he deduces that the canon's discourse "is intended to persuade me that there never were any knights-errant in the world, and that all the books of chivalry are false, lying, mischievous and useless to the State, and that I have done wrong in reading them, and worse in believing them, and still worse in imitating them" (De Cervantes, 2013, pp. 369–370).

Once again, the dialogue becomes truly Socratic. "[…] you deny that there ever were Amadises of Gaul or of Greece, or any other of the knights of whom the books are full". The canon agrees, falling into a trap of his own making. "It is all exactly as you state it."

These premises will serve as the foundation of a rigorous discussion intending to prove that myth and the epic tale are crucibles for truth. It is important to consider them not in terms of their likelihood, but in terms of their practical and symbolic efficiency, to revive speech when it has been betrayed, through *mythos* and *epos*, which both mean speech in ancient Greek.

Myths and epic tales shed light on different facets of the same psychodynamic process, depending on the language game being played.

This process is epic when it refers to human history, and is mythical at other times, when it deals with surviving images which haunt us. The name of the goddess of Fate, Atê, comes from the verb *aô*, which means to drive somebody mad—and this kind of madness is indeed transmitted from one generation to another, as a duty to overcome fate.

The confusion always made is between the mythical origin of the symptoms—a stain, *mancha*, inaccessible by definition—and the epic, sometimes tragi-comic way of making it through, which most often takes the form of a joust—*agon*.

As the loyal son of an elite soldier, Don Quixote aims straight at the target, at the confusion between the so-called objective cause of madness and its intersubjective aim, that of inscribing denied truths between people. "You also went on to say that books of this kind had done me much harm, inasmuch as they had upset my senses, and shut me up in a cage, and that it would be better for me to reform and change my studies, and read other truer books." He then goes on to demonstrate that such a confusion is deliberately fostered to prevent madness from producing knowledge.

What kind of knowledge are we talking about? Don Quixote places himself resolutely outside the realm of academic knowledge collected in libraries for the learned, where the cleric expects to confront him. He focuses at the same time on an excess of knowledge which makes one crazy, bringing on a madness "owing to some ancient blood-guiltiness" and which must be "[considered] in every light", as Socrates says in the *Phaedrus* (Plato, 2003). For this reason, he valiantly defends the therapeutic use of myths and epic tales, for those who have been changed by certain events.

To bring someone out of depersonification, an epic song is needed, whose rhythm animates the body and the memory. As Martin Cooperman, analyst of madness at Austen Riggs says: "I have seen more than I can see, and nothing I have read can do justice to what I have lived." A survivor of the Pacific War, he had been aboard the sunk aircraft carrier *The Wasp* and spoke like my father, a veteran of the same age, who interrupted me while I was stubbornly trying to write this book:

> Do you think you can say it?
> Do you think you can say it like it was?
> Do you think you can face it? And the tax collector—although
> they are not my favourite people—whom they were forcing

> to run, and the young German they were forcing to fire, who
> was wetting his pants and was the same age as your sons are
> now … It's impossible to describe.

Once again, he was getting angry one night, in the Alps, during the interval between Christmas and New Year, when I was toiling on at my *Don Quixote*. "My word, she is writing again!", while in the crispness of the air around him he still heard the echoes of voices refusing to be erased by objective reports. "But it's no use, they all had false names anyway."

School for advanced studies in epic sciences

The discussion becomes more heated. Don Quixote launches a sudden counter-attack. Sword drawn, he defends the epic tale. "[…] to my mind it is you who are the one that is out of his wits and enchanted, as you have ventured to utter such blasphemies against a thing so universally acknowledged and accepted as true that whoever denies it, as you do, deserves the same punishment which you say you inflict on the books that irritate you when you read them" (De Cervantes, 2013, p. 370).

The canon is accused of the crime of negationinsm, of denying proven facts. In truth, the psychotherapy of trauma is evident, even in "foreign realms". Myths and epic tales proved themselves therapeutic long before Wittgenstein attacked ethnologist James Frazer with Quixotic fervour, accusing him of being "much more savage than most of his savages, for they are not as far removed from the understanding of spiritual matters as a twentieth-century Englishman" (Wittgenstein, 1979a, p. 67).

Therefore, Don Quixote's criticism becomes virulent, and his attack against the canon merciless, since the knight judges him to be out of touch with actual events. His demonstration is built on a comparative analysis of history and literature, displaying remarkable erudition.

Having come to the end of his journey, out of the cage where he was imprisoned for the freedom of his speech, he defends the right of madness to be listened to in a cathartic context, which means:

- The right of legend to claim its grain of truth: "For to try to persuade anybody that Amadis […] never existed, would be like trying to persuade him that the sun does not yield light, or ice cold, or earth

nourishment [...]; and if it be a lie, it must be a lie too that there was a Hector, or Achilles, or Trojan war, or Twelve Peers of France, or Arthur of England."
- The right of oral transmission to invent creatures of language for children and adults.

When describing his picture atlas named Mnemosyne, Aby Warburg referred to it as "a ghost story for truly adult people" (Warburg, 1923). Don Quixote would certainly have agreed with this perspective, as we see when he points out to the canon that it is useless to call apocryphal "the loves of Tristram and the Queen Yseult, as well as those of Guinevere and Lancelot, when there are persons who can almost remember having seen the Dame Quintañona [...]. I recollect a grandmother of mine on the father's side, whenever she saw any dame in a venerable hood, used to say to me, 'Grandson, that one is like Dame Quintañona', from which I conclude that she must have known her, or at least had managed to see some portrait of her". Suffice it that the Dame remains present in the words of a grandmother and in our thoughts, linking us to myths that it would be criminal to erase.

- The right of ancestors to exist and to play a role in transmission, even if the story defies logic, like "the pin with which the valiant Pierres guided the wooden horse he rode through the air". This pin is the connection to The Second Part, in which the flying horse Clavileno the Swift embodies the knight's decidedly visionary obsession with flying machines. For the time being, this "pin" pins him to his own ancestors: "[...] whence we may infer that there were Twelve Peers, and a Pierre, and a Cid [...]. Or perhaps I shall be told, too, that there [were no] adventures and challenges achieved and delivered, [...] in Burgundy, by the valiant Spaniards Pedro Barba and Gutierre Quixada (of whose family I come in the direct male line)" (De Cervantes, 2013, p. 371). But the canon, "amazed to hear the medley of truth and fiction Don Quixote uttered, and to see how well acquainted he was with everything relating or belonging to the achievements of his knight-errantry", asks nevertheless, what kind of truth is transmitted in these books of chivalry. In more recent times, we might ask what kinds of truth were those contributed by such eccentric Nobel prize winners as John Nash and Kurt Gödel, to cause these visionaires, "endowed with such a good understanding" (De Cervantes, 2013, p. 372) to be locked up.

The right to catharsis: the lake of bubbling pitch

When all is said and done, at the last minute Don Quixote has thwarted his father's last attempt to make him disappear. Perhaps the aim was to make the reader lose interest. No such luck! The knight sets out to prove brilliantly that the analysis of madness and trauma is a cathartic practice he describes as the crossing of "a lake of bubbling pitch".

Instead of arguing with the canon about abstract concepts, he uses the visionary method advocated by T. S. Eliot in his introduction to Dante's *Divine Comedy* (Eliot, 1929).

In 1593, four years before the hero was conceived, Philippe II had given the Escorial Monastery Jerome Bosch's triptych *The Garden of Earthly Delights*. Called the "Strawberry painting" at the time, the altarpiece was transported from the Netherlands to the chapel, where it can be seen behind the altar. A parishioner becoming bored with the service could always contemplate, depending on his mood, either the worst tortures of Hell, the delights of Paradise, or the Garden of Delights in the central panel.

Among other delights, a certain detail may have inspired Cervantes. Mermaid-like knights, whose bodies end in dolphin tails, are wading in the Fountain of Youth, painted in the geometric centre of the triptych. A very small step is needed to go from this to imagining that these knights are being regenerated, returning to an embryonic state after the horrors of war. Don Quixote takes this step by describing the stages of the veteran's catharsis.

First, the knight must plunge, without thinking, into a foul-smelling lake filled with terrifying creatures which inhabit the survivor's hell. "For, come, tell me, can there by anything more delightful than to see, as it were, here now displayed before us a vast lake of bubbling pitch with a host of snakes and serpents and lizards, and ferocious and terrible creatures of all sorts […]." A baroque depiction of the bloody mess of the frontlines, where the soldier rushes in without thinking, to face inevitable death. Indeed, the knight hears "a plaintive voice saying: '[…] if thou would win the prize that lies hidden beneath these dusky waves, […] cast thyself into the midst of its dark burning waters'."

But the puzzling question: "Can there be anything more delightful?" causes us to wonder if there is not a hint of masochism—or jouissance, as it has become fashionable to say today—in this description. In truth, what possible pleasure can be found in the following scene, in which the knight "without stopping to consider, without pausing to reflect upon the danger to which he is exposing himself, [...] plunges into the midst of the boiling lake, [...] when he little [...] knows what his fate is to be"? (De Cervantes, 2013, p. 373).

The pleasure lies in the anticipation of the catharsis: "[...] he finds himself among flowery meadows [...]. The sky seems more transparent there, and the sun shines with a strange brilliancy." The universe destroyed by chaos is reborn. All the senses are revived one after the other: the wind in the trees, the song of birds, the fragrance of the woods, the murmur of the brook and, in the centre of the scene, a castle appearing suddenly, solid like the mountains—a most reassuring spectacle.

The liminal space open to regeneration allows beauty to triumph over horror at last (Lacan, 1997). Like Jerome Bosch, who tames monsters with his brushes and captures beauty, the knight sees "a bevy of damsels [come] forth from the gate of the castle in gay and gorgeous attire". Contrary to what we might expect, they do not perform the dance of the seven veils for the pleasure of the returning warrior. "[...] she who seems to be the first among them all takes the bold knight who plunged into the boiling lake by the hand, and without addressing a word to him leads him into the rich palace or castle, and strips him as naked as when his mother bore him" (De Cervantes, 2013, p. 374). Once again, what follows is not what we expect.

The agency of the Lady is initially maternal. She bathes him and anoints him all over, as if he truly was the infant he resembles just then. Sweet scents replace the stench of corpses, and a silk shirt replaces the tar that stings and sticks to the body. She lavishes upon him music and victuals, reviving all his senses, "all in profound silence". Far from the noise of battle and from trivial chatter, he is now sated and, blissfully happy, is "picking his teeth perhaps as [is] usual". It may be that given our present-day liberated mindset, we were not expecting to come down in such a prosaic manner from the erotic promise of the scene.

But our objective is not to see whether or not the knight makes the grade among all these beauties, for another damsel enters, in third place, after those who resuscitated him when he was left for dead, "much lovelier than any of the others".

She speaks to him, not to give him comfort, but to request his assistance. Held enchanted in the castle, she asks him to free her. She is the Dulcinea who will give him back his "whereof", the object of the tyrant's envy, according to La Boétie (De La Boétie, 2012). Not the "whereof" to accumulate property, but the "whereof" to give, the equivalent of the "give away" of the Plains Indians, and what is called "potlatch" on the Pacific Coast. By practicing "the duty of liberality", he will be able to give his word once again, to renew the broken social link.

With great panache, the knight reviews how books of chivalry have proven their effectiveness through the centuries. "[...] take my advice, sir, and, as I said before, read these books and you will see how they will banish any melancholy you may feel and captain your spirits should they be depressed." Researchers attempting to find answers to the universal torment of depression would do well to take note, and so would the public service campaigns so often launched on this subject. A short video clip could present the following testimony: "For myself, I can say that since I have been a knight-errant I have become valiant, polite, generous, well-bred, magnanimous, courteous, dauntless, gentle, patient, and have learned to bear hardships, imprisonments, and enchantments" (De Cervantes, 2013, pp. 374–375).

Bolstered by this catharsis declared in public, despite his humiliating confinement in a cage, Don Quixote states once again his desire to honour Sancho. He grants him *aristeia*, excellence, recognising him as "one of the best squires that ever knight-errant had, just as Patroclus was, according to Homer, the best *therapon*—ritual double and second in combat—for Achilles, the best of the Achaeans" (Nagy, 1999).

Games of slaughter, gallant last stand

Thus, the plural body has proven its ability to resist, despite the breakdown of ideals, inevitably brought about by war. Now, Cervantes joins his hero in his cathartic folly and enters the fray, amusing himself delivering blows left and right. Taking careful aim, he begins by demolishing the pastoral romance, then heroism, and finally a religious ceremony. Does this mean that in his iconoclastic zeal he destroys *in fine* everything he once loved? In truth, this sport is familiar to the analyst, who witnesses the disappearance—when the work is ending and "melancholy has lifted"—of all the scaffolds that seemed essential.

The last episode of traumatic revival sets as its objective the triumph of Quixotic intelligence over stupid ideologies. The simpleton illustrating the point is a goatherd, Eugenio—whose name means "well-born". He also loves nature, is seduced by the pastoral life and tells his little goat, Spotty, a moral tale on the model of Mr Seguin's Goat—about beautiful Leandra who went off into the mountain with a big bad wolf in the guise of a seductor who, "without robbing her of her honor, had taken from her everything she had" (De Cervantes, 2013, p. 380).

The youth is surprised by Don Quixote's offer to be of service. He is among those who judge superficially. "[...] noticing Don Quixote's sorry apearance and looks", he quickly makes up his mind that "this gentleman has empty lodgings in his head." The gentleman in question is not one to take this sitting down. "[...] it is you who are empty and a fool. I am fuller than ever was the whore son bitch that bore you" (De Cervantes, 2013, p. 382).

Fortunately, the circus starts again, to everyone's satisfaction. Once their trials are over, all everyone wants is to be entertained, like today, with games and betting. In the rink of the prairie, the goatherd and the knight fought like brutes, while the audience hissed. Sancho rushes in and attacks the goatherd, leaving him "with his face covered with blood", so that the lad, "on all fours [feels] about for one of the table-knives to take a bloody revenge" (De Cervantes, 2013, p. 383). The audience is capering with delight, "bursting with laughter [...] and [hissing] them on as they do dogs that are worrying one another in a fight". The pastoral genre has taken a turn from romanticism to biting cynicism.

After the innocence of the eclogue, it is heroism in battle that is demolished by a swaggerer returning from war in Italy, Vincente de la Roca, a brash youth who "showed marks of wounds, which, [...] could not be made out" (De Cervantes, 2013, p. 379). He is a behind-the-lines braggart, a bit of a poet and musician, but above all a seducer of willing maidens, including the one whose heart the goatherd hoped to win. This damsel then, the beautiful Leandra, was not only willing, but "fell in love with him before the presumption of making love to her had suggested itself to him; and as in love affairs none are more easily brought to an issue than those which have the inclination of the lady" (De Cervantes, 2013, p. 380), she ran away with him.

But Leandra could be said to be a Zoraida who turned out badly, a rather empty-headed damsel who falls for the promises of fabulous riches the boastful lad dangles before her. "[...] at the end of three days they found the flighty Leandra in a mountain cave, stripped to her shift, and robbed of all the money and precious jewels she had carried away from home with her". Thus, the world reverts to its usual ways when Don Quixote grows tired of putting things right.

The last Quixotic mission aims at freeing no less than the Virgin Mary, whose image, draped in black, is carried by a procession of penitents across the fields, to implore God for rain. The drought devastating the earth can be equalled only by the state of the knight devastated by the betrayal of his companions. For this reason, he uses his last strength to fight a battle no longer to avenge his father, but to overcome his friend's betrayal.

Not only did the illustrious guests at the inn refuse to accompany him to his village, but they consented to the scheme hatched to deprive him of his freedom. Thus, "in a hoarse, excited voice" he asked the penitents dressed in white who carried the image: "You who hide your faces, perhaps because you are not good subjects, pay attention and listen to what I am about to say to you" (De Cervantes, 2013, p. 384). And, like an experienced rider, "he brought his legs to bear on Rocinante—for he had no spurs", and makes a gallant last stand to free the lady in mourning.

For the last time, the episode illustrates the canonic precepts, summed up by Cervantes for our benefit:

- Surviving image "of that worthy lady [...] borne captive [...] against her will [by] villains and discourteous thieves".
- Sancho's warning: "Where are you going, Señor Don Quixote? What devils have possessed you to set you on against our Catholic faith?"
- Coma. After his last sally, he is really left for dead, and mourned by his squire, whose funeral eulogy describes him as a "scourge of the wicked" and "enemy of the mean", in short, knight-errant, which is all that can be said" (De Cervantes, 2013, p. 385).
- Talking cure, for this eulogy brings the knight out of his coma, after the beating by the penitent, who—a scene creating an impression of déjà-vu—"fancying he had killed him, [...] hastily hitched up his tunic under his girdle and took to his heels across the country like a deer" (De Cervantes, 2013, p. 385).

– Invocation of the Lady. Don Quixote's first words when he awakens are addressed to her: "He who lives separated from you, sweetest Dulcinea, has greater miseries to endure than these. Aid me, friend Sancho, to mount the enchanted cart, for I am not in condition to press the saddle of Rocinante, as this shoulder is all knocked to pieces."

Does this resurrection announce a third sally? It is doubtful, for Cervantes is now fifty-eight and is perhaps asking himself if he can stay in the saddle long enough to write a sequel. But Sancho does not doubt it. A true forerunner of Salmon and his principles, he immediately brings into play, in the proximity of their friendship, the principle of expectancy: the hope of returning to the frontlines of knight-errantry, after recovering from his wounds. "[…] let us return to our village with these gentlemen, who seek our good, and there we will prepare for making another sally, which may turn out more profitable and creditable to us." Don Quixote ends up consenting to be hospitalised at home until he recovers.

The five hundred pages of exertion to which his father compelled him—which lasted eight months altogether—have so exhausted him that, for the moment, he places himself in the hands of his niece and his housekeeper, who "took him in and undressed him and laid him in his old bed. He eyed them askance, and could not make out where he was" (De Cervantes, 2013, p. 387). We can wager that he would have preferred to find himself naked among the sublime maidens on the other side of the Lake of Bubbling Pitch. In fact, Cervantes himself seems embarrassed to leave him like this. The best he can do is provide "epitaphs and eulogies of his life" written by "clowns, boasters, eccentrics, blunderers and oddballs". While we await a third sally, Cervantes brings the story to a close with a verse from Aristotle: "Perhaps another more talented poet will recount his deeds" (De Cervantes, 2013, p. 391).

Fortunately, the ruffian Avallenada took this proposition literally, just as others still take literally the condemnation of books of chivalry. We know that his insolent daring impelled him to take up the lyre and compose an inept sequel to the knight's adventures. Always ready to defend the old soldiers, Cervantes writes in The Author's Preface of The Second Part, published ten years later, when he was sixty-eight (one year before his death): "What I cannot help taking amiss is that [Avellaneda] charges me with being old and one-handed; or as if the loss of my hand had been brought about in some tavern, and not on the grandest occasion the past or present has seen, or the future can hope to see. If my wounds have no beauty to the beholder's eye, they are, at least, honorable in the estimation of those who knew where they were received" (De Cervantes, 2013, p. 397).

CHAPTER TWELVE

"Bella ciao! ciao! ciao!"

"Françoise!" This call drew me away from the incredible ceremony that had just ended. Across from me, at a distance, the Rutor glacier waterfalls had not suspended their motion. Behind me, the Mont Blanc mountain chain, the Grandes Jorasses, the Dent du Géant, and a little nearer the Aiguille des Glaciers, the Tré-la-tête glacier and the Montvalezan on the right were still there. The French and Italian standard-bearers were putting the flags back in their sheaths. The six Alpine "chasseurs" were leaving the marble stele covered with flowers, which was henceforth inscribed with the names of the twenty-eight hostages. The "call of the fallen" had been carried out, so that their relatives could answer, when the names were called one by one: "Fallen for France". My father, his head bowed, was still sitting on the grass next to the stele. Across from the young "chasseurs" dressed in ceremonial white, he had whispered "Emile".

I had brought him there without telling him where we were going. He would have refused to come with me to this place where he had never once returned in sixty-three years. He had been startled when his own name was mentioned at the end of the speech given by the host of the event.

Two days earlier, I had taken him on my annual pilgrimage, to the Col du Petit Saint-Bernard and to the cromlech, a circle of about fifty standing stones laid out three thousand years before the Roman road spanning the mountain and going to Aoste was built. Very recently, the road has been rebuilt to go around the old circle after having cut through it heedlessly for ages, for the circle lies on the border, with one half in France and the other in Italy. No one can guess that underneath there is a bunker built by the Nazis, which during the war was equipped with an optical system making it possible to see strategic locations in the whole valley.

As usual, I had gathered some flowers, pink and white yarrows that grew in abundance behind the inn, brought there perhaps by the wind, from Abbot Chanoux' Alpine garden nearby, in front of the old Hospice famous for using St. Bernard dogs to rescue lost travellers in the snow, a tradition on the Great St. Bernard Pass to Switzerland. I always hung the flowers on the small plaque that had been placed on the wall only a dozen years ago. The plaque only mentions the massacre of the twenty-eight men who should have numbered at least twenty-nine, and many more.

The innkeeper's wife was bringing plates of soup, cheese, and cold cuts. Suddenly, when I least expected it, I asked her who had hung the plaque on the wall. Perhaps because this time my flowers were next to a withered bouquet tied with a ribbon displaying the colours of Italy. Or perhaps because, for the first time since the war, my father was here with me. He had wanted to see the war landmarks in his mountains again.

The innkeeper's wife could not answer my question. But she did tell me that the following Sunday there would be a ceremony for the inauguration of a new monument at the place where the hostages were killed, in front of the grave they had dug themselves.

"Where?"

– At Terre Noire. Terra Nera, she corrected herself, on the Piedmontese side.

Stunned, I poured myself another glass of Mondeuse wine. Terre Noire! This mythical name was that of a real place?

"At what time?"

She did not know. But she could tell me how to get there, to the other side of the border, on the Italian side: you turn right, across the old Customs building converted into a hotel.

We left at once on a scouting mission, taking the road along the lake, on the other side of the border, then making a hairpin turn onto a narrow road; we kept going at random on slopes equipped with ski lifts, for such a distance that soon we found ourselves stuck in black, slaty soil. A Piedmontese truck driver came miraculously to our rescue, and showed us the place we were looking for.

We had bypassed the small enclosure without seeing it, and had not seen the pit full of water in the middle of it either, nor the two steles. The first, a cairn of white stone, had been built very early by the inhabitants of the Italian town of La Thuile, who found the place invaded by a swarm of flies when the snow melted, the following spring. This memorial bore a date, until then unknown to me: August 1944. The second stele was brand new: a large grey marble plaque inscribed, at last, with the twenty-eight names, listed according to their place of origin in the valley; it awaited its unveiling on the following Sunday. Of course we would come back that day! At the same time, I felt it would be a colossal effort to cross an invisible wall as thick as the span of its sixty-three years.

The twenty-ninth on the list, my father, had been able to escape with a few others, one hour before the rest were pushed up to the mountain pass. A fluke of fortune he had never stopped telling me about, as if a part of him was travelling endlessly towards the pass with the others, all the way to the pit they had dug.

To understand, we must go back to the summer of 1942. The chalets were burning in the mountains, in retaliation for the population's refusal to give food to Resistance fighters. The Resistance was just organising itself into different groups and the mountaineers were reluctant to give away food to all of them.

My father was the organiser of the cooperatives called "fruitières", meaning that they produced the "common fruit", Beaufort cheese, and he was also the director of the adjoining school, the "École fruitière" for young cheese makers, most of whom had joined the underground.

The cooperatives created to ripen the cheese produced in the mountains during the summer became a central point for the distribution of food supplies to Resistance fighters. After having consulted trustworthy mountaineers like the uncle of the writer Frison-Roche, and contacted General Challe, the head of the Secret Army in Grenoble, my father created a system of clandestine vouchers with a code that changed every week. Only his assistant, Lepain, knew of the plan. The supplies were exchanged against these bits of paper, on the simple promise of receiving payment when the war ended. When would that be? Some fine day, no one really knew when. He put up all he owned as a guarantee—not much, in truth—and everything his parents-in-law possessed. The houses stopped burning down instantly, and the banks lended money.

This is how it came about that the cellars of the Beaufort "fruitière" in Bourg Saint Maurice, where I was born, served as a hiding place for all kinds of food supplies and people. The school enrolled a few young Jews under assumed names. A crossing point providing easy escape, our kitchen was used by the "Maquis" to hold their meetings. Among the visitors, there were two men in blue, one tall and one short, about whom no one except my father knew that they belonged to another network, the "Reseau Alliance"—as I happened to learn recently—working for the English. The garage owner who was our neighbour, Aristide Ayet, hid weapons and repaired them, in the angle of fire of the German machine gun aimed at the intersection, from the window of a house about a hundred yards away.

After the war, the vouchers were repaid to the last penny, and living conditions in the valley improved thanks to the cross-border contraband with our Piedmontese cousins: salt for rice, vermouth, and silk stockings given out at the town hall. I received an Italian doll which was so beautiful that I was afraid to play with it.

But let us go back to the end of August, 1944. For the past three days, the barracks of the Alpine troops had been used as a prison for over fifty hostages crowded in without food or water, with not even enough room to lie down. But the lack of food was most cruelly felt by the German troops. They held the mountain passes in order to be able to withdraw, and they fought fiercely until May 1945. The SS officer and the mayor summoned my father. Pierced with a hard, cold stare, he expected to be shot like the pharmacist who had been killed the day before in front of him, when he tried to run away. This memory is always associated for him with the screams of the waiter from the café, who was being buried alive. For me, these screams are part of an undated, unending memory.

The SS officer and the mayor demanded that my father bring them food, because they knew that he was supplying the Resistance. He refused the German truck they offered to provide, quickly chose three or four men whose names he no longer remembers and, once they got across the national highway, they ran for their lives straight to a Resistance leader who gave them contraband pastis, hid them and forbid them to go home. One hour later, pursued by Alpine troops advancing up the valley, the German soldiers headed towards the pass, to Italy, pushing before them the exhausted hostages. My mother saw them passing under the window of the cheese dairy, and thought that my father was among them.

It was only when I read the date inscribed on the stele that I realised that I had already been there, somewhere, for over fifteen months. Some of the hostages died along the way, shot if they showed the least weakness; others, who knew the mountain paths well, were able to escape under cover of darkness. When the bodies were taken out of the pit, half-empty bottles of wine were found in their pockets, probably slipped to them by local inhabitants along their terrible march, a climb of some thirty kilometres.

"It's all in the past: your mother, who was not from Savoy, didn't want to hear any more about it. And she was right, after everything she had endured in prison, pregnant with you! I still see her, in her little checkered dress, at the gate of the barracks, with the basket of food she was trying to pass me, in vain. She knew from experience that when the doors close, it's all over." He had worshipped her, like one would a Dulcinea. His goddess forbade, among other things, access to the mountains and its native people—all my relatives, as the Sioux Indians say—except for skiing and walking in the summer, to take in the invigorating mountain air. After the war, this air had restored my health, which did poorly on the plain.

Crossing the invisible frontier established by my mother, I visited the mountain pass each year in secret, and not at all like a tourist. I had a vague sense of something that was like a crazy idea, between obsession and paranoia. Indeed, in 1974, I spotted, at the same inn, decorated differently then, a German my father's age, who came in and sat at a table alone. I had a strong desire, which I did not dare to act on, to ask him if by any chance he had not killed some hostages at the mountain pass. My silence bothered me for a long time. As if this stranger, whose accent produced a ghostly effect on me when he ordered cold cuts and cheese, was the sole carrier of that day which no one ever mentioned to me on the French side. And this was why I didn't even know, and neither did my father, if I was already born when those events had taken place.

"Events turned to dust"! I must say, as Fernand Braudel did about the Battle of Lepante, when he insisted on *"l'histoire de la longue durée"* (history in the long run), as opposed to *"l'histoire evenementielle"* (history constituted by events). What was the use? And yet, every year I stubbornly went back to this site with its prehistoric splendour, without ever daring to ask any questions.

Breaking the wall of silence requires the strong intervention of knights-errant. When I learned about the ceremony that would be held shortly, I called the Tourist Offices in the region, on both sides of the mountain. Courteous voices showed great surprise at my request. They had no idea what it was that I was telling them. When I hung up, I had the impression that these mountains were quite able to welcome two types of visitors, who knew nothing about each other: the skiers, climbers, and hikers; and then the phantom warriors who climb, walk across and come down the same trails. Between these two groups, the rocks, the marmots, the eagles, the little fawn Tarentaise cows with long black lashes, the yarrow and the gentians surely knew about these events, passed down from father to son, from mother to daughter. And I had just discovered that I also knew.

That Sunday at the end of July 2007, standing on that mountain, I did not dare look at my father, who sat beside me. The name of the seventeen-year-old lad he talked to me about all the time had just been called. Wounded in the leg, he had thought that his "Chantiers de la jeunesse" uniform would save his life. He was shot before the others, because his wound slowed him down; a shepherd found his body the following spring on the French side. Led to the corpse by flies, like in La Thuile, he found the stump of an arm sticking out, devoured by birds. When his name was inscribed on the stele sixty-three years later, it was impossible to imagine that he would have been eighty years old now.

During the ceremony, several officials from Savoy and from Piedmont—united until 1860—spoke eloquently. A politician born in the region had obtained the funds for the new stele. The organiser of the ceremony had also joined the Resistance at seventeen. Another man, older than him, who had been an officer in the Secret Army, made that day come to life, standing, without any notes, describing the events hour by hour, speaking in the present tense, in a firm voice that defied his age, the rhythm of his speech interrupted by intervals of silence, his voice choked with emotion. I had the impression of hearing Homer for the first time, even though I had so often translated him in my youth.

My father was still sitting on the ground, his misty eyes covered by the visor of his cap. When he heard his own name he was startled and lifted his face in disbelief. Then, after we heard the song of the Allobroges, hymns from Savoy and Piedmont, national anthems, the songs of French and Italian partisans—all in this majestic scenery that was the last thing the hostages saw before their execution, the ritual came to an end. Groups of people formed to talk among themselves.

That is when I heard my name being called. Running towards us down the slope, we saw the youthful figure of a lively, energetic man who helped my father rise to his feet. He kissed us, sobbing, repeating "Oskich, Oskich!" like a password.

I instantly remembered the black car, a Hotchkiss, in which I would wait at night for my father, while he had secret meetings with the lieutenant de France, who was soon assassinated. Long ago had become today!

When he called himself by his family name, Gabriel Ayet, the garage owner next to the *fruitière*, I recognised the son of my father's best friend in the underground, so often mentioned. Breathlessly, he went on telling stories I knew by heart: the nights spent in the cellars, where we all slept together under the concrete slab that had been reinforced to accommodate trucks. The weapons hidden and repaired in the garage, the sabotage of German vehicles. The shells and the bullets, suddenly clearly present. His memory was full of scenes recorded in full detail. At the time, he was seven and I was two. We had not seen each other since.

Our fathers were friends for life, for better or for worse. My father now confessed to him that they had taken each other by the hand one night, like two children, when on their way back from a secret meeting after curfew they flattened themselves against a wall, in the corner of a door, to avoid being seen by a patrol who would have shot them on the spot. Gabriel went on and on, there was so much to say: the hiding places, the pursuits, the escapes, the parachuting of weapons to La Plagne and to Les Saisies, the denunciations, the assassination of Captain Bulle, the signed denunciatory letters, the informing, the neighbour who received a visit from German officers—whose gesture

Gabriel mimicked when they took off their caps—and would have had her head shaved had both our fathers not intervened. I knew all these stories.

My father turned to me and said: "It's true, I would never have come if you had told me where we were going, but I am not ashamed to be here. You see, I haven't lied to you."

Again and again, I kept hearing in my head the song the Italian partisans sang to their Dulcineas, its echoes coming from a village whose name I refused to remember for a long time: *Bella ciao, bella ciao! bella ciao! ciao! ciao!*

REFERENCES

Amadas and Ydoine (13th century). Arthur, R. G. (Trans.), Routledge Revivals, 2014.

Apollinaire, G. (1964). "The breasts of Tiresias". In: Benedickt, M. & Wellwarth, G. E. (Ed.), *Modern French Theatre*. New York: E. P. Dutton and Co.

Apuleius (1999). *The Golden Ass or Metamorphoses*, Kenney, E. J. (Trans.). Lolndon: Penguin Classics.

Arendt, H. (1951). The secret police. In: *The Origins of Totalitarianism*. Cleveland: The World Publishing Company.

Artaud, A. (2009). *The Theatre and Its Double*. Corti, V. (Trans.). London: Oneworld Classics.

Barrois, C. (1993). *La Psychanalyse du guerrier* (Psychoanalysis of the Warrior). Paris: Hachette.

Bataillon, M. (1961). *La Célestine selon Fernando de Rojas*. Paris: Didier.

Bédier, J. (2011). *The Romance of Tristan and Iseult*. Belloc, H. (Trans.). Oxford: Fonthill Press.

Benedetti, G. (1998). Les images transformantes et la transformation des images. In: *Le Sujet emprunté*. Érès.

Bennassar, B. & Bennassar, L. (2001). *Les Chrétiens d'allah. L'histoire extraordinaire des renégats, XVIᵉ–XVIIᵉ siècle*. Paris: Perrin.

263

Bigeard, M. (1972). *La Folie et les fous littéraires en Espagne, 1500–1650*. Paris: Centre of Hispanic Research.

Binswanger, L. & Warburg, A. (2007). *La Guérison infinie. Histoire clinique d'Aby Warburg*. Stimili, D. (Ed.). Paris: Rivages.

Bion, W. R. (1982). *The Long Week-End (1897–1919)*. London: Karnac.

Bion, W. R. (1997). *Taming Wild Thoughts*. London: Karnac.

Bloch, M. (1999). *Strange Defeat*. New York: W. W. Norton.

Bogonet, U. (2005). *Section Paganon. Dans les crimes pour la liberté*. Montmélian: La Fontaine de Siloé.

Braudel, F. (1995). *The Mediterranean and the Mediterranean World in the Age of Philip II*. University of California Press.

Canavaggio, J. (1949). Trans. and Introduction *Don Quichotte*. In: Pléiade. Paris: Gallimard.

Canavaggio, J. (1977). *Cervantès dramaturge, un théâtre à naître* (Cervantes Dramatist: A Theatre to Be Born). Paris: PUF.

Canavaggio, J. (1991). *Cervantes*. New York: W. W. Norton.

Carroll, A. (Ed.) (2006). *Operation Homecoming, Iraq Afghanistan, and the Home Front, in the words of US Troops and Their Families*. New York: Random House.

Caruth, C. (1996). *Unclaimed Experience. Trauma, Narrative, History*. Baltimore: Johns Hopkins University Press.

Cassou, J. (1953). *La Mémoire courte*. Paris: Mille et une nuit, 2001.

Chernow, R. (1994). *The Warburgs*. New York: Vintage Books.

Clément, R. (1952). *Forbidden Games* (dir.).

Coignet, C. (1850). *Mémoire d'un officier de l'Empire*. Paris: Éditions Deux Trois.

Cooperman, M. (1983). Some observations regarding psychoanalytic psychotherapy in the hospital setting. The Psychiatric Hospital.

Damasio, A. (2005). *Descartes' Error*. London: Penguin Books.

D'Aranda, E. (1997). *The History of Algiers and its slavery*. Davies, J. (Trans.), 1666. London: Printed for John Starkey.

D'Arras, J. (1400). *Melusine*. Donald, A. K. (Ed.). London: Kegan Paul Trench Tribner & Co., 1895; Le Goff, J. Melusine: mother and pioneer. In: *Time, Work and Culture in the Middle Ages*. Chicago: University of Chicago Press, 1980.

Davis, R. C. (2004). *Christian Slaves, Muslim Masters: White Slavery in the Mediterranean, the Barbary Coast and Italy, 1500–1800*. Basingstoke: Palgrave Macmillan.

Davoine, F. (2014). *Mother Folly: A Tale*. Miller, J. G. (Trans.). Stanford: Stanford University Press.

Davoine, F., & Gaudillière, J. -M. (2004). *History Beyond Trauma*. New York: Other Press.

De Cervantes, M. (1615). *El Rufian Dichoso*. Ediciones Catedra, 2000.

De Cervantes, M. (1615). *The Vigilant Sentinel*. Flores A. & Liss, J. (Trans.). New York: Dover Publications, 1991.

De Cervantes, M. (1617). *The Trials of Persiles and Sigismunda*, Weller, C., & Colahan, C. A. (Trans.). Cambridge, MA: Hackett Classics, 2009.

De Cervantes, M. (1867). *Galate: A Pastoral Romance*, Gyll, G. W. J. (Trans.). Whiefish: Kessinger Publishing, 2008.

De Cervantes, M. (2001). *Don Quichotte*, French translation under the supervision of Jean Canavaggio, with an Introduction by Jean Canavaggio, 1949. In: Pléiade. Paris: Gallimard.

De Cervantes, M. (2013). *Don Quixote*, Ormsby, J. (Trans.). Canterbury: Canterbury Classics/Baker & Taylor.

De Coster, C. (1867). *The Legend of Ulenspiegel and Lamme Goedzak*. Atkinson, F. M. (Trans.). Nabu Press, 2010.

De Haedo, D. (1998). *Topographie et histoire générale d'Alger*. Saint-Denis: Bouchène.

De la Barca, P.C. (2012). *Life Is a Dream*. SMK Books.

De La Boétie, E. (2012). *Discourse on Voluntary Servitude*. Atkinson, J. B. & Sices, D. (Trans.). Cambridge, MA: Hackett Classics.

De Molina, T. (1986). *The Trickster of Seville*. Edwards, G. (Trans.). Oxford: Aris & Phillips.

De Pizan, C. (1405). *The Book of the City of Ladies*. London: Penguin Classics, 2000.

De Rojas, F. (2009). *Celestina*. Peter Bush (Trans.). London: Penguin Books.

De Ronsard, P. (2002). *Hymn to Demons* (Les Daimons). London: Penguin Classics, p. 144.

De Sade, M. (2013). *Justine or the Misfortunes of Virtue*. Oxford: Oxford University Press.

Descartes, R. (2003). *Discourse on Method and Meditations*. Haldane, E. S. & Ross, G. R. T. (Trans.). New York: Dover Philosophical Classics.

De Troyes, C. (1997). *Lancelot: The Knight of the Cart*. Raffel, B. (Trans.). Yale: Yale University Press.

Devos, R. (1989). *À plus d'un titre*. Paris: Olivier Orban.

Doi, T. (1973). *The Anatomy of Dependence*. Bester, J. (Trans.). Tokyo: Kodansha International.

Dubard, P. (1945). *Patrouilles à la mer*. Paris: Éditions de la Nouvelle France.

Dufourmantelle, A. (2007). *La Femme et le sacrifice*. Paris: Denoël.

Eliot, T. S. (1922). The waste land. In: *The Complete Poems and Plays*. London: Faber & Faber Poetry, 2004.

Eliot, T. S. (1929). *Dante*. London: Faber & Faber.

Erasmus (2013). *In Praise of Folly*. Literary Licensing.

Feldman, S. & Laub, D. (1992). *Testimony. Crisis of Witnessing in Literature, Psychoanalysis and History*. New York: Routledge.

Felman, S. (2002). 'The storyteller's silence: Walter Benjamin's dilemma of justice. In: *The Juridical Unconscious*. Cambridge: Harvard University Press.

Flacelière, R. (1961). *Devins et oracles grecs*. Paris: PUF; *Que sais-je?*, No. 939.

Fourcade, M. -M. (1968). *L'Arche de Noé. Réseau Alliance 1940–1945*. Paris: Plon, 1998.

Freud, E. L. (Ed.) (1970). *Letters of Sigmund Freud, 1873–1939*. Stern, T., & Stern, J. (Trans.). London: Hogarth.

Freud, S. (1907a). *Delusions and Dreams in Jensen's Gradiva. S.E. 9*. London: Hogarth.

Freud, S. (1921c). *Group Psychology and the Analysis of the Ego. S.E., 1*: pp. 103–114. London: Hogarth.

Freud, S. (1955 [1939a]). *Moses and Monotheism*. Jones, K. (Trans.). New York: Vintage Books.

Fritz, J. -M. (1992). *Le Discours du fou au Moyen Âge*. Paris: PUF.

Gaide, G., Mérendet, O., & Penna, J. -L. (1996). *Le Petit-Saint-Bernard. Un col, des hommes*. Montmélian: La Fontaine de Siloé.

Garcés, M. A. (2002). *Cervantes in Algiers. A Captive's Tale*. Nashville: Vanderbilt University Press.

Garin, J. -P. (1946). *La Vie Dure*. Lyon: Audin.

Gouhier, H. (1997). *Biographie d'Auguste Comte*. Paris: Librairie J. Vrin, Ch. VIII, Un épisode cérébral (Mental Illness).

Graves, R. (1958). *Goodbye to All That*. Anchor.

Homer (1924). *The Iliad, Book 22*. Murray, A. T. (Trans.). London: William Heinemann Ltd.

Horace (2002). *Horace Odes III*. West, D. (Trans.). Oxford: Oxford University Press.

Ionesco, E. (1965). Amedee or how to get rid of it. In: *Plays, Volume 2*. London: John Calder.

Isotti, M. (1978). *Armour, mon ennemi*. Faugeras, P. (French Trans.). Erès, 1996.

Jackson, J. (2000). *The Fall of France*. Oxford: Oxford University Press.

Jéquier, C. (1993). Portrait du fou avec gourdin et fromage. *Paragone, No. 39–40*; Fritz, J. -M. (1992). *Le Discours du fou au Moyen Age*, Paris: PUF: Fromage et littérature, le fromage au fol.

Kandel, E. (2006). *In Search of Memory. The Emergence of a New Science of Mind*. New York: Norton.

Klossowski, P. (2015). *Living Currency*. Smith, D. W. (Trans.). London: Bloomsbury Academic.

La Boétie, É. (1548). *Discourse of Voluntary Servitude*. Kurz, H. (Trans.). Columbia: Columbia University Press, 1942.

Lacan, J. (1997). *The Seminar of Jacques Lacan: The Ethics of Psychoanalysis (Book VII)*. London: W. W. Norton & Company.

Laub, D. (1991). Bearing witness on the vicissitudes of listening. In: Feldman, S. & Laub, D. *Testimony*.

Le Goff, J. (1986). *The Birth of Purgatory*. Chicago: University of Chicago Press.

Mascarenhas, J. (1993). *Esclave à Alger (1621–1626)*. Paris: Chandeigne.

Missios, C. (1985). *Lucky You Died Young*. Athens: Grammata.

Molho, M. (1968). *Romans picaresques espagnoles*. Paris: Gallimard, Pléiade.

Nagy, G. (1996). *Poetry As Performance*. Cambridge: Cambridge University Press.

Nagy, G. (1999). *The Best of the Achaeans*: Baltimore: The Johns Hopkins University Press.

Nakagawa, H. (2007). *Mémoires d'un "moraliste passable". Le pied gauche et la vie droite d'un professeur japonais*. Ferney-Voltaire, Centre international d'études du XVIIIe siècle.

Nasar, S. (2011). *A Beautiful Mind*. New York: Simon & Schuster.

Offenback, J. (1864). *La Belle Hélène*. Libretto Meilhac, H. and Halévy, L. Paris: Édition Keck.

Pergaud, L. (1942). *La Guerre des boutons* (1912). Paris: Rombaldi.

Plato (2003). *Phaedrus*. Newburyport, MA: Focus Publishing/R. Pullins Co.

Plato (2007a). *The Republic*. London: Penguin Classics.

Plato (2007b). *Timaeus*. Jowett, B. (Trans.). BiblioLife.

Plato's Theaetetus (1955). Jowett, B. (Trans.). New York: The Liberal Arts Press.

Potter, H. C. (1941). *Hellzapoppin* (dir.).

Proust, M. (1993). *Time Regained*. Mayor, A. & Kilmartin, T. (Trans.). New York: The Modern Library.

Recamier, P. -C. (1992). *Le Génie des origines. Psychanalyse et psychose*. Paris: Payot.

Ridington, R. (1982). Telling secrets. Stories of the vision quest. *The Canadian Journal of Native Studies*, Vol. II, No. 2.

Roy, J. (1946). *La Vallée heureuse*. Paris: Gallimard.

Sahlins, P. (1994). *Forest Rites. The War of the Demoiselles in the Nineteenth Century in France*. Cambridge: Harvard University Press.

Salmon, T. (1917). *The Care and the Treatment of Mental Diseases and War Neuroses (Shell Shock) in the British Troops*. New York: War Work Committee of the National Committee for Mental Hygiene.

Savall, J. (2005). *Don Quijote de la Mancha, Romances y Músicas*, Hesperion XXI, La Capella Real de Catalunya, Edición commemorativa de la reapertura del corral de comedias de Alcalá de Henares, Alia vox—Communidad de Madrid.

Schmitt, J. -C. (1983). *The Holy Greyhound: Guinefort, Healer of Children Since the Thirteenth Century*. Cambridge: Cambridge University Press.

Schur, M. (1972). *Freud: Living and Dying*. Madison, CT: International Universities Press.

Shay, J. (1995). *Achilles in Vietnam, Combat Trauma and the Undoing of Character*. New York: Touchstone Books.

Shibiku, M. (1005–1013). *The Tale of Gengi*. Seidensticker, E. G. (Trans.). London: Vintage Classics, 1990.

Sterne, L. (1999). *The Life and Opinions of Tristam Shandy, Gentleman*. London: Wordsworth Editions.

Sullivan, H. S. (1974). *Schizophrenia as a Human Process*. London: W. W. Norton & Co.

The Gateless Gate (Wu-men kuan) (1229). In: *Fifty Eastern Thinkers*. Collinson, D., Plant, K. & Wilkinson, R. London: Routledge, 2000.

Tissier, A. (1984). *Farces du Moyen Âge*. Paris: Garnier-Flammarion.

Vilar, P. (1971). The Age of Don Quixote. *New Left Review, No. 68, July–August*, 1971.

Villon, F. (1489). Ballad of dead ladies. Rossetti, D. G. (Trans.). In: *Ballads Done into English from the French of François Villon*, Portland, Maine: Thomas B. Mosher, 1904.

Villon, F. (1489). The ballad of proverbs. In: *The World's Wit and Humor in 15 Volumes* (1906). Vol X.

Virgil (1952). *The Aeneid of Virgil*. Humphries, R. (Trans.). New York: Charles Scribner's Sons.

Von Goethe, J. W. (1782). The Erl-King. Bowing, E. A. (Trans.). In: *The Poems of Goethe*, New York: Thomas Y. Crowell Co., 1882.

Warburg, A. (1923). A lecture on serpent ritual. Mainland, W. F. (Trans.). *Journal of the Warburg Institute 2, 1938–1939*: 277–292.

Wilder, B. (1959). *Some Like It Hot* (dir.).

Winnicott, D. W. (1971). *Playing and Reality*. London: Tavistock Publications.

Winnicott, D. W. (1974). Fear of Breakdown. *International Review of Psycho-Analysis, Vol. 1* (1–2).

Wise, R. (1965). *The Sound of Music* (dir.).

Wittgenstein, L. (1918). *Tractus Logico-Philosophicus* 6.52 2. London: Psychology Press & Routledge Classic Editions, 2001.

Wittgenstein, L. (1929). *A Lecture On Ethics*. London: John Wiley & Sons, 2014, p. 42.

Wittgenstein, L. (1934–1936). Notes for lectures on "private experience" and "sense data". In: the *Oxford Handbook of Wittgenstein*. Oxford: Oxford University Press, 2011.

Wittgenstein, L. (1979a). Remarks on Frazer's *Golden Bough*. Beversluis, J. (Trans.). In: *Wittgenstein, Sources and Perspectives*. C. G. Luckhardt (Ed.). Cornell University Press.

Wittgenstein, L. (1979b). *Notebooks: 1914–1916*. Chicago: University of Chicago Press.

Wittgenstein, L. (2010). *Philosophical Investigations (1945–1949)*. London: Wiley-Blackwell.

Wood, S. (1935). *A Night at the Opera* (dir.).

Zumthor, P. (1978). *Le Masque et la Lumière. La poétique des grands rhétoriqueurs*. Paris: Seuil.

INDEX

FIGHTING MELANCHOLIA
Don Quixote's Teaching

Françoise Davoine

Translated by Agnès Jacob

KARNAC

First published in 2016 by
Karnac Books Ltd
118 Finchley Road
London NW3 5HT

British Library Cataloguing in Publication Data

A C.I.P. for this book is available from the British Library

ISBN-13: 978-1-78220-365-0

Typeset by V Publishing Solutions Pvt Ltd., Chennai, India

Printed in Great Britain by TJ International Ltd, Padstow, Cornwall

www.karnacbooks.com

"Strive, too, that in reading your story
the melancholy may be moved
to laughter [...]"

Don Quixote, The Author's Preface, p. 7

To the old soldiers